SOFTWARE ENGINEERING

Kassem A. Saleh

Copyright © 2009 by J. Ross Publishing, Inc.

ISBN-13: 978-1-932159-94-3

Printed and bound in the U.S.A. Printed on acid-free paper
10   9   8   7   6   5   4   3   2

Library of Congress Cataloging-in-Publication Data

Saleh, K. A. (Kassem A.)
Software engineering / by Kassem A. Saleh.
    p. cm.
  Includes bibliographical references and index.
  ISBN 978-1-932159-94-3 (hardcover : alk. paper)
  1. Software engineering. I. Title.

QA76.758.S25 2009
005.1—dc22

                                           2009021860

Direct all inquiries to J. Ross Publishing, Inc., 5765 N. Andrews Way, Fort Lauderdale, FL 33309.

Phone: (954) 727-9333

Fax: (561) 892-0700

Web: www.jrosspub.com

Dedications

To God who blessed me with the ability
to learn and increase my knowledge
To my father's soul
To Maha, May, Hasan, Mazen, and Wasim

Contents

Acknowledgments

I would like to thank my wife Maha and my children May, Hasan, and Mazen for supporting me during this project. Thank you, May, in drawing most of the difficult figures for this book. Special thanks to Tim Pletscher for his patience and encouragement, and to Charles Ashbacher whose feedback helped improve the content of this book. Additionally, I would like to thank the many students at Kuwait University and the American University of Sharjah who pointed out errors in earlier versions of the book.

Foreword

Software and software systems are omnipresent in our lives. They help us perform many of our daily tasks. We rely on them for banking, shopping, learning, communicating, and commuting. They are embedded in hardware such as home appliances, mobile devices, cars, and medical equipment. There is a growing need to develop increasingly complex software systems. Moreover, there is a shortage of highly-qualified professionals specializing in development and maintenance, that is, the engineering of software systems.

During the many years I spent at NASA's Jet Propulsion Laboratory, I personally witnessed the importance of software and the effort we expend in the development of reliable and highly-dependable safety-critical software systems to accomplish our space exploration missions.

In this book, Kassem Saleh introduces the principles and techniques that can be used to develop and maintain high-quality software systems. The book builds on the 25 years he has spent as a software practitioner, researcher, educator, trainer, and consultant. The ten chapters flow seamlessly, are easy to read, and are focused. The book introduces the most popular and industry-proven techniques used for engineering and managing high-quality software. Chapters 1 through 8 address requirements, specifications, design, coding, and testing as they pertain to the engineering side of software development. Maintenance techniques are presented in Chapter 9 with issues related to this important yet often ignored and disrespected area of software engineering. The final chapter discusses software project management techniques for the cost-effective and timely production of software, software risk management, and estimation. I believe the book fills a void in this important area and provides a strong foundation for future software engineers. Moreover, educators, trainers, graduate students, researchers, and practitioners undoubtedly will benefit. I am certain that you will find that it enriches your professional training and career.

Charles Elachi

Vice President, California Institute of Technology

Director, NASA's Jet Propulsion Laboratory

Preface

About the Book

This book on software engineering is written in a simple and concise manner to cover all aspects of software development and maintenance. *Software Engineering* provides the software engineering fundamentals, principles, and skills needed to develop and maintain high-quality software products. The software engineering processes and techniques covered include requirements specification, design, implementation, testing, and management of software projects. This up-to-date book is modeled on the recommendations and guidelines prescribed in the 2004 version of the *Guide to the Software Engineering Body of Knowledge* (SWEBOK), published by the IEEE Computer Society, and the 2004 *Software Engineering Curriculum Guidelines for Undergraduate Degree Programs in Software Engineering* published by the IEEE Computer Society and the Association for Computing Machinery Joint Task Force on Computing Curricula.

At the end of each chapter, the reader is able to perform tangible software engineering tasks by applying the learned techniques and methods, to review and become more familiar with the terminology, to understand the principles by mastering the subjects, to analyze existing task deliverables and compare and critique those techniques. The book is designed as a text for an undergraduate first course in software engineering and graduate bridging courses in information technology. In addition, *Software Engineering* can be used by practitioners who need to refresh their knowledge with the latest in software engineering techniques and processes. The prerequisite to use this text is a background in an object-oriented programming language.

Structure

Chapter 1 **Software and Software Engineering** presents introductory information and background on software, software engineering, stakeholders, and the code of ethics for software professionals.

Chapter 2 **Software Development Life Cycle Models** contains well-known industry-proven life cycle models for software development and maintenance that are used to deal with the complexity as well as quality issues of the software we produce.

Chapter 3 **Software Requirements** discusses the development of both functional and non-functional software requirements and the related deliverable documentation.

Chapter 4 **Software Specification** deals with the specification of software requirements, using various formal specification techniques and formalisms for the modeling of data, behavior, and processes.

Chapter 5 **Software Design** introduces the basics of software design. The various desirable features of both high-level and detailed designs are discussed. In addition, the graphical user interface design and its beneficial features are presented.

Chapter 6 **Object-Oriented Design** features concepts in object-oriented design, software design patterns, design reusability, and software architectural patterns.

Chapter 7 **Software Implementation** considers software implementation issues, including fault tolerant software, coding styles, software reuse, and secure software.

Chapter 8 **Software Testing and Quality Assurance** covers the various techniques for testing software. It includes white box- and black box-based techniques for unit-level testing and system-level testing. In addition, the chapter discusses integration testing among other testing types, and quality assurance-related issues.

Chapter 9 **Software Maintenance** presents the various software maintenance activities and change management issues, including version control, regression testing, and software configuration management.

Chapter 10 **Software Project Management** discusses software project management activities, including risk management, metrics and estimation, scheduling, tracking, and documenting the software project management plan.

Intended Users

This book can be used as a textbook for a first course in software engineering in computer science, computer engineering, software engineering, and management information systems programs. The book can also be used for training courses on software engineering. Software engineering practitioners who would like to refresh their knowledge will also find this book useful and informative.

Available Resources

PowerPoint notes covering the book chapters are available for download from the WAV section at the publisher's website www.jrosspub.com. Students and instructors can also communicate with the author by sending an e-mail to saleh.software@yahoo.com.

About the Author

Dr. Kassem A. Saleh is currently a professor in Information Sciences at Kuwait University. He received his BS, MS, and PhD in computer science from the University of Ottawa in Canada. Dr. Saleh worked as a computer systems specialist at Mediatel, Bell Canada, from 1985 to 1991, and was on the faculty of Concordia University during 1991-1992, Kuwait University from 1992 to 2000, and American University of Sharjah from 2000 to 2007. Dr. Saleh is also a Certified Information Systems Security Professional (CISSP). He is a senior member of IEEE and a professional member of the ACM.

The *Journal of Systems and Software* has ranked Dr. Saleh among the top scholars in the field of systems and software engineering in seven of its annual assessments published from 1996 to 2003. His research interests include software engineering, requirements engineering, and information security. Dr. Saleh has published more than 120 refereed journal and conference papers and has presented numerous tutorials and lectures at international conferences and universities worldwide. Dr. Saleh is currently editor-in-chief of the *Journal of Software*.

Web
Added
Value™

Free value-added materials available from
the Download Resource Center at www.jrosspub.com

At J. Ross Publishing we are committed to providing today's professional with practical, hands-on tools that enhance the learning experience and give readers an opportunity to apply what they have learned. That is why we offer free ancillary materials available for download on this book and all participating Web Added Value™ publications. These online resources may include interactive versions of material that appears in the book or supplemental templates, worksheets, models, plans, case studies, proposals, spreadsheets, and assessment tools, among other things. Whenever you see the WAV™ symbol in any of our publications, it means bonus materials accompany the book and are available from the Web Added Value™ Download Resource Center at www.jrosspub.com.

Downloads for *Software Engineering* consist of PowerPoint slides available to instructors covering the book chapters, figures and examples.

Software and Software Engineering

Software is omnipresent in the lives of billions of human beings around the globe. Today, humans rely heavily on software-intensive systems. Software runs many aspects of our daily life. It helps us communicate, socialize, and perform daily tasks at work and at home. Most importantly, software is a player in the emerging knowledge-based service economy. However, there are many concerns about the quality and reliability, and hence the trustworthiness, of the software we produce and consume. Existing software is plagued with thousands of defects. Some of the defects are known and have already been detected; others have not manifested and are yet to be uncovered. The defects have caused many disasters, leading to financial losses, physical harm to humans, and life threatening situations. The main reasons for the current state of software technology are the lack of adequately trained software professionals and the lack of tools and techniques that can scale up to the complexities of the needed software. In this chapter, we introduce the concepts of software, software engineering, and the stages in software development. We then present the types of software and their stakeholders. Education and training issues in software engineering and an existing code of ethics for software professionals are discussed. We also present the disciplines related to software engineering and analogies to other engineering disciplines. Finally, we present some pioneers in the field of software engineering and their main contributions.

Learning Outcomes

In this chapter you will learn:
- Historical origins of software, software engineering, and the related disciplines
- Types of software applications and system software
- Stakeholders in software products
- Three Ps in software engineering
- Software engineering as a discipline and its code of ethics and professional practice
- Recurring concepts in software engineering and the desirable software capabilities
- Pioneers in software engineering and their main contributions

1.1 SOFTWARE, SOFTWARE ENGINEERING, AND THE SOFTWARE CRISIS

Software is omnipresent in the lives of billions of human beings. It is an important component of the emerging knowledge-based service economy. Software or computer software consists of the computer program and its related documentation. The word *software* was coined by John Tukey in 1958. However, the theoretical foundations behind the concept of a computer program were established by Alan Turing in the 1930s. The concept of a program as a sequence of steps to solve a problem is a realization of the concept of algorithm, which was introduced by Muhammad Al-Khawarezmi, a 9th century mathematician. An algorithm became concrete when it was programmed by Ada Lovelace, the first computer programmer. A computer program consists of instructions that perform certain tasks on computer hardware. Instructions are written at different levels of closeness to the hardware, ranging from low level instructions written in machine or assembly language to high-level instructions written in high-level programming languages. Documentation plays a crucial role in the success of software and is of interest to the people using the software and to the people developing and maintaining it. User manuals, installation procedures, and operating manuals are written mainly for the software users. They are written in a user-friendly language appropriate to the competency levels of the target users. The documents are crucial for the usability of the software and, hence, are useful for achieving the economic viability and marketability of the software. However, internal developmental documents such as specification, design, and testing documents are written at a level that is appropriate to the people developing, reviewing, and maintaining the software. The timeliness and correctness of the documents are critical over the long term. Software development and maintenance activities form the basis of a steadily growing industry—worth more than $250 billion—and characterizes the emerging knowledge-based economy.

Software engineering is a term that was coined during the October 1968 NATO Software Engineering conference held in Garmisch, Germany. The term was introduced by Friedrich Bauer, the conference chairman. There are many definitions for software engineering. One definition refers to software engineering as the application of a disciplined approach for the development and maintenance of computer software. The Institute of Electrical and Electronics Engineers (IEEE) states that it is software engineering that deals with the establishment and use of sound engineering principles to economically obtain software that is reliable and works efficiently on real machines. This definition touches on both the technical and management aspects involved in software engineering. The technical aspect of this definition refers to the reliability and performance of the target software product, whereas the management aspect refers to the economic feasibility related to both time and money. Software engineering encompasses the use of tools, techniques, and methods that are useful during the execution of the steps needed for the development of the software and its future maintenance.

The NATO conference discussed the software crisis and was characterized by the inability of existing techniques, tools, and processes to deal with the increasing complexity of the needed software. It was identified that the main reasons for the crisis were due to the complexity of the software, changing and misunderstanding of requirements, and the lack of tools and skilled professionals. Consequently, the produced software is of low quality, is not maintainable, and does not meet the stakeholder's requirements. In addition, software projects were frequently running over budget and over time, and many did not deliver a functioning product.

Unfortunately, many of the symptoms of the software crisis are still present. According to the Standish Group, a software market research firm, 17 percent of software projects were complete failures in 2002. Moreover, 50 percent of projects were not completed within the planned schedule, ran over budget, or were missing some of the required features. There are many concerns about the quality and reliability of the software we use. Existing software is plagued with millions of defects. Some of the defects are known and have already been detected; others are yet to be uncovered. The defects have caused many disasters, leading to financial losses, physical harm to humans, and life threatening situations. The software engineering profession is still in its infancy, therefore tools, techniques, standards, and appropriate software engineering education programs at all levels are needed. In the United States alone, it was reported in 2004 that approximately 750 thousand software engineers are employed compared to an estimated 1.5 million practitioners in all other engineering disciplines. It was also reported that most software practitioners do not hold degrees in software engineering. Currently, most people working as software engineers hold either a degree in computer science or computer engineering. It is worth mentioning that the first bachelor program in software engineering was established in the United States as recently as 1996.

1.2 TYPES OF SOFTWARE

There are two categories of software that are currently in use: system software and applications software. **Systems software** typically deals with interfacing with hardware and provides services to **applications software**. Examples of system software include operating systems, language compilers, assemblers, device drivers, debuggers, and networking tools and software. Application software, also referred to as end user software, allows users to perform their tasks. In the following, we list some of the main applications software categories:

- Games and entertainment: Software games for handheld devices, including mobile phones, PC or stand-alone games, and distributed collaborative games.
- Intelligent: Applications that include specialized domain-specific expert systems, mobile agent systems, learning systems, robot vision software, business decision and intelligence software, and mining software.
- Modeling and simulation: Applications that include domain-specific modeling and simulation packages for military, financial, medical, educational, and training uses.

- Real-time: Applications that include industrial plant monitoring and control systems, missile control systems, air traffic control systems, telephony software, and network security software such as firewalls and intrusion detection systems.
- Embedded: Applications that include home appliance controllers, mobile phone software, and vehicle controllers.
- Productivity: Applications that include tools that implement proven methods and techniques to help specific types of users execute their tasks with ease and maximum productivity. For example, AutoCAD software facilitates architects and engineers, Rational Rose aids software developers in performing their tasks, project management software packages allow project managers to perform their tasks efficiently, and word processing tools help users produce thorough and accurate documentation. Other types of software in this category, also known as information worker software, are time and resource management software, data management software, and distributed collaborative software.
- Enterprise: Applications that include business workflow management software, customer relation management software, and supply chain management software.
- Web-based: Applications that include content management software, web publishing software, electronic commerce software, web services, web portal software, and web browsers.
- Educational: Applications that include school and university management, online and distance learning, training management, and educational software for children.
- Multimedia: Applications that include software for video, image and sound editing and management, 3D and animation, and virtual reality.
- Domain-specific: Applications that include domain-specific software systems such as banking, finance and stocks, accounting, medical, airline reservation, hospital management, and human resource management.

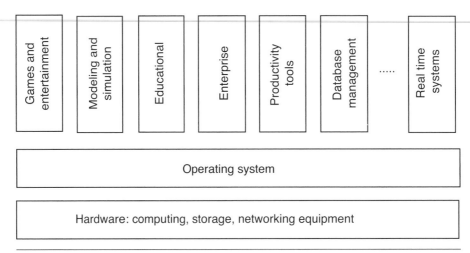

Figure 1.1 A layered view of hardware and software

It is considered that systems software provides the proper interface through which applications software makes use of the information and other hardware resources to provide services or functions to respective application users. Figure 1.1 illustrates the layering of hardware and the two types of software products.

1.3 GENERIC STAGES IN SOFTWARE DEVELOPMENT

As stated earlier, software engineering encompasses the use of a disciplined and systematic approach for the development and maintenance of computer software. The goals of software engineering are to deal with the software complexities, increase the reliability, and enhance the quality of the produced software.

One of the main features of a disciplined approach is to deal with complexity in a staged manner. In the initial stages, the software is tackled in different phases and at higher levels of abstraction. In the subsequent phases, the software is tackled at lower levels of abstraction by providing more details so that a proper implementation is obtained in the second stage. This process is also called top-down and stepwise refinement.

The three generic stages of software development and maintenance activities consist of the (1) **definition stage**, (2) **implementation stage**, and (3) **maintenance stage**. The definition stage is comprised of the **requirements phase** and the **specifications phase** in which user requirements are collected and analyzed to obtain a formal software specification. During the implementation stage, at a lower level of abstraction, the **design phase** refines the specifications to obtain a basis for a concrete implementation of the software. Coding of the design is performed and then tested for conformance to the specifications. The maintenance stage deals with software change requests to correct software errors, adapt, or expand the software. The software changes could involve a rework of the requirements, specifications, design, and implementation followed by a complete or regression testing to ensure the proper implementation of the needed software changes. The details of the generic stages are discussed in Chapter 2 in the context of specific industry-proven software development life cycle models. Figure 1.2 illustrates the three generic stages for software development and maintenance, and their respective phases.

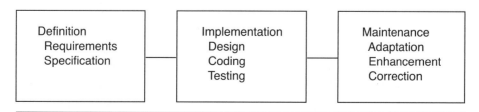

Figure 1.2 The three generic stages for software development and maintenance

1.4 SOFTWARE ERRORS

Existing software is plagued with a significant number of errors. Some of the errors are known because they have been discovered by the software developers or reported by users. However, there are errors that are yet to be discovered. The errors have eluded discovery during testing and will probably manifest only after the software is deployed. The exact number and severity of the errors is unknown. Reported software failures reveal that the unidentified errors can be safety-critical, affecting the physical well being of individuals, and business-critical, affecting the financial well being of individuals and institutions. Moreover, many software companies, to avoid embarrassment and a negative reputation, do not publicize the errors. In an article on software risks published in 2000, Peter Neumann states that risks have monotonically become worse both relative to increased vulnerabilities and threats and their consequent domestic and worldwide social implications with respect to national stability, electronic commerce, personal well-being, and many other factors.

Software errors can be traced back to the various phases of the software development process. In a taxonomy of software errors reported by Beizer in 1990, approximately 25% of the errors are requirements and specifications, 25% are design, 10% are implementation, 10% are integration, 25% are data-related, and 3% are testing. The remaining are unspecified errors. It has also been reported that, as a general rule of thumb, if it takes $1 to fix a bug during the development phases, it will cost $100 or more to fix the same error after the software has been deployed. In a recent study published by the National Institute of Standards and Technology in 2002, it is estimated that if it costs $1 to fix a defect during the requirements phase, it will cost $90 to fix it during testing and $440 to fix it during operations.

Requirements and specifications errors include incorrectly captured or missing requirements, incomplete functions or features, and input/output domain specifications. If the errors are not discovered early in the development process, they lead to expensive maintenance or, possibly, even project failures. Moreover, missing functionality in a safety-critical system could lead to human harm and other serious problems. For example, a specification error in a flight simulator for pilot training led to a crash and the death of the pilot when he was faced with a situation that was overlooked in the training simulator.

Design errors include errors in the specification of the algorithms and their related data structures. A design error in a banking software application led to the duplication of transfer instructions, resulting in the transfer of billions of dollars and a substantial cost incurred to recover the transferred amounts.

Coding errors include memory access violation, buffer overflows, arithmetic overflow or underflow, loss of precision, typographical errors, or data flow-related errors. A coding error in AT&T telephony switch software in 1990 led to a breakdown in long distance communications in many states and resulted in the loss of hundreds of millions of dollars. Another coding error led to the self-destruction of Ariane-5, a satellite carrier rocket, resulting in the loss of $7 billion. More dramatic is the Scud missile failure, during the Gulf War, due to an arithmetic instruction coding error, resulting in the loss of 28 lives and the injury of hundreds.

Integration errors include parameter mismatches, run-time stack errors, compatibility errors, interoperability problems, and timing and synchronization problems. For example, it was reported that many space shuttle missions were delayed due to software/hardware interfacing problems. Data-related errors include errors in data definition, input file data, and data access and handling. Finally, testing errors involve erroneous test cases leading to the wrongful flagging of an error or the misinterpretation of the test results and, thus, reaching an incorrect test verdict.

Known software errors lead to vulnerabilities that could be exploited by computer criminals. The security of computer information systems is now affected by the security of the software running on the systems. A taxonomy of known software security errors is available and is updated regularly.

A disciplined approach to software development should ensure that errors are detected and dealt with early in the development process. The long-term economics of software reveals that spending more time early in the process helps reduce the cost of software maintenance in the long term.

1.5 SOFTWARE BEHAVIOR, STRUCTURE, AND ARCHITECTURE

Like any system, a software system can be viewed as a static and dynamic entity that evolves over time after it has been subjected to both internal and external events from its executing environment.

The fixed set of instructions that makes a program provides the static structure of the software. This aspect of the software can be modeled at different levels of abstractions. Flowcharts can be used at the implementation level, structured charts or class diagrams can be used at the design level, and use case diagrams can be used at the requirements specifications level.

When subjected to internal events from timers and interrupts or external inputs from other systems, devices, or users, the software behaves according to the behavioral specification by changing its internal state and by triggering the appropriate internal or external events. Software is mostly state-oriented. The reaction of the software to the various events depends on the state at which the software exists when the event occurs. All possible software reactions determine the behavior of the software. Software **behavior** can be modeled by diagrams, including state, sequence, timing, and activity diagrams and Petri nets. The diagrams and models can be used at different levels of abstraction. Software behavior reflects the dynamic aspects of a software system.

Finally, the architectural aspect of software addresses some of the non-functional issues such as robustness, performance, resiliency, and security. Solutions affecting the software architecture include concurrency, distribution, synchronization, and multithreading. This aspect is

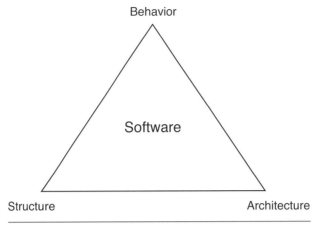

Figure 1.3 The software triad

gaining more attention because one of the main reasons for software failures is the misunderstanding or the lack of handling of the non-functional requirements affecting the software architecture. Software **architecture** can be modeled by package and component diagrams. Figure 1.3 illustrates the three aspects of the software triad.

To gain a better understanding of the software we develop, the behavioral, structural, and architectural issues of the software must be modeled and analyzed. The three aspects of software should be part of any disciplined approach to software development.

1.6 SOFTWARE STAKEHOLDERS

Software products are complex to develop and maintain because of the many internal interactions within the software development group and the interactions with the external environment, including the various software stakeholders. Software development **stakeholders** are those people who can affect or be affected by the software product that is to be developed (see Figure 1.4).

The software stakeholders include:

- Software developers: People involved in the development of the software. A software developer might be involved in the various phases of the software development project, including requirements, specification, design, coding, and testing of the software.
- Software maintainers: People involved in the post delivery and installation of the software, including maintenance, deployment, and configuration management.
- Technical writers: People involved in writing the various technical and user documentation that are needed to ensure the deployment of highly usable and maintainable software systems and applications.

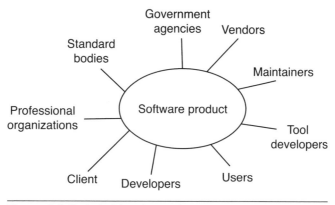

Figure 1.4 Stakeholders in a software product

- Software vendors: People responsible for marketing and selling the software application and who use various distribution channels.
- Software users: Intended users of the software who can be classified according to the functionality offered to them and based on their roles or responsibilities. Possible types include normal, administrative or privileged, executive management, and maintenance users.
- Government bodies: Entities that might set and enforce rules and regulations to which the software must conform. Examples of such government bodies include environmental agencies, health agencies, and financial agencies.
- Professional organizations and societies: Entities involved in overseeing the state of the discipline and its body of knowledge and in setting and maintaining the **code of ethics** for the profession. Moreover, professional organizations help in the life-long and continuous development of software professionals through administering professional certifications and organizing conferences, workshops, and other continuing education programs.
- Standards bodies: Entities that are setting standards for software development, software environments, and software/hardware interfaces. In addition, standard bodies might be involved in setting application or context-specific standards in areas that include health, banking, and environment, and, possibly, working in tandem with governmental agencies and professional organizations and societies.
- Tool developers and vendors: People who develop and maintain software development tools and integrated development environments to facilitate the production of high-quality software products. The tools have an influence on the quality of the software produced.
- Clients: People who pay for the software that is developed. They are interested mainly in the success of the project, both financially and technically. They have a substantial

Table 1.1 The stakeholders in a banking software

Stakeholder	Description
Client	Bank (paying for the software)
Developer	Software Company X (selected to develop the software)
Users	Bank customers having online access
Technical writers	Can be employees of the bank or the software company
Government bodies	Banking regulations related to privacy protection
Standard bodies	Basel II for IT risk management
Professional organizations	Banker's association
Software maintainers	Can be the bank, the software company, or a third party

stake in faithfully reflecting the users' needs while ensuring a return on investment in terms of users' productivity.

The specific list of project stakeholders for a particular application depends on the complexity of the needed software and its application domain. For example, in a context in which a bank needs to outsource the development of a web-based application to provide value-added services to its customers, the stakeholders of this banking software might include those shown in Table 1.1.

1.7 RELATED DISCIPLINES

Software is typically developed by teams of various sizes. The composition of a team depends on the size, type, and complexity of the software. The team must possess expertise in the various areas of software development and must include an expert in the particular application domain of the software. In addition, software engineering as a discipline is related to various other disciplines including:

- Mathematics: A mathematics background is needed if the software product is meant to solve complex engineering problems. In addition, regardless of the type of applications, a background in discrete mathematics is useful in producing efficient and optimized software designs.
- Computer science: The study and development of algorithms, and the analysis of their complexities, play an important role in the selection or design of an appropriate algorithm and its data structures when the software is in the design phase. The relationship of the field of computer science to software engineering is analogous to that of the field of chemistry to chemical engineering.

- Computer engineering: A computer engineering background might be needed for the successful development of some types of software products. The proper interfacing and synchronization between software systems and hardware components is crucial for embedded software, real-time, and systems software such as operating systems. Hardware/software co-design deals with making the appropriate and efficient balance and tradeoffs between what can be implemented in software or hardware.
- Psychology: Skills related to the understanding of human behaviors and their learning levels help in developing highly-usable software products. Many software companies advertise for jobs requiring degrees in human/computer interactions and psychology.
- Economics: A background in the economics of the product and the financial feasibility of the software product being developed is crucial for the success of the product.
- Management: Skills in varying levels of management are needed at different phases in a software development environment. The software project manager must be able to manage the complexity of a software project, including the technical and human resource aspects of the project complexities. A software project manager is often involved in conflict resolution, human resource management, quality management, and risk management. In addition, software developers must have some basics of management. For example, time management skills are needed as a precondition for the successful completion of the tasks at hand.
- Knowledge of the application domain: For a successful analysis of the software requirements and the production of accurate specifications, the software analyst must be knowledgeable in the application domain of the product being developed. Examples of specific application domains include banking, financial, health, insurance, travel, education, gaming, simulation, training, inventory, and supply chain management.

Figure 1.5 shows the various disciplines related to software engineering.

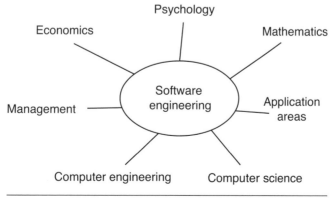

Figure 1.5 Software engineering and related disciplines

1.8 SOFTWARE ENGINEERING EDUCATION, TRAINING, AND CERTIFICATION

Software engineering is a relatively young discipline. Progress in the discipline is continuous and progresses at an accelerated pace. In addition to a formal undergraduate education in software engineering, the software engineering professional should always aim to upgrade the knowledge and skill set in the various areas of the discipline. Many venues can be pursued to achieve continuous professional development: obtaining a graduate certificate or graduate degree in software engineering; attending software engineering conferences, workshops, tutorials, and short courses; studying vendor-specific software engineering productivity tools; and securing certification as a software engineering professional.

The certified software development professional (**CSDP**) is a professional certification for software engineers managed by the IEEE Computer Society. Unlike other vendor-specific software certification programs, the CSDP is comprehensive and covers most of the areas of software engineering.

Various software engineering conferences are held worldwide. The largest and most established ones are the IEEE International Conference on Software Engineering (ICSE) with all the parallel workshops and tutorials, and the International Computer Software and Applications Conference (COMPSAC) held annually in Chicago since 1977. In addition, there are many regional software engineering conferences in Europe and Australasia.

The body of knowledge of the software engineering discipline defines the areas around which software engineering curricula must be built. This body of knowledge was developed by the collective efforts of hundreds of software researchers and practitioners in both industry and academia.

1.9 CODE OF ETHICS AND PROFESSIONAL PRACTICE

The software engineering code of ethics and professional practice was developed and recommended by an IEEE-CS/ACM joint task force. The committee consisted of members from academia, industry, and government. The code addresses the expectations of the society from the software professionals and vice versa, the expectations of the professionals from each other and from themselves, and the expectations regarding the quality of the products they produce.

The code contains a short version consisting of eight guiding principles. The eight principles of the code are clustered into four categories: the public, peers and self, the product, and the profession:

- Public
    1. Software engineers shall act consistently with the public interest.
    2. Software engineers shall act in a manner that is in the best interests of their client and employer, consistent with the public interest.

- Product
  3. Software engineers shall ensure that their products and related modifications meet the highest professional standards possible.
- Profession
  4. Software engineers shall advance the integrity and reputation of the profession consistent with the public interest.
- Peers and self
  5. Software engineers shall maintain integrity and independence in their professional judgment.
  6. Software engineering managers and leaders shall subscribe to and promote an ethical approach to the management of software development and maintenance.
  7. Software engineers shall be fair to and supportive of their colleagues.
  8. Software engineers shall participate in lifelong learning regarding the practice of their profession and shall promote an ethical approach to the practice of the profession.

A full version of the code is also given and provides details on how the eight principles can be implemented.

1.10 PROJECT, PROCESS, AND PEOPLE

Software development involves the participation of people in project teams for the purpose of developing a software product using sound and proven processes. On the other hand, as stated earlier, software engineering is related to the use of a disciplined approach to software development. The three cornerstones needed to produce a successful software product are people, projects, and processes (three Ps). Processes are part of a software life cycle model or software methodology. Project tasks are developed based on the adopted process model or methodology. People are assigned to specific tasks of the project and are adequately managed to successfully complete the assigned tasks on time and within budget. The developed product must possess good qualities guaranteed by the processes used to develop it. Failure in any of the three cornerstones leads to the partial or even the total failure of the product. For example, failure in project management leads to late and over budget projects. Failure in recruiting the most appropriate people for the project tasks lead to a low-quality product. Finally, failure in the selection and adoption of the most relevant process model and software development methodology also affects the quality of the delivered product. The proper use and management of the three cornerstones of a software product plays a vital role in the success of the product in terms of its desirable qualities and functionalities. Figure 1.6 shows the three cornerstones of a software product.

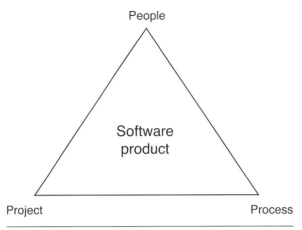

People

Software
product

Project   Process

Figure 1.6 The three cornerstones of a software
product

1.11 DESIRABLE SOFTWARE CAPABILITIES

The software capabilities determine the overall quality of the software product. Unfortunately, there is no quantitative assessment of such overall quality. However, the desirable capabilities should contribute positively to the overall software quality. When developing software, the desirable functionality of the product aimed for should always be kept in mind. Knowing the capabilities in advance helps promote more effective practices in software development and maintenance. The features that concern the developer or maintainer are flexibility, interoperability, maintainability, portability, reusability, and testability. The features that are more relevant to the users are availability, correctness, efficiency, integrity, reliability, scalability, and usability.

User-centered software capabilities:

Availability is the degree to which the software system is available when its services are required. It can be quantified as the ratio of the actual availability of the software services to the expected availability during the same period.

Correctness is the degree to which the software meets its requirements specifications. Correctness is affected positively by the completeness, consistency, and traceability of the software. Accuracy is a qualitative assessment of correctness.

Efficiency is the degree to which the software system performs its functions using the least amount of computational and memory resources.

Integrity is the degree to which the software system prevents unauthorized access to information or programs. Both integrity and availability contribute to the security of the software system.

Reliability is the ability of a software system to perform its function under stated conditions and for a specified period of time. Reliability can be quantified using the mean time between failures. Reliability is affected positively by error recoverability and fault tolerance, modularity and simplicity, and other quality factors.

Scalability is the ability of the software system to handle a growing number of user requests up to a certain specified limit.

Usability is the degree of ease with which the software system can be used. Usability is positively affected by learnability, readability, understandability, and other quality factors.

Developer-centered software capabilities:

Flexibility is the measure of how easily the software system can be extended or expanded. Flexibility is positively affected by the simplicity, generality, and modularity of the software, and other quality factors.

Interoperability is the ability of the software system to exchange information with other external systems.

Maintainability is the measure of how easily the software system can be modified to fix errors, to improve its functions, or to adapt it to different environments. Maintainability is positively affected by adaptability, simplicity, modularity and traceability, and other quality factors.

Portability is the ease with which the software system can be moved to a different software or hardware environment or platform. Portability is positively affected by generality and modularity and other quality factors.

Reusability is the measure of how easily a software component can be reused in the same software system or utilized to build new systems. Reusability is positively affected by generality and modularity and other quality factors.

Testability is the measure of how easily the test cases can be selected and executed to test the software. Testability is positively affected by modularity, simplicity and traceability, and other quality factors.

Chapter 5 discusses the recurring concepts in software design that will make the desired software capabilities possible.

1.12 PIONEERS IN SOFTWARE AND SOFTWARE ENGINEERING

Many individuals made significant contributions to the development of the fields of software and software engineering. Following, the names of the individual researchers and practitioners are listed along with their main contributions:

Alan Kay is known for his pioneering work on window-based graphical user interfaces. He is also known for coining the term *object-oriented programming* in 1966.

Ali Mili contributed to the formalization of software fault tolerance that is currently a major concern for developing secure software systems.

Barry Boehm contributed to software engineering economics and software metrics. He also introduced the spiral model for software development.

Bill Joy contributed to the development of the Unix operating system and the Java programming language.

Brian Kernighan and Dennis Ritchie were instrumental in developing the Unix operating system and the C programming language.

C. A. R. Hoare introduced the concepts of assertions and program proof of correctness, designed and analyzed well-known algorithms, and developed communicating sequential processes, a formal language for the specification of concurrent processes.

David Parnas introduced the concepts of information hiding, software interfaces, and software modularity. He also contributed to software engineering education and the ethical responsibilities of a software engineer.

Donald Knuth is known for the design of many well-known computer algorithms and the use of rigorous mathematical techniques for the formal analysis of the complexity of algorithms.

Edsger Dijkstra introduced the concept of structured programming and carried out in-depth studies of the problems of concurrency and synchronization needed in complex distributed systems.

Erich Gamma with Richard Helm, Ralph Johnson, and John Vlissides introduced the concept of object-oriented design patterns to facilitate software design reuse.

Fred Brooks contributed to the development of the OS/360 operating system software. He is also known for introducing the mythical man-month in software project management.

Friedrich Bauer introduced the use of stacks for the evaluation of expressions in programming language compilers. He also contributed to the development of the ALGOL programming language. Moreover, he coined the term *software engineering* at the 1968 NATO conference held in Germany.

Grace Hopper contributed extensively to the first compiler and the COBOL programming language in 1959.

Grady Booch is known for his method for object-oriented analysis and design and his co-development of the unified modeling language (UML).

John Backus is well known for the invention of FORTRAN, compiler optimization, and the Backus-Naur Form for the formal description of programming language syntax.

Michael Fagan contributed extensively to the area of software inspection.

Niklaus Wirth introduced the Pascal programming language and other languages and contributed to the idea of decomposition and stepwise refinement.

Ole-Johan Dahl and Kristen Nygaard introduced the Simula language, which was the first object-oriented programming language.

Peter Naur is known for his contributions to the creation of the ALGOL programming language and the introduction of formal syntax description language.

Tom DeMarco and Edward Yourdon introduced the structured analysis and design approach for specifying and designing software systems.

Watts Humphrey is known for his work on the capability maturity model developed by the software engineering institute and the personal software process.

Winston Royce contributed the well-known model for the management of large software systems, which was later named the Waterfall model.

The *Journal of Systems and Software* publishes an annual article that includes an assessment of the top software systems and engineering scholars and institutions. The annual assessment considers the most published scholars in six software engineering journals during a sliding window of five years. The first and the last five-year assessment covering the years 1993-1997 and 2001-2005, appeared in 1998 and 2007, respectively. The nine scholars who appeared five or more times in the nine assessments published so far, along with their affiliations and areas of research expertise, are listed below in decreasing order of appearance frequency:

Robert Glass, Computing Trends, is a software visionary interested in strengthening discipline, software practice, and project failures.

Barbara Kitchenham, Keele University, specializes in empirical methods in software engineering, software cost estimation, and software metrics.

Richard Lai, LaTrobe University, specializes in web services, component-based software engineering, protocol engineering, and software testing.

Kassem Saleh, Kuwait University, specializes in distributed systems, communications software engineering, software testing, and information systems security.

T. Y. Chen, Swinburne University of Technology, specializes in software testing, debugging, and software quality.

Victor Basili, University of Maryland, specializes in empirical software engineering and model building.

Johnny Wong, Iowa State University, specializes in system and network security, information assurance, and multimedia and medical applications.

Jeff Tian, Southern Methodist University, specializes in testing and quality improvement, measurement and risk management, and web-quality engineering.

Khaled El Emam, University of Ottawa, specializes in software measurements and quality improvement.

1.13 ANALOGY TO OTHER ENGINEERING DISCIPLINES

Although software engineering is a relatively young profession, it has many similarities to other engineering disciplines. For example, the well-established building engineering discipline is

Table 1.2 Analogy between software and building development

Phase	Software as a product	Building as a product
Requirements specification	Requirements specifications	Owner's requirements
Design	Design	Design
Implementation	Coding or construction	Construction
Testing	Testing and integration	Pre-delivery approval
Maintenance	Maintenance	Maintenance

defined as the use of engineering principles and technology in building design and construction. Analogously, software engineering encompasses the use of a disciplined (engineering) approach to software development. The phases involved in software development are analogous to those phases used in building development. The generic phases include requirements specifications, design, construction, and testing. In addition, similar to software products, once the building is handed over, the maintenance phase starts. Table 1.2 summarizes the similarities between the development and maintenance of software and a building.

One distinct difference between software and hardware products is related to the nature of and need for the maintenance activities. In software, the developed program does not change over time. The software remains the same and performs the same functions every time. However, in hardware devices and physical entities, including buildings or electromechanical products, defects are introduced over time. They wear out or degrade due to environmental and external reasons such as weather conditions, humidity, and excessive use. In the case of software products, known or unknown defects exist the moment the software is initially deployed in the market. Defects are not introduced because of usage over time. We say that software defects are uncovered during the software's operation. It is important to note that if an application does not start or run as usual, it is not because it has changed. This malfunction can be caused by the wearing out or degradation of the storage medium in which the software resides. Under certain circumstances, a virus could destructively alter the behavior of an application and prevent it from starting properly.

1.14 OVERVIEW OF THIS BOOK

Chapter 1 has served as a summary of the growth and change in software. The remaining chapters offer important information for anyone pursuing this career path.

Chapter 2 presents some well-known, industry-proven life cycle models for software development and maintenance that are used to deal with the complexity and quality issues of the software we produce.

Chapter 3 deals with the development of both functional and non-functional software requirements and the related deliverable documentation.

Chapter 4 discusses the specification of software requirements using various formal specification techniques and formalisms for the modeling of data, behavior, and processes.

Chapter 5 introduces the basics of software design. It discusses the various desirable features of both high-level and detailed designs. In addition, it discusses the graphical user interface design and its features.

Chapter 6 presents concepts in object-oriented design, software design patterns and design reusability, and software architecture.

Chapter 7 deals with software implementation issues, including coding styles, software libraries and reuse, fault tolerance and exception handling, and writing secure software.

Chapter 8 discusses the various techniques for testing software. It includes techniques for unit level testing, system level testing, and integration testing.

Chapter 9 discusses software maintenance issues, including maintenance processes, maintenance management, configuration management, change management, and software maintenance techniques.

Chapter 10 discusses software project management issues, including risk management, metrics and cost estimation, scheduling, tracking, and documenting the software project management plan.

SUMMARY

Software engineering is a disciplined approach for the development of high-quality software products given both time and budget constraints. This disciplined approach consists of techniques, methods, standards, guidelines, and practices that can be used during the software development process. The main objective of software engineering is to allow the software practitioners to deal with the increasing complexity of needed software products. There are various stakeholders in software products. The proper capturing and mediation of the various, and sometimes conflicting, stakeholders' concerns is an interesting challenge to deal with in software engineering. Software systems can exhibit complex behaviors and structures, and, frequently, require solid architectures to deal with concerns such as scalability and performance. Desirable software capabilities, including developers- and users-centered capabilities were discussed. Software engineering is a relatively young profession for which many standards continue to be developed. A code of ethics for software practitioners, the body of knowledge for software engineering programs, and professional certification for software developers have been developed by professional computing organizations, including the IEEE and the ACM. Pioneers in the field of software systems and software engineering were introduced. Also, the related fields to software engineering and an analogy to other engineering disciplines were presented.

KEY TERMS

applications software	efficiency	requirements phase
architecture	flexibility	reusability
availability	implementation stage	scalability
behavior	integrity	software engineering
code of ethics	interoperability	specification phase
correctness	maintainability	stakeholders
CSDP	maintenance stage	systems software
definition stage	portability	testability
design phase	reliability	usability

REVIEW QUESTIONS

1. List two definitions for software engineering.
2. List the differences between software engineering and software development.
3. List five types of productivity software tools.
4. List the stages of software development and maintenance and their respective phases.
5. What is involved in the maintenance stage?
6. List three software pioneers and their main contributions to software engineering.
7. List the principles of the code of ethics that deal with the need to be up to date in the software field.
8. Define three of the software capabilities that are more relevant to the software users.
9. List the possible stakeholders in chemical factory control software.
10. Discuss why architectural considerations are important in software products.

EXERCISES

1. Which of the principles of the code of ethics deals with user's privacy concerns? How?
2. Search on the Internet for software faults that led to the loss of human lives. Discuss the problem and how it could have been prevented.
3. Is a software fault the responsibility of one developer? Why? Discuss your arguments.
4. List the categories of software security errors.
5. Provide an analogy between software behavior, structure and architecture, and bridge behavior, structure, and architecture.
6. List the areas of the CSDP certification.
7. List the main areas of the software engineering body of knowledge.

BIBLIOGRAPHY

Books

Beizer, B. *Software Testing Techniques*, 2d ed., Boston, MA: International Thomson Computer Press, 1990.

Booch, G. *Object-Oriented Analysis and Design with Applications*, 3d ed., Reading, MA: Addison-Wesley Professional, 2007.

Broy, M., and E. Denert, eds. *Software Pioneers: Contributions to Software Engineering*, Berlin: Springer, 2002.

Glass, R. *Computing Catastrophes*, Seattle, WA: Computing Trends, 1991.

Hoffman, D., and D. Weiss, eds. *Software Fundamentals: Collected Papers by David Parnas*, Reading, MA: Addison-Wesley, 2001.

Humphrey, W.S. *A Discipline for Software Engineering*, Reading, MA: Addison-Wesley, 1995.

Marciniak, J. J. *Encyclopedia of Software Engineering*, 2d ed., New York: Wiley & Sons 2002.

Meyer, B. *Object-Oriented Software Construction*, 2d ed., Englewood Cliffs, NJ: Prentice-Hall, 1997

Pfleeger, S. L. *Software Engineering: Theory and Practice*, 2d ed., Englewood Cliffs, NJ: Prentice-Hall, 2001.

Pressman, R. S. *Software Engineering: A Practitioner's Approach*, 6th ed., New York: McGraw-Hill, 2004.

Proceedings of the Workshop on the Future of Software Engineering held in 2000 in conjunction with the 22d International Conference on Software Engineering.

Schach, S. R. *Object-Oriented and Classical Software Engineering with UML and C++*, 6th ed., New York: McGraw-Hill, 2004.

Sommerville, I. *Software Engineering*, 7th ed., Reading, MA: Addison-Wesley, 2005.

Papers

Glass, R. L., and T. Y. Chen. "An assessment of systems and software engineering scholars and institutions," *Journal of Systems and Software*, vol. 76, (2005) 91–97.

Gotterbarn, D., K. Miller, and S. Rogerson. "Computer society and ACM approve software engineering code of ethics," *IEEE Computer*, (October 1999) 84-88.

Gurchiek, K. "Influential men and women in software," *Crosstalk: The Journal of Defense Software Engineering*, (December 1999) 26–27.

Meyer, B. "Software engineering in the academy," *IEEE Computer*, (May 2001) 28–35.

National Institute of Standards and Technology. *The Economic Impacts of Inadequate Infrastructure for Software Testing*, Gaithersburg, MD, 2002.

Naur, P. and B. Randell, eds. Software Engineering: Report on a Conference sponsored by the NATO Science Committee, Garmisch, Germany, (October 1968).

Neumann, P. "Risks in retrospect," *CACM*, vol. 43, no. 7, (July 2000).

Parnas, D. "Software aspects of strategic defense systems," *CACM*, vol. 28, no. 12, (December 1985) 1326–1335.

Vaughan-Nichols, S. "Building better software with better tools," *IEEE Computer*, (September 2003) 12–14.

Standards

IEEE Standard Glossary of Software Engineering Terminology, IEEE Standard 610.12–1990.

Software Development Life Cycle Models

To manage the increasing complexity of software project activities and to increase the quality of the produced software, industry-proven models for software development and maintenance must be adopted and followed. Software engineering **life cycle models** provide systematic and well structured approaches that software development organizations can follow. A model includes a high-level definition of the phases. At a more detailed level, the activities, techniques, methodologies, and deliverables that are associated with each phase of the model are identified. A software development model should be flexible and adapt to different types and complexities of software applications. Well-known models that are adopted by the software industry are supported by tools that facilitate their effective use. The level and depth of adaptation of a model depends greatly on the type and complexity of the application that is to be developed and the maturity of the software development firm. Maturity assessment methodologies for life cycle models and implemented processes are developed and used to classify the development organization as well as for the purpose of process improvement.

Learning Outcomes

In this chapter you will learn:
- Software development life cycle models and their importance
- Pre-development and ongoing life cycle activities
- Phases, activities, and deliverables of a life cycle model
- Waterfall model and its variations
- Object-oriented software development model
- Rationale Unified Process model (RUP) and the Unified Modeling Language (UML)
- Software engineering standards
- Assessment of quality and capability maturity of a software development organization

2.1 LIFE CYCLE MODELS

A **software development life cycle model** defines the framework under which a software product is going to be developed. A life cycle model defines, at a high-level, the phases that the product under development will go through. At a lower level, the activities involved in each of the model phases and their respective deliverables are identified.

The development of a life cycle model and its constituent phases, activities, and deliverables is the result of the efforts of various stakeholders from industry and academia. A successful model is one that has been adopted by the software industry and has undergone many modifications and enhancements to improve its efficiency and applicability. An ideal life cycle model is generic, flexible, adaptable, and scalable. Depending on the size of the adopting software development company, its maturity level, and the complexity of the software to be developed, a life cycle model can be tailored to suit the particular needs of the company and its development team. The model should be flexible to allow a different emphasis to be placed on activities and deliverables of the model, depending on its application context. Finally, the model must have the capacity to scale up to large and complex software development projects.

There are many industrial-strength and popular software development models that have been used to develop software products of varying complexities and in a wide variety of application domains. The models include the waterfall or SDLC, the prototyping model, the spiral model, the object-oriented model, the incremental and iterative model, the extreme model, and the component-based model.

Prior to embarking on the activities and phases of the software life cycle development model, there are some pre-development activities and deliverables that must be performed to enable the proper startup of the software development project. Again, the need and the extent of the pre-development activities depend on the complexity and type of software being developed. For a software system to be implemented as a part of a complete system, including software, hardware, and people, the allocation of functions to the software component of the system and the interactions and boundaries between the software and other system elements must be clearly identified.

There are activities that do not belong specifically to a particular phase and that must be performed during the various phases of the life cycle model. The activities are also referred to as **umbrella** or ongoing activities. They are related to project management, risk management, quality assurance, verification, validation and reviews, configuration management, and software documentation.

2.2 PRE-DEVELOPMENT ACTIVITIES AND DELIVERABLES

Before starting the activities of the software development life cycle, important prerequisite pre-development activities must be completed. The pre-development activities include activities related to concept exploration, system allocation, software allocation, and initial project management activities.

Concept exploration activities start with the identification of new ideas and the various stakeholders' needs. Alternative approaches to address the new idea or needs are then investigated and documented. Both technical and economic feasibility assessments are performed for each of the alternative approaches. Finally, a formal statement of need is refined and documented.

The system allocation activities begin with an analysis of the functions described in the statement of need. The allocation of the functions on the three system elements—software, hardware, and people—is performed. This allocation is based on both feasibility and performance assessments of the needed functions. Some functions might be performed more efficiently by software, others by hardware or people. System allocation activities lead to the development of a system architecture in which boundaries and interfaces between the various system elements are clearly identified.

The software allocation activities begin with the identified software functions obtained after completing the system allocation activities. The software functions are analyzed in terms of the feasibility of developing them in-house, outsourcing them, procuring them as off-the-shelf packages, or adapting and reusing existing software. A document outlining how the identified software functions will be obtained is developed as a result of the software allocation activities.

The project management activities needed prior to starting the development phases culminate in an initial **project management plan**. Initially, a life cycle model is adopted for the project. The activities, milestones, and deliverables of the initial project plan are specified according to the selected life cycle model. Software estimation techniques are used to estimate the effort needed to develop the software functions. Risks are identified and prioritized, and a plan to deal with them is developed. Appropriate human, financial, and physical resources are specified for each of the identified project plan activities. Moreover, metrics, documentation, and quality requirements are defined so that metrics collection, documentation writing, and quality assurance reviews can start early in the development phases.

Table 2.1 summarizes the deliverables of the pre-development activities needed prior to starting the phases of a software development model.

Table 2.1 Pre-development activities and deliverables

Activity type	Deliverables
Concept exploration	Statement of need 　Alternatives and feasibility assessments
System allocation	Hardware, personnel, and software requirements System interfaces requirements
Software allocation	Requirements for reused or off-the-shelf software
Project management 　Initiation 　Planning	Metrics specification Selected and adapted life cycle model specification 　Phases and deliverables Initial project plan document 　Estimation, risk planning, resource allocation, and scheduling

2.3 WATERFALL MODEL DEVELOPMENT PHASES, ACTIVITIES, AND DELIVERABLES

The System Development Life Cycle (SDLC) model, also called the **waterfall model**, is one of the most popular development models used in the software industry. The original version of this model was first presented by Winston Royce in 1970. Royce described a model structured around phases and argued that the sequential nature of the model is unrealistic and flawed. He stated that iterations are needed after each phase to deal with corrections before proceeding to the subsequent phase. The structured and sequential nature of the model he presented, and then criticized, was later called the waterfall model for software development. The phases of the model include requirements analysis, design, implementation, testing and integration, and operations and maintenance.

Analysis

The **analysis phase** includes the requirements and specifications activities. The main activities involved in this phase include the definition of both functional and non-functional requirements, the definition of the various interfaces between external entities and the software function to be developed, and a prioritization of the identified software requirements. The main deliverables of the analysis phase are the software requirements specifications document, the acceptance test plan document, and the scope and vision document. A revised project plan may also be needed to deal with newly-discovered risks or modified software functions.

As a result of the analysis phase activities, the functional and non-functional software requirements are well defined and agreed upon by the various software stakeholders. The deliverables of this phase are considered binding documents that guide the rest of the software development activities. It is imperative to spend enough time in this phase to ensure that all aspects of the software are considered, including constraints, assumptions, functionalities, user needs, developmental context and environment, risks, quality requirements, among many other aspects. Studies have shown that most of the serious software errors are those errors that are not captured during the analysis phase. Fixing errors originating from the analysis phase is costly if the errors are not discovered until subsequent phases or during the software operations. Therefore, the deliverables of this phase must be carefully reviewed and verified (tested) for completeness, correctness, and consistency among other quality requirements.

Design

Once the deliverables of the analysis phase are reviewed and accepted by the appropriate stakeholders, the **design phase** is initiated. The design activities include the high-level architectural, database, interface, and detailed designs. The main deliverables of the design phase include the high-level design and the detailed design documents. Design documents are reviewed for quality, completeness, and correctness with respect to the software requirements specifications document.

The high-level architectural design concentrates on the identification of software modules and their interfaces. In addition, concerns related to design robustness, scalability, security, fault-tolerance, and testability are addressed in the high-level design.

The detailed design document provides details on each of the modules identified in the high-level design. The details include the data structures and algorithms needed to implement each module.

The database design presents a detailed description of the database schema needed to support the high-level and detailed design. The database design considers the data model described in the software requirements specifications document of the analysis phase.

The interface design consists of the design of the graphical user interface components and artifacts needed to support the human interaction with the software system. In addition, all interfaces between the system and other external software and hardware systems, components, and devices are clearly designed.

Building executable design models and prototypes allows the designer to automate the verification of the design. This eventually leads to software designs of better quality. In addition, prototyping designs allows experimentation with various design alternatives and the selection of the most suitable design.

Implementation

Once the design deliverables are finalized and approved by the various stakeholders, the activities of the **implementation phase** start. The main activity of this phase is the transformation of the high-level design into an executable code. The code is developed according to the coding standards adopted by the development firm. In addition, the database design is implemented and properly integrated with the produced code. If required, the created database is also populated with some initial data.

Testing and Integration

Once the modules of the executable code are tested individually, the developed modules are integrated with external modules, systems, and components. The **integration test plans** are executed. The obtained test results are analyzed and errors are dealt with accordingly. The deliverable of this phase is the integrated software.

Installation

Once the software is properly integrated, it is delivered to the client premises and installed according to the **installation and deployment plan**. The client runs the acceptance test plan and, ideally, accepts the software. The deliverables of this phase are the official acceptance document signed by the client and the properly installed software system.

One of the strengths of the waterfall model is that it is well structured with clearly identified phases. Each phase has well-specified inputs and deliverables and is composed of a set of activities. In addition, as a result of the activities of the waterfall model phases, a large amount of documentation is produced. Although it seems that this amount of documentation is excessive and costly, in the long term, the detailed documents reduce future maintenance cost.

An ideal realization of the waterfall model implies that once a phase is completed and its deliverables are approved, the subsequent phase can start. The development activities are executed in sequence without a need to repeat any of the preceding activities. However, in practice, although a phase is complete, errors discovered in later phases might be traced backward to an already completed phase. Hence, a realistic waterfall model is more iterative in nature, allowing the revisiting of preceding phases if necessary. For example, if, during the design phase, an ambiguity in the software requirements is discovered, the designer has to report this error to the manager, and the analysis team has to deal with this ambiguity. Ignoring this error during the design might have severe consequences, including higher repair cost to deal with the same error in the future. In addition, it would be irresponsible and unethical for the designer to ignore or neglect reporting this analysis error in a timely fashion and through the proper reporting channels. Similarly, while in the coding phase, the programmer might discover a flaw in the detailed design. This flaw must be reported to the designers and the appropriate actions must take place to address the error. Figure 2.1 illustrates, with dashed arrows, the iterations needed from one

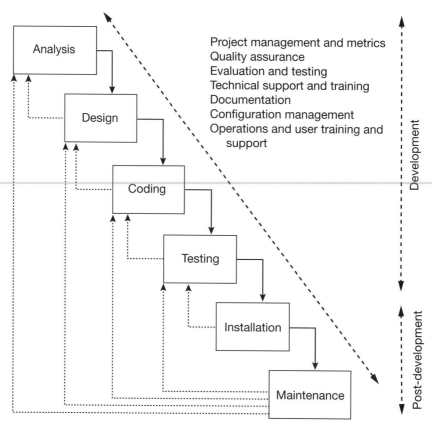

Figure 2.1 Waterfall model phases and its ongoing umbrella activities

Table 2.2 Software life cycle development phases and corresponding deliverables

Life cycle phase	Deliverables
Analysis 　Requirements 　Specifications	Vision and scope Requirements Software requirements specifications User interface specification Acceptance test plan
Design	High-level design Detailed design Database design User interface design Test plans 　Unit 　Stress and load 　Performance 　Integration
Implementation	Documented code Unit test plans execution
Testing	Execution and result analysis report Integration test
Installation	Installed software Official acceptance of the software

phase to its preceding phases. Table 2.2 shows the phases of the waterfall model and their corresponding deliverables.

2.4 SOFTWARE MAINTENANCE ACTIVITIES

After the proper installation and acceptance of the software, its intended users begin running the software by invoking its functions or services. Software maintenance activities include the management of software improvement requests, the identification, categorization, and prioritization of needed improvements, and the scheduling and execution of the needed improvements.

The management of requests is facilitated implementing a user-friendly system for requesting software improvements and reporting software faults. The system is used by software users, software developers, and the client to report software faults and to request enhancements to the software. The requests and error reports are then analyzed by the maintenance team. The scheduling of the execution of the requests depends mainly on their complexity and urgency. There are different types of maintenance activities including corrective, preventive, perfective, and adaptive activities.

Corrective maintenance activities are triggered by software faults encountered during the use of the software. They involve simple fixes, such as cosmetic changes to the user interface, or more complex fixes such as redesign of a module or the re-introduction of a missing functionality.

In the former case, only the code is revisited and limited testing is needed. However, in the latter case, all phases are applied again beginning at the requirements specifications in the analysis phase and proceeding to the proper integration testing or regression testing prior to the re-installation of the software.

Preventive maintenance activities involve dealing with weaknesses and vulnerabilities identified by the development team during or after deploying the software and that were not dealt with in the installed software. Prior to the users reporting them, the maintenance group might want to start working on removing the identified weaknesses.

Perfective maintenance activities involve dealing with requests to improve the efficiency of the algorithms and data structures, as well as user interface interactions in the design.

Finally, **adaptive maintenance** activities involve requests from software stakeholders to adapt the software to different operating environments, user interface styles, social contexts, or new government regulations and standards.

Again, the phases and activities of the development model that need to be performed depends on the severity and type of the requested maintenance activity. For example, adaptive maintenance activities typically need to perform activities of all development phases of the life cycle model.

2.5 CONTINUOUS LIFE CYCLE ACTIVITIES AND DELIVERABLES

In addition to the well-defined software engineering phases and their deliverables, there are important and critical activities that must be performed continuously during the execution of the software development phases. Each of the ongoing activities, also called umbrella activities, is needed to support the proper execution of the development phases and to ensure the production of high-quality software. The ongoing life cycle activities are project management, quality assurance, evaluation and testing, configuration management, documentation, and user training. Post-development phases include software installation and maintenance. Obviously, development activities are also performed during the maintenance phase because the same activities are performed when maintaining the software. In addition, operations, support, quality assurance, and training activities are continuous activities that are performed during the post-development maintenance phase.

Project Management

During the progress of the life cycle activities, the project manager continuously performs project management-related activities. The progress of the activities is closely monitored using an appropriate reporting procedure. Risks are continuously monitored and corrective actions are taken when needed. In addition, new risks are identified and monitored. The project schedule is updated regularly as needed. Project- and process-related metrics are regularly collected and assessed. In addition, human resource management and project management activities, including delegation and evaluation, are performed.

Quality Assurance

During each phase and at the end of each phase, the quality assurance group performs its activities, including the review of the deliverables of each phase and ensuring the use of and conformance to internal and external standards. Reviews of parts of the deliverables are conducted during the phase execution and after the deliverables are produced. Quality reports and logs are maintained and relevant metrics are collected according to the metrics collection plan. The **quality assurance plan** is executed and updated if needed. Moreover, process improvement recommendations are provided by the group after completion of the project.

Evaluation and Testing

Evaluation and testing processes and activities, including validation and verification activities, are performed all along the various product development phases. At the end of each phase, the phase deliverable is evaluated and tested. Once the deliverable is approved, the next phase starts. Formal and informal processes are used for evaluation and testing purposes. The processes are performed by the developers themselves and by independent groups such as quality assurance. Informal evaluation processes include reviews that might involve walkthroughs, inspections, and audits. Formal evaluation processes include the use of formal techniques and automated tools for the verification of phase deliverables. Tools and techniques for design verification and code testing can be used for these purposes. Formal product validation techniques and methods can also be used to generate and document effective tests, automate the validation process, and analyze and validate the results.

Configuration Management

Configuration management activities initially include the identification of all software documents, deliverables, and artifacts that will be produced, manipulated, and maintained during the development and maintenance of the software. Configuration control activities are then performed continuously during the software development and post-development phases. Configuration management deals mainly with the management of the software resources and the overall support and control of the software development and maintenance processes. The configuration management control activities include revision and version control, process and workflow control, build control, and change control. Ideally, the control activities are performed using an integrated and automated configuration management tool for revision, version, build, and change management. Finally, a periodic configuration management audit and status report is generated by the automated tool. The report is then analyzed by the appropriate management team.

Technical Support and Internal Training

During the development and maintenance of a software product, the developers might require some technical support and training. Support technicians help the developers in solving technical problems that arise while developing the software. The activities help improve the efficiency and productivity of the development and maintenance teams. A plan can be devised as part of a project plan to deal with the training of technical staff on the development process, standards to be followed, or new tools and technologies that are needed during the development phases.

Documentation

During product development, various documents that target different audiences are produced. Some of them are internal technical documents that are needed for future software maintenance activities. Other documents target external users and include user manuals, installation manuals, and operations manuals. Standards and standard templates are normally used to guide the writing of the software-related documents. Technical writers are involved with the production of the external documents. Internal documents are typically written by the software developers themselves. The documents are evaluated by internal review processes for quality and involves various stakeholders, including software development team members and representatives of the software quality assurance group.

Operations, Support, and User Training

After installing the software, its operations are supported by providing customer help desk support, technical assistance, training, and consultation. Help desk request logs and fault report logs are maintained and appropriate metrics are generated. Fault reports are used to trigger the appropriate maintenance activities.

Table 2.3 summarizes the life cycle activities performed continuously during the software development and post-development phases, and includes the respective deliverables.

2.6 PROTOTYPED WATERFALL MODEL

One of the weaknesses of the waterfall model lies in the initial phases related to the requirements specifications. Reliance on written documentation for the description of requirements might be inappropriate for software systems that are user-centered. Industrial experience shows that approved written requirements are volatile and subject to numerous revisions and changes later in the development process. It is clear that visualizing the requirements specifications helps in obtaining an approval of the requirements from the stakeholders more quickly and is given with greater confidence. Prototyping the requirements by building a visual and executable model is considered to be an effective way to review and approve requirements. Requirements prototyp-

Table 2.3 Ongoing life cycle activities and deliverables

Activity type	Deliverables	
Project management 　Monitoring 　Planning (update) 　Control	Updated project plan Metrics collection plan Metrics database maintained Project log maintained	
Quality assurance	Quality assurance plan Quality assurance review reports	
Evaluation and testing	Test data Test execution reports Test metrics and logs	Test plans Fault reports Review plans and reports
Technical support and internal training	Training plan Tech support reports	Training programs Training manuals
Documentation	User manual Installation and operations manuals	Various technical documents
Configuration management	Configuration identification Change logs Updated configuration management plan	
Operations, user training, and support (only post-development)	Help desk request logs Fault report logs User training plan and training material	

ing reduces the risks of requiring changes after approving the requirements. This leads to fewer revisions and iterations during software development, hence contributes to the reduction of the development and maintenance costs and avoids delays in the delivery of the final software product. Prototyping requirements, then, reduce the risks.

A **prototype** is an executable program that mainly implements the functional aspects of the software being developed that are related to the graphical user interface. Showing the client the graphical interfaces and the user interactions with the software allows the client to make a better assessment of what is missing and what needs to be modified or removed. However, prototypes can also address non-functional concerns such as performance, security, and fault-tolerance.

Typically, a prototype should only be used for the purpose of getting an agreement on requirements. It must be easy to develop and easy to modify to reflect the client's changes to requirements prior to obtaining an agreement. A prototype must not be used further as a basis to build the software unless it is an accurate reflection of the customer's desires. Because of the investment made to produce the prototype, an ill-informed manager might be tempted to continue the software development phases by building on the top of the prototype. Experiences show that using a prototype frequently leads to a software project failure. Avoiding the reuse of the prototype is an ethical responsibility of the manager and the development team. Figure 2.2 shows the waterfall model, including the prototyping of requirements.

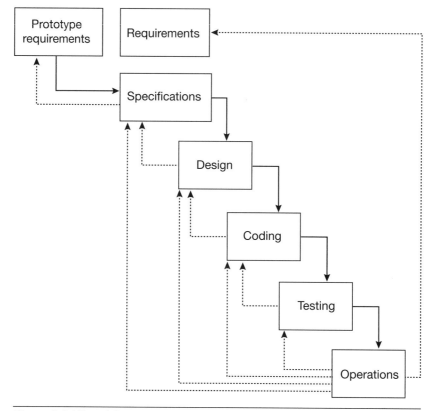

Figure 2.2 Waterfall model with prototyped requirements

2.7 OBJECT-ORIENTED MODEL

The object-oriented software development model is centered on the object concept in software systems. The model consists of four phases: the object-oriented (1) analysis, (2) design, (3) implementation, and (4) testing.

To deal with the complexity of software systems, the object-oriented analysis starts by identifying the types of objects needed in the software system to cover all the requirements. Objects are typically real-life physical and logical objects needed to build the analysis model. Objects and their respective attributes and their visibilities are identified. For each object, the methods that are needed to create, define, modify, and destroy an object are also identified. Object relationships are then identified. The three main types of relationships among objects are the aggregation, inheritance, and communication relationships. The aggregation or composition relationship states that one object is made of one or more objects in the analysis model. The communication relationship among two objects indicates that one object is sending a message to the other object, normally to change or enquire about the state of that object. Methods for object communications are then identified as part of the object analysis model. The inheritance relationship among two objects indicates that one object expands the attributes and methods of the other object. In addition, the object-oriented analysis includes the sequencing of interactions between the external users and systems and the software system to be developed. A scenario-like specification of the interactions can be used and an executable prototype can be built to visualize the interactions.

Object-oriented design consists of the identification of classes and their interrelationships from the given analysis model. The detailed descriptions of the methods identified in each class are provided. A class is a template from which an object is created. Classes can be entity, interface, and behavior classes. Entity classes represent real-life physical and logical objects that need to remain in persistent store. The classes are used to obtain a database design that can be implemented in a relational, object-oriented, or object-relational database system. Interface classes are used to define and manipulate graphical user interface artifacts and components needed to interface between the software and its external users, and to communicate between systems. Interface objects are normally not needed to remain in persistent store. Finally, behavior or control classes include methods that are needed to encode the business logic necessary to manipulate the entity objects through interface objects. Existing object-oriented design patterns can also be reused to build the design model.

Once an object-oriented design is completed, it is mapped to an implementation using an object-oriented programming language. Object-oriented testing and integration techniques are then used to test the implementation and integrate it with other components and systems.

Unified Modeling Language (UML) is used to develop and document the object-oriented analysis and design models using various modeling artifacts and diagrams. The UML is incrementally introduced in detail in the subsequent chapters that also include object-oriented analysis and design.

2.8 INCREMENTAL AND ITERATIVE MODEL

In the **incremental and iterative model**, the software requirements are prioritized. High priority requirements are considered first as an initial release of the software. A life cycle is started to develop this initial software version or build. Depending on available resources, the project manager might be able to start the development of the second release, perhaps containing the medium priority requirements. Similarly, a third release might contain low priority requirements. Figure 2.3 shows the scheduling of high, medium, and low priority requirements. The figure shows the phases of the waterfall model exercised during the development of each release. However, note that any software development model can be used in combination.

The incremental and iterative model accelerates the early deployment of high priority software functionalities. In addition, a careful scheduling of the different releases can lead to an efficient use of the available resources.

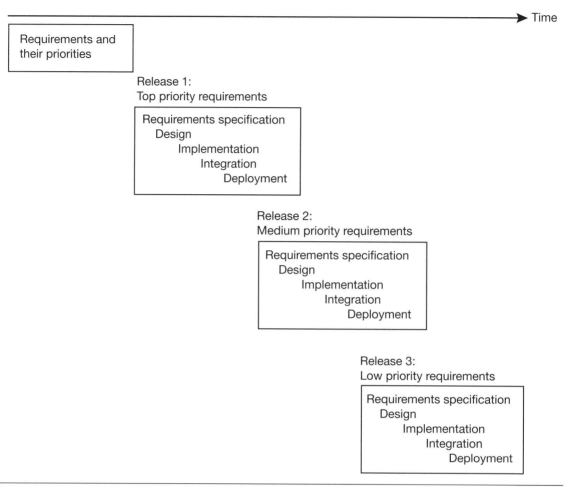

Figure 2.3 Incremental and iterative model for software development

2.9 SPIRAL MODEL

The **spiral model** for software development was introduced by Barry Boehm in 1988. The model addresses the weaknesses of the waterfall model with respect to the treatment of software development risks. The phases of the waterfall model do not include any reference to risk management. **Risk management** is considered an ongoing activity that is part of the project management activities.

The spiral model embeds risk management activities within the development activities. The model provides a risk-driven approach to software development. Software risks and the lack of a clear and continuous risk management strategy are the main reasons for software project failures. Therefore, formal and continuous consideration of risks embedded within the software development process contributes to enhancing the quality of software. In addition, it contributes to the successful completion of the software project leading to complete and correct product functionalities developed within the given budget and time constraints. The success of software projects is closely related to how well the software risks are managed. Each cycle in the spiral model shown in Figure 2.4 involves the repeated execution of four steps at each level of abstraction or phase of a development process. At a given level or phase, the steps include first, the identification of objectives, alternatives, and constraints that are relevant at that phase; second, the evaluation and assessment of the identified alternatives with respect to constraints and identified potential risks; third, development of the phase deliverable by performing its activities followed by a review of the deliverables; and fourth, preparation and planning for the following phase. The preparation might prescribe the partitioning of the remaining work into

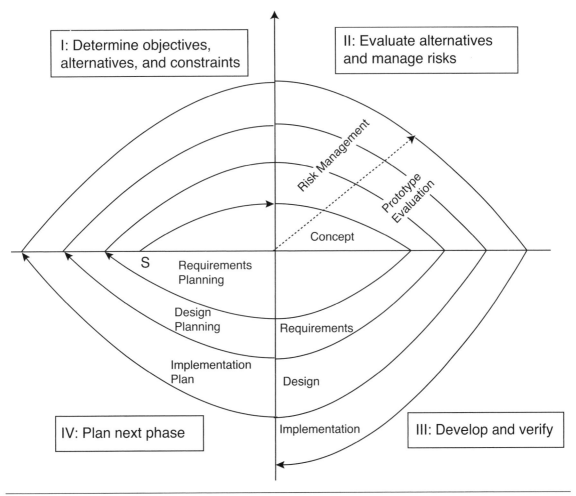

Figure 2.4 Spiral model for software development and maintenance

different sequential or parallel software increments, leading to concurrent spiral model execution of the remaining phases of the software. The four steps are shown in the four quadrants of the spiral in Figure 2.4. The spiral model execution starts at point S in the figure. The spiral model applies to both the development and future maintenance of the software product.

2.10 RATIONAL UNIFIED PROCESS

The **Rational Unified Process** (RUP) is a software engineering process management tool encapsulating best practices in software development and maintenance. The best practices that are implemented and supported in RUP include the iterative and incremental development of software, requirements management, software components reuse, visual modeling, software quality verification, and configuration and change management. The RUP is a configurable product that can be adapted to software products of different types and complexities.

RUP consists of well-defined sequential phases for the iterative development of software. The RUP phases include **inception**, **elaboration**, **construction**, and **transition phases**.

During the inception phase, the development team develops the business context and scope of the project. In addition, stakeholders of the product are identified and their interfaces with the software to be developed are determined. All use cases are also identified and partly developed and prototyped. A risk management plan and cost as well as schedule estimations are developed. The main deliverables of the inception phase include a vision and scope document, an initial use case model, an initial project plan, including a risk management plan, and an initial prototype. The financial and technical feasibility of the project is carefully assessed at this point and a go/no go decision is made.

In the elaboration phase, the use case model is formalized and an executable prototype of the most complex and critical use cases is implemented. The deliverables of the elaboration phase include a use case model, non-functional requirements specifications, a revised and complete project plan, including revised risk management plan, more accurate estimates of the cost and time needed to complete the project, and an executable prototype. The inception and elaboration phases of RUP correspond to the software requirements specification or analysis phase of the prototyped waterfall model.

In the construction phase, the software is designed, implemented, and integrated prior to its deployment in the transition phase. Various software releases might be constructed concurrently to accelerate the deployment of high priority features of the software product. The deliverables of the construction phase include the software design document, the software product, and all related documentation, including installation and user manuals.

In the transition phase, the software product is deployed and made available to its intended user population. The product is validated against the requirements. Necessary database conversions are performed. Training of software users and operators is provided. Finally, the product is distributed to its intended users using the appropriate distribution channels.

In addition to the description of its sequential phases, the RUP can also be described by activities that are clustered into different workflows. Each workflow culminates in one or more deliverable. The nine workflows that are clearly identified in RUP are:

1. Business modeling
2. Requirements
3. Analysis and design
4. Implementation
5. Test
6. Deployment
7. Project management
8. Configuration and change management
9. Environment

The activities of one workflow can span more than one phase of the RUP. For example, project management, change and configuration management, and environment activities are spread over all four phases of the RUP. The three workflows are called **core supporting workflows**. The other six workflows are called **core process workflows**. The relationship between phases and workflows are best shown in a two dimensional diagram in which the phases are listed along a horizontal axis and the workflows are listed along a vertical axis.

2.11 SOFTWARE DEVELOPMENT AND MAINTENANCE TEAMS

To perform the activities of an adopted life cycle model, the human resources in a software development organization must be broken into various teams. People can be organized by functional teams, each specializing in one phase of the software development cycle. This functional organization is suitable for a medium or a large software organization that is continuously undertaking software development projects. The main advantage of such organization is the specialized nature of the team members due to the expertise in the processes used over time. The main problem is for the manager to allocate tasks to the different teams and team members to make an efficient use of their time. A typical functional team structure in a medium to large size software development firm is shown in Figure 2.5.

Another team organization is a project-based organization in which the same developer can be scheduled to work on the various phases of the project. The project team structure is used in software organizations that are created solely to develop a single software product. The disadvantage of this team organization is the possible lack of expertise of one developer in one or more of the development phases. However, the developer's time is used more effectively and, hence, the team productivity is higher.

A third team organization is a hybrid between functional- and project-based structures. The hybrid organization is typically used in large organizations working on multiple software

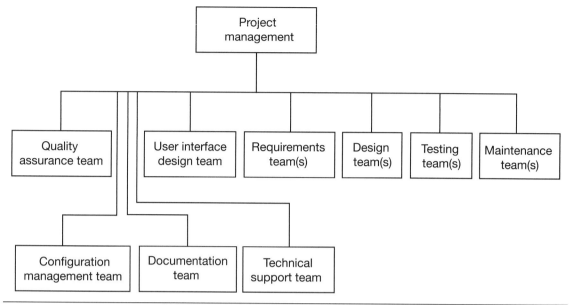

Figure 2.5 Typical functional team organization of a software firm

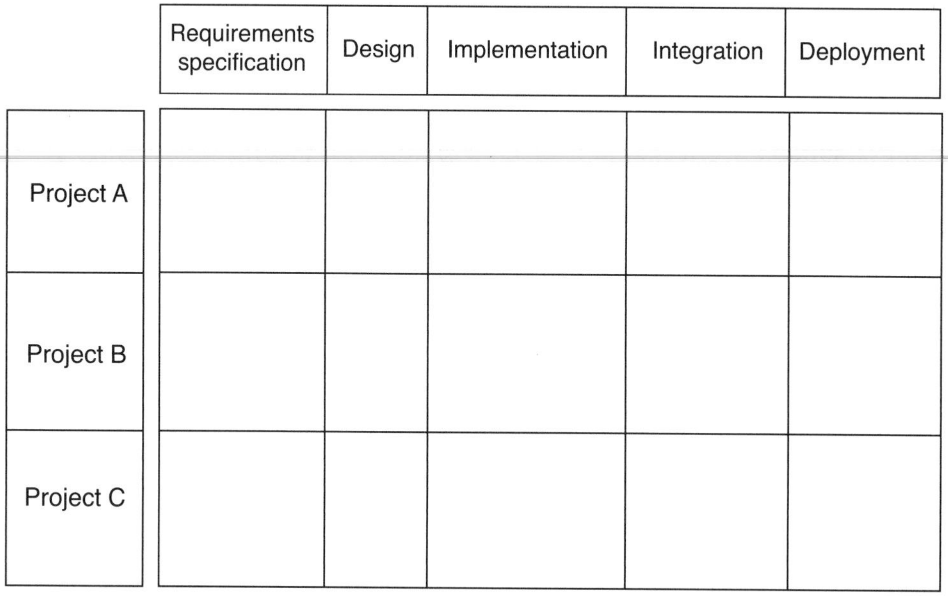

	Requirements specification	Design	Implementation	Integration	Deployment
Project A					
Project B					
Project C					

Figure 2.6 Hybrid functional- and project-based team organizations

projects concurrently. The hybrid organization has the advantages of both functional and project organization. A developer can have expertise in one or more development phases and can therefore be scheduled on one or more phases of different projects. Obviously, this hybrid organization requires more complex scheduling constraints. It can also lead to reporting conflicts. It has to be decided whether the developer reports to a project leader or to a team leader. The hybrid organization can be illustrated using a two dimensional table as illustrated in Figure 2.6. In this figure, we are assuming that there are three concurrent projects of similar complexity and project schedules undertaken by the software firm.

2.12 SOFTWARE ENGINEERING STANDARDS AND TOOLS

As the software engineering discipline is becoming more mature, various practices related to software engineering phases and activities are now either standardized or being standardized. The Institute of Electrical and Electronics Engineers (IEEE) is the most active professional organization involved in the standardization of software-related activities. Many of the standards have undergone several revisions to reflect the maturity level of the software engineering processes. Standards provide guidance for the software developers and managers using the best practices in the various software development and maintenance areas. Table 2.4 shows the correspondence between the various software engineering phases and activities and the existing **IEEE standards**. In addition, the table includes the ISO standard related to the quality of software systems. Recently, many of the IEEE standards listed in the table have been superseded by the International Standardization Organization/International Electrotechnical Commission (ISO IEC) standards. For example, the IEEE 1540 standard was superseded by ISO IEC 16085 in 2006.

Tools supporting the various software engineering methods, techniques, and standards are needed to make them feasible, practical, and automated. Integrated software development tools encapsulating various techniques and spanning most, if not all, of the life cycle activities are referred to as computer aided software engineering (**CASE**) tools. The IEEE provided few standards for the selection, assessment, and design of CASE tools. CASE tools must be user-friendly, configurable, and adaptable to software projects of varying types and complexities. Currently in the market there are many industrial-strength CASE tools that are being used extensively in software production shops. Many of the tools automate or semi-automate the software development activities from project management and configuration management to requirements specifications and management, up to code generation and maintenance. Normally, a CASE tool is designed around an adopted life cycle model; the waterfall, the RUP, or an object-oriented model. Another type of tool that mainly assists in the implementation, testing, and debugging of software is called an integrated development environment (IDE). The tools are functionally a subset of the more comprehensive CASE tools.

Table 2.4 Correspondence between software phases and activities and IEEE standards

Phase or activity group	Number	Standard title
Requirements specification	IEEE 830 IEEE 1233 IEEE 1320	Recommended practice for software requirements specifications Guide for developing system requirements specifications Functional modeling language
Design	IEEE 1016 IEEE 1471	Software design descriptions Recommended practice for architectural description of software-intensive systems
Implementation, acquisition and tools	IEEE 1062 IEEE 1462 IEEE 1175	Software acquisition Guideline for the evaluation and selection of CASE tools Guide for CASE tool interconnections
Testing	IEEE 829 IEEE 1008 IEEE 1012 IEEE 1059 IEEE 1028 IEEE 1044	Software test documentation Software unit testing Software verification and validation Guide for software verification and validation plans Software reviews and audits Classification for software anomalies
Maintenance	IEEE 1219	Software maintenance
Project management	IEEE 1058 IEEE 1228	Software project management plans Software safety plans
Documentation	IEEE 1063	Software user documentation
Risk management	IEEE 1540	Software life cycle processes—risk management
Metrics	IEEE 1061	Software quality metrics methodology
Configuration management	IEEE 828 IEEE 1042	Software configuration management plans
Quality assurance	IEEE 730 IEEE 1298 ISO 9001 ISO 9003	Software quality assurance plans Software quality management system Quality systems—model for quality assurance in design, development, production, installation, and servicing Quality systems—model for quality assurance in final inspection and test
Life cycle processes	IEEE 1074	Developing a software life cycle process

2.13 SOFTWARE PROCESSES CAPABILITY MATURITY MODEL

The **Capability Maturity Model** (CMM) was developed by W. Humphrey at the Software Engineering Institute at Carnegie Mellon University for the assessment of the development processes at software development companies. CMM was succeeded by the CMM Integration (CMMI) as a generalized model to assist in the assessment of the process maturity of different types of organizations and in various areas such as systems engineering, project management, and supply-chain management. The CMM does not recommend any particular set of mature processes to be followed by an organization. However, the CMM can be used to assess the maturity of existing processes. The basis for the placement at a particular level is based on the availability of specific process areas defined for that level. As a result of the process maturity assessment, an organization is placed at one of five maturity levels: (1) initial, (2) repeatable, (3) defined, (4) managed, (5) and optimized, the best of which is obviously the optimized level.

Level 1: Initial

The processes used are ad hoc, informal, and not documented. The knowledge and experiences are not archived and documented. Project success relies heavily on the efforts of some of the team members. However, due to the lack of documented development methodologies and experiences, it might be impossible to repeat success in new projects of similar types and complexities. Completed projects in organizations at the initial level of maturity are characterized by low quality, numerous errors, and running over time and over budget.

Level 2: Repeatable

The development methodology and all its phases are partially documented. The processes involved in the documented phases are repeatable, but the successful application of the processes is not guaranteed every time they are followed. The rigorous application of the documented phases varies from project to project. Project management techniques and tools are used to track project progress in terms of cost, schedule, and project deliverables. Software quality assurance is considered for the documented processes.

Level 3: Defined

The development processes are documented and well defined. Internal standards and documented methodology are used uniformly across the organization and in all development projects undertaken. The documented processes have also been updated over time using past experiences to improve performance. However, past experiences are assessed and documented qualitatively. Moreover, the documented processes are adapted to take into consideration the project complexity and context. Organizations at this level thoroughly consider all aspects of project management.

Level 4: Managed

Developmental metrics are collected during the execution of the project to provide a quantitative basis for software quality management. The metrics allow the project manager to predict the future performance of the remaining phases of the project. The predictions allow the manager to closely track and control the project based on quantitative assessment. Consequently, this allows the manager to manage the risks more effectively and take the necessary and timely actions should any risk occur.

Level 5: Optimized

Using metrics collected during the execution of the project phases, and using the documented standards and processes, modifications to both standards and processes are implemented

Table 2.5 Summary of the characteristics of the five maturity levels

Maturity level	Characteristics
1. Initial	Ad hoc, informal, and nondocumented processes
2. Repeatable	Processes and standards partially documented
	Software quality assurance considered
	Requirements management and project tracking in place
3. Defined	Development methodology and standards documented
	Risk management and qualitative assessment of project performance in place
4. Managed	Metrics on processes collected
	Quantitative assessment of process performance and software quality management in place
5. Optimized	Optimal processes and workflows in place
	Continuous process and standards improvements in place

continuously. The changes are also triggered by technology changes, the adoption of which can lead to improved performance. Performance indicators are developed and monitored. Changes to processes and standards show improvements in performance from project to project. Process and technology change management systems are in place to deal with changes in processes and in available technology. As the software development organization is maturing and gaining experience, the collected metrics are used to optimize the processes and the organization workflow leading to increased productivity while maintaining the product qualities.

An organization placed at a particular level is an indication that it meets all the requirements for that level and is showing clear indication that it is progressing toward the next higher level. The Software Engineering Institute (SEI) is maintaining a database of appraised organizations. The SEI Appraisal System (SAS) contains the appraisal results of hundreds of IT organizations at levels 2 to 5. The characteristics of the five maturity levels are summarized in Table 2.5.

2.14 UNIFIED MODELING LANGUAGE

The **unified modeling language** (UML) is a de facto software industry standard modeling language for visualizing, specifying, constructing, and documenting the elements of systems in general and software systems in particular. UML has well-defined syntax and semantics. It provides a rich set of graphical artifacts to help in the elicitation and top-down refinement of object-oriented software systems from requirements capture to the deployment of software components. UML is typically used in an object-oriented software development life cycle model, including the object-oriented analysis and object-oriented design phases.

In UML, systems can be modeled by considering three aspects: behavioral, structural, and architectural. Each aspect is concerned with both the static and dynamic views of the system. The static view represents a projection on the static structures of the complete system description. However, the dynamic view represents a projection on the dynamic behavior of the system. Views are communicated using a number of diagrams containing information that emphasizes a particular aspect of the system. Following, the various aspects, views, and diagrams and their relationships are described. The RUP model for software development uses the UML as a tool for the visual modeling of software artifacts.

Aspects

Three aspects of systems can be recognized when modeling software systems: behavioral, structural, and architectural. The **behavioral aspects** involve the functionalities provided by the system (static behavioral aspects) and their associated interactions, timings, and orderings (dynamic behavioral aspects). **Structural aspects** involve the class structures of the object-oriented software and the interrelationships among the classes (static structural aspects), and the algorithmic details of object life cycles and their interactions (dynamic structural aspects). **Architectural aspects** are related to the deployment and distribution of software and hardware across the various distributed system components.

Views

Aspects of systems are covered by various static and dynamic views: use case, design, process, implementation, and deployment. The use case view focuses on the behavioral aspects of a system. Primarily, it reflects the user's concerns and requirements. This view considers the system as a black box. Normally, users, testers, and requirements analysts are interested in the use case view. The design and process views are the concern of the development team, including the analysts, designers, and implementers. They describe both the static and dynamic structural aspects of the system. The design view is concerned with objects, classes, and collaborations, whereas the process view is concerned with software architecture issues such as concurrency, multithreading, synchronization, performance, and scalability issues. The implementation view describes the files and components needed to assemble and release the system. The deployment view describes the ways to distribute, deliver, and install the system components and files across the distributed nodes of the system.

Diagrams

A diagram contains model elements such as classes, objects, nodes, components, and various types of relationships described by graphical symbols. Moreover, a diagram can be used to describe certain system aspects at different levels of abstraction. For example, a state diagram can describe system level input/output interactions and can also be used to show state changes of a particular system object across multiple use cases. The UML diagrams are clustered under behavioral, structural, and architectural modeling diagrams.

Behavioral Modeling

The **use case diagram** describes the functions of the system and its external users and defines their interfaces. This diagram shows a number of external actors and their connection to the use cases representing the services provided by the system. Use cases can be inherited by another use case, allowing reusability of use cases. Also, use cases can be associated using the *include* relationship, allowing the modularization of use cases. Similarly, use cases can be associated with the *extend* relationship to deal with certain exceptional or abnormal conditions or situations that can disrupt the normal execution of the use case. The use case diagram is used to model the static behavioral aspects of the use case view of the system to model. It is mainly used to capture and document functional software requirements.

A **statechart diagram** describes the possible behavior of an object using state changes. It can also be used as a system level diagram showing system state changes during the operation of the system. Therefore, this diagram can be used to model both the dynamic behavioral aspects of the use case view and the dynamic structural aspects of the design and process views of the system to model.

Sequence diagrams show the interactions between a number of objects and their time ordering. In other words, this diagram describes a scenario involving various interacting objects. This diagram can be used to model the dynamic behavioral aspects of the use case view if the interacting objects are interface objects or actors. However, if the interacting objects are internal ones, this diagram would then be used to model the dynamic structural aspects of the design and process views of the system to model.

An **activity diagram** shows a sequential or concurrent flow from one activity to another activity. An activity diagram consists of action states, activity states, and transitions between them, and usually spans more than one use case (or functionality). Similar to interaction diagrams, an activity diagram can be used to model both the dynamic behavioral aspect of the use case view in addition to the dynamic structural aspect of the design view of the system to model.

Communication diagrams show the objects and the messages they exchange. Messages are numbered to provide a time ordering of the message. Similar to a sequence diagram, a communication diagram can be used to model both the dynamic behavioral aspect of the use case view in addition to the dynamic structural aspect of the process view of the system to model. It is worthwhile to mention that one can easily produce a sequence diagram from the communication diagram and vice versa. Both sequence and communication diagrams are also referred to as interaction diagrams.

A **timing diagram** merges a sequence and a state diagram to provide a timeline showing the changes of the state of an object over time. The timing diagram also shows the messages or interactions exchanged as well as the time and duration constraints attached to the interactions.

The **interaction overview diagram** is a variation of an activity diagram in which the activities represent an interaction diagram. An interaction diagram can be a sequence, a communication, or a timing diagram.

Structural Modeling

Class diagrams show the static structure of classes and their possible relationships (i.e., association, inheritance, aggregation, and dependency) in the system. This diagram is used to model the static structural aspects of the design and process views of the system to model.

Object diagrams are a variant of a class diagram and uses almost identical notation. An object diagram can be an example of a class diagram that shows possible instantiations of classes during system execution. This diagram is used to model the static structural aspects of the design and process views of the system to model.

A **composite diagram** shows the internal structural composition of a class. It also includes the interaction points that are also called ports through which the component interacts with the other parts of the system.

The **component diagram** shows the physical structure of the code in terms of code component. Components can be composed of a source code, a binary, or an executable component. A

Table 2.6 Aspects of an object-oriented model and UML diagrams

Aspects/views	Diagrams
Behavioral (functional)/use case	Static model Use case

	Dynamic model
	  Sequence
	  Activity
	  State chart
	  Timing
	  Interaction overview
	  Communication

Structural (design)/design and process	Static model
	  Class
	  Object
	  Composite structure
	  Component

	Dynamic model
	  Sequence
	  Activity
	  Statechart

Architectural/implementation and deployment	Deployment Package

component contains information about the logical class or classes it implements, thus creating a mapping from the design view to the component view. A component diagram is used to model the static architectural aspects of the implementation view of the system to model.

Architectural Modeling

Package diagrams show the packages existing in the software and their relationships. A package can contain components, class diagrams, and use case diagrams among other UML diagrams. Packages can be composed of other packages and two packages can be merged.

The **deployment diagram** shows the physical architecture and distribution of the hardware and software components in the system. A deployment diagram is used to model the static architectural aspects of the deployment view of the system.

Table 2.6 shows the three aspects of an object-oriented model and their supporting UML diagrams.

SUMMARY

To deal with the development and management of complex software projects, structured and well-documented processes must be clearly defined and used by the development team. Industrial-strength and scalable software development and maintenance life cycle models have been introduced. A typical model consists of sequential phases, including analysis, design, implementation, testing, and integration. In addition to the sequential phases and related activities, important continuous activities must be performed, including project management, validation and verification, configuration management, quality assurance, and documentation. The chapter briefly introduces three software industry standards and tools. The unified modeling language (UML) is primarily used with the object-oriented life cycle model, the rational unified process (RUP) is a structured software engineering process model, and the capability maturity model (CMM) is used to assess the maturity of the processes in a software development organization. In addition, the chapter lists the various IEEE standards related to the software development activities.

KEY TERMS

activity diagram	CASE	construction
adaptive maintenance	class diagram	core process workflows
analysis phase	communication diagram	core supporting workflows
architectural aspects	component diagram	corrective maintenance
behavioral aspects	composite diagram	deployment diagram
Capability Maturity Model	configuration management	design phase

elaboration	object diagram	software development life
IEEE standards	object-oriented design	cycle model
implementation phase	package diagram	spiral model
inception	perfective maintenance	statechart diagram
incremental and iterative	preventive maintenance	structural aspects
model	project management plan	timing diagram
installation and deployment	prototype	transition
plan	quality assurance plan	umbrella activities
integration test plans	Rational Unified Process	unified modeling language
interaction overview diagram	risk management	use case diagram
life cycle model	sequence diagram	waterfall model

REVIEW QUESTIONS

1. Define the typical phases of a software development model.
2. List the four types of maintenance activities.
3. List three types of ongoing software development activities.
4. List the advantages and disadvantages of the waterfall model.
5. List the advantages and disadvantages of the prototyped waterfall model.
6. List the types of activities performed during each software development phase.
7. What is the main advantage of the spiral model?
8. Define the levels of the capability maturity model.
9. Describe the three types of team organizational structures in a software firm.
10. Describe the phases and workflows of the rational unified process.
11. Describe and classify the diagrams in the unified modeling language.

EXERCISES

1. Consider a software development company of your choice and describe the development life cycle model they use.
2. List software development life cycle models that were not discussed in this chapter. Consider one of them and provide a concise description of it.
3. Obtain from this chapter the diagram showing the phases and workflows of the rational unified process model. Explain the graph related to the requirements workflow.

BIBLIOGRAPHY

Books

Boehm, B. W. *Software Engineering Economics*, Englewood Cliffs, NJ: Prentice Hall, 1981.

Booch, G., J. Rumbaugh, and I. Jacobson. *Unified Modeling Language User Guide*, 2d ed., Reading, MA: Addison-Wesley, 2005.

Bruegge, B., and A. Dutoit. *Object-Oriented Software Engineering: Using UML, Patterns and Java*, 2d ed., Englewood Cliffs, NJ: Prentice Hall, 2003.

Hughes, B., and M. Cotterell. *Software Project Management*, 4th ed., New York: McGraw Hill, 2005.

Humphrey, W. *Managing the Software Process*, Reading, MA: Addison-Wesley, 1989.

Humphrey, W. *Introduction to the Team Software Process*, Reading, MA: Addison-Wesley, 1999.

Jacobson, I., G. Booch, and J. Rumbaugh. *The Unified Software Development Process*, Reading, MA: Addison-Wesley, 1999.

Larman, C. *Applying UML and Patterns: An Introduction to Object-Oriented Analysis and Design and Iterative Development*, 3d ed., Englewood Cliffs, NJ: Prentice Hall, 2004.

Lethbridge, T., and R. Laganiere. *Object-Oriented Software Engineering*, 2d ed., New York: McGraw Hill, 2005.

Marciniak, J. *Encyclopedia of Software Engineering*, 2d ed., New York: John Wiley and Sons, 2002.

Moore, J. W. The *Roadmap to Software Engineering: A Standards-Based Guide*, New York: Wiley and Sons, 2006.

Peters, L. *Getting Results from Software Development Teams*, Redmond, WA: Microsoft Press, 2008.

Schach, S. *Object-Oriented Software Engineering*, New York: McGraw Hill, 2007.

Papers

Boehm, B. "A spiral model for software development and enhancement," *IEEE Computer,* (May 1988) 61–72.

Royce, W. "Managing the development of large software systems," *Proc. IEEE WESCON*, (Aug. 1970) 1–9.

Standards

IEEE 610.12, IEEE Standard Glossary of Software Engineering Terminology, 1990.

IEEE 730, IEEE Standard for Software Quality Assurance Plans, 1998.

IEEE 828, IEEE Standard for Software Configuration Management Plans, 1998.

IEEE 829, IEEE Standard for Software Test Documentation, 1998.

IEEE 830, IEEE Recommended Practice for Software Requirements Specifications, 1998.

IEEE 1028, IEEE Standard for Software Reviews, IEEE, 1997.

IEEE 1042, IEEE Guide to Software Configuration Management, 1993.

IEEE 1045, IEEE Standard for Software Productivity Metrics, 1992.

IEEE 1058, IEEE Standard for Software Project Management Plans, 1998.

IEEE 1059, IEEE Guide for Software Verification and Validation Plans, 1993.

IEEE 1061, IEEE Standard for a Software Quality Metrics Methodology, 1998.

IEEE 1062, IEEE Recommended Practice for Software Acquisition, 1998.

IEEE 1074, IEEE Standard for Developing Software Life Cycle Processes, IEEE, 1997.

IEEE 1219, IEEE Standard for Software Maintenance, IEEE, 1998.

IEEE 1233, IEEE Guide for Developing System Requirements Specifications, 1998.IEEE 1298, IEEE Standard for Software Quality Management System, Part 1: Requirements, 1992.

IEEE 1540, IEEE Standard for Software Life Cycle Processes-Risk Management, 2001.

ISO 9001, Quality systems—Model for quality assurance in design, development, production, installation, and servicing, 1994.

ISO 9001, Quality Management Systems-Requirements, 2000.

ISO 9003, Quality systems—Model for quality assurance in final inspection and test, 1994.

Software Requirements

As part of the software development activities, the first stage of the **software analysis** phase deals with the development of software requirements. Software requirements must reflect the user's view of what the software system must do. Requirements should be both design and implementation independent and easy to read and understand. Requirements must be developed, managed, and documented in a way that facilitates future maintenance of the software. Requirements must be elicited from all possible stakeholders of the software in a systematic way. Once written, requirements should also be analyzed and refined prior to the start of the design phase. The complete analysis and refinement of software requirements is normally included in an SRS document. Techniques that are used to refine and clarify software requirements and develop software specifications are presented in Chapter 4.

Learning Outcomes

In this chapter you will learn:
- Basic terminology in software requirements
- Product vision and project scope document
- Difference between functional and non-functional requirements (NFRs)
- Types of NFRs
- Requirements engineering process steps
- Techniques for requirements elicitation
- Development of a use case model
- Validation of software requirements
- IEEE standard for writing a software requirements specifications document

3.1 SOFTWARE ANALYSIS

The first phase of a generic software development life cycle model is the software analysis phase. In this phase, we concentrate on the definition of what the software under development is supposed to do. Software analysis involves defining the scope of the software to be developed, capturing and documenting its users' requirements, knowing the various constraints that have to be met, and understanding the interfaces with external systems, entities, and users. The analysis model should be neither abstract nor constraining in terms of forcing specific design or implementation choices. It should be sufficiently detailed to unambiguously understand the requirements so that a designer does not have to return frequently to the software analyst, client, or users for clarifications. After developing an initial analysis model, the model must be validated and officially approved by the client's and the developer's representatives. The people who should be involved in the review of the software requirements include representatives from the clients and users, the design and testing teams, and the software quality assurance team as well as the software analyst. The software project plan is updated if changes to the project's milestones and activities are needed. The analysis model concentrates on the specification of functional and non-functional software requirements.

To build an effective analysis model, we should adopt and use a well-structured requirements engineering process. The requirements engineering process starts normally from the given product vision and project scope document accepted by the various product stakeholders. In this chapter, we adopt a use case model-based approach to develop the software requirements.

3.2 PRODUCT VISION AND PROJECT SCOPE

A **product vision** and **project scope** document facilitates in establishing the business requirements and aligning them with the **software requirements specifications (SRSs)**. Clear vision and scope aid in accelerating the convergence toward more focused software requirements. The product vision provides the business limits and focus to the project scope. A typical vision and scope document template includes three main sections: (1) business requirements and context, (2) product vision, and (3) project scope and limitations.

The section on business requirements and context includes a brief description of the rationale and business opportunity for the product being developed. It also includes the main business objectives and some quantifiable success criteria for the objectives. The business objectives can refer to either financial or technical benefits to the target customers that are preferably quantifiable. An example of a quantifiable financial benefit is: *The product helps reduce the customer support cost by 30 percent during the first year of operations.* An example of a quantifiable non-financial and technical benefit is: *The average delay to deal with and service a customer complaint is approximately eight hours.* This section also contains the business risks associated with the business requirements and their management, which include risk assessment, prioritization, monitoring, mitigation, and control. (Detailed elaboration on the technical and non-technical project risks is included in the software project plan document and is discussed in Chapter 10.) In addition, this section identifies and describes the types of product users and other stakeholders. Finally, this section describes the context and environment in which the product will be operating. The operating context and environment will determine many of the non-functional product quality requirements such as security, performance, availability, and business continuity requirements.

The section on product vision provides a clear statement of the product goals. Writing such a statement is challenging because it has to capture the views of many potential stakeholders and types of users, and has to clearly show the financial and non-financial business benefits over other existing systems. In addition, this section identifies the main functionalities and features of the product being developed. The detailed functional requirements that are developed later must be traceable back to this section of the vision and scope document. Finally, this section lists all the assumptions that are made and the dependencies that exist. Normally, dependencies are related to external conditions that have to be met, for example, the availability of a hardware device with which to interface. Stating the assumptions and dependencies helps to identify and reduce the risks and to clarify the constraints to the various project and product stakeholders.

The section on project scope and limitations explicitly lists the functionalities and features that will be included in different releases or versions of the product. The scope for each release is developed in line with the stakeholders' objectives and priorities. This also lessens the chance of future misunderstandings between the developers and the clients. The limitations include the functionalities and features that will not be provided by the product in any of its future releases. Clearly stating the limitations helps clarify the expectations and functional boundaries of the product and reduce possible future conflicts between the various product stakeholders. Table 3.1 illustrates a template for a software product vision and project scope document.

Table 3.1 Template for a software product vision and project scope document

```
Title page
Change history
Preface
Table of contents
1. Business requirements and context
     1.1   Product rationale and business opportunity
     1.2   Business objectives
     1.3   Business risks
     1.4   Stakeholders
     1.5   Context and environment
2. Product vision
     2.1   Statement of product goals
     2.2   Main features
     2.3   Assumptions and dependencies
3. Project scope
     3.1   Scope of current release
     3.2   Scope of future releases
     3.3   Limitations
Annexes
Index
```

3.3 REQUIREMENTS ENGINEERING

Obtaining good software requirements is a crucial step toward building reliable and usable software systems. Studies show that one of the main reasons for software project failures is due to poor requirements, consequently leading to unusable software products. Additionally, accurate requirements save time and money later in the software development and maintenance activities. We should always remember that finding an error at the requirement phase costs much less in resources than if the same error is uncovered during the maintenance phase or after the software is released. Therefore, there is a need to use structured and well-defined processes to develop requirements. In addition, well-defined processes for the management of requirements are needed. Requirements engineering is a subset of software engineering that deals with the use of sound techniques for the development and management of software requirements.

Requirements development includes four main steps:

1. Elicitation
2. Analysis
3. Specification
4. Maintenance

Requirements elicitation uses various proven techniques for seeking, extracting, acquiring, and documenting software requirements. Requirements elicitation is discussed later in this chapter. Requirements analysis and specification and the various techniques that are used to complete the requirements specification document are discussed in detail in Chapter 4.

Requirements management deals with project management issues as part of the overall software project management. In addition, it deals with some technical issues supporting the proper management of requirements. These issues include prioritization, maintenance and change management, negotiation, and quality assurance of requirements. Issues related to software project management are detailed in Chapter 10.

A typical list of key requirements management activities includes:

- Defining the appropriate requirements development processes
- Determining the outcomes and deadlines of the requirements engineering phase
- Negotiating and finalizing the software requirements
- Prioritizing the requirements and evaluating the risks
- Tracking and controlling the requirements development steps
- Acquiring and training on requirements management tools
- Managing the requirements library
- Controlling its use and defining a change management mechanism
- Determining and collecting key metrics statistics
- Ensuring the quality of the software requirements

Software projects fail because of errors made during the development of the software requirements. Some of the causes for the failures include:

- Lack of a formal process by which the requirements are collected or elicited
- Breakdown in personal communications between the requirements stakeholders and particularly between the client and user representatives and the analyst
- Absence of a formal requirements validation process
- Failure in the management of the requirements engineering processes
- Ineffective use of tools to deal with requirements for large software projects
- Inexperience of application domain on the requirements development team

Requirements include functionalities and services that are needed by the users to meet their needs and to achieve their business objectives. These requirements are called **functional requirements**. While offering tangible and observable functionalities, other requirements constraining the provision of functionalities must also be specified. These types of requirements are called **non-functional requirements** or quality requirements. NFRs are either system-wide or function-specific and are discussed later in more detail.

3.4 ELICITATION OF FUNCTIONAL REQUIREMENTS

The **elicitation** of requirements engineering is a crucial step toward obtaining effective software requirements. It results in clearly understanding and learning the needs of the software users and then communicating those needs to the software developers. The process of elicitation involves the extraction, discovery or invention, acquisition or elaboration of the stakeholders' needs. The person performing the elicitation step is called the system analyst, business analyst, requirement engineer, or requirement facilitator. Elicitation relies heavily on cognitive and human communications skills to obtain the proper requirements. In addition to practical experience in the application domain, the requirements engineer must be knowledgeable in group and social dynamics, organizational skills, and knowledge engineering. The proper elicitation of the requirements is often a challenging task. The under-specification of requirements can allow a serious defect in the software product and has to be discovered during the validation step of the requirements. Although over-specification of requirements is not as harmful as under-specification, it can be eliminated as a result of requirements prioritization and validation. If it goes undetected, over-specification leads to wasted effort and the provision of unwanted functionalities.

The initial activities undertaken by the requirements engineer include the understanding of the application domain and the current environment or system, the identification of the sources of requirements and the stakeholders, and the selection of appropriate techniques to use for requirements elicitation. Requirements elicitation requires inputs from the problem owner or client, the stakeholders, the various documentation and standards from the application domain,

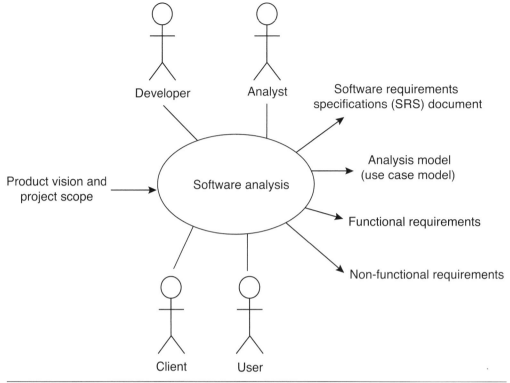

Figure 3.1 Inputs to and outputs from the software analysis phase

the interface information from other systems and the existing system in case the requirements are not developed from scratch. The stakeholders include the software users and developers and all those who are going to be affected or are going to benefit in one way or another from the software under development. Figure 3.1 shows the inputs to and outputs from the software analysis phase that includes the requirements elicitation stage.

Elicitation Techniques

The requirements elicitation step relies heavily on the communications skills and the dynamics of the interactions among the various participants. There is a variety of elicitation techniques that can be used to produce requirements. The use of one of them or a combination of techniques depends on the requirement analyst's preference, the type of system under development, and the type of stakeholders and other participants in the process.

The main elicitation techniques that are used include:

- Interviews or questionnaires
- Task analysis and scenarios

- Preliminary requirements and domain analysis
- Brainstorming
- Workshops, meetings, and/or observations
- Ethnographic assessment
- Practicing
- Prototyping

The **interviewing** technique is an informal technique that is used at the beginning of the elicitation process to engage the various participants. The individual interviews are used to establish the initial mission statement and goals of the system being developed. Interviews can be structured, unstructured, or hybrid. Structured interviews require a set of questions prepared ahead of time and can be distributed to the participants before the interview. In unstructured interviews, questions are developed dynamically as the interview progresses. Hybrid interviews are formatted with a set of fixed questions and impromptu questions that are asked during the interviews. Overall, the formulation of the interview questions and the way they are presented demands thought so that there is not a negative impact on the participants.

The **questionnaire** technique is also used at the beginning of the elicitation process to poll the participants and stakeholders and to obtain their thoughts on issues related to the system. The questions have to be clear, concise, and appropriate to the issues of the project. They can be multiple choice, true and false, or open-ended questions. The answers to questions can be used by the requirements engineer to identify initial conflicting requirements requests that need to be resolved later.

The **task analysis** technique is based on the identification of the uses of the system and the description of the interactions between the users and the system. The interactions can be described using scenarios or flow of events. Additionally, task analysis can be performed in a top-down manner in which initially high-level system tasks are identified. High-level tasks are then refined into lower level tasks and sub-tasks for which scenarios have to be elicited. Task analysis requires domain knowledge expertise and an understanding of the tasks performed by similar systems.

Preliminary requirements and domain analysis techniques start from an initial set of requirements. The preliminary requirements are proposed by the expert requirements engineer and are passed to the various stakeholders for discussion. In this case, the engineer must be an authority in the domain of application.

Group meetings that include all participants and stakeholders are also useful to start the elicitation process. The formation of the group and the dynamics of the interactions among group participants are crucial for the success of this technique. Cohesiveness, openness, and transparency are key communications features during group meetings.

Brainstorming sessions are informal meetings in which stakeholders meet and discuss the various desirable functionalities and services to be offered by the system. Normally, inventive ideas that might or might not be feasible are generated. The meetings are not meant to make decisions or discuss the feasibility of the ideas proposed. All ideas are encouraged and the merits are discussed by the requirements analyst and other participants later in more formal settings. The end product of a brainstorming session is an initial set of software requirements.

Requirement **workshops** are formal settings that are used to elicit software requirements. Participants in the workshop include a facilitator, a technical writer, the requirements engineer, and representatives from the clients' and users' groups. The aim of a requirements workshop is to reach an agreement on a working draft of the software requirements. The workshops must be prepared thoroughly ahead of time and expectations from each participant must be explicitly known. One of the main activities performed during the workshop is to elicit best case and worst case scenarios and fit them in the various use cases of the use case model.

Ethnographic assessment is another requirement elicitation technique that is used by the requirements engineer to gain a greater understanding of the problem domain. It relies on the active or passive participation of the engineer in the working of similar systems and their user interfaces. The engineer can learn from the users' activities by going through the various scenarios and business flows. Also, the engineer can be a passive participant observing the users' activities without any interference. In this technique, the engineer acts as the apprentice and the user acts as the master or supervisor.

Prototyping the graphical user interface is considered an effective tool for eliciting and validating requirements. The requirements engineer, with possible inputs from the users, can develop an initial **prototype** of the system. A prototype should show the main elements of the system functionalities. A prototype must be easy to develop and modify. The investment in time and other resources must be kept at a minimum. The prototype must be evaluated and modified interactively with the users' input. Experience proves that prototype-based requirements are faster to elicit. They also include fewer errors than requirements developed using other elicitation techniques. This observation is certainly valid for systems that are mainly graphical user interface-driven systems. Clients and users like this technique because they feel they are actively engaged in the development of the system they will use later. The main drawback to prototyped requirements is the tendency of non-technical managers to consider them overhead. Consequently, they are tempted to use them as a basis for building the actual system. Additionally, non-technical managers tend to consider a semi-working prototype to be an indication that the project is nearly complete.

During the various elicitation activities, including interviews, group meetings, and workshops, videotaping is a useful tool. Participants must be informed that they are being videotaped. Participants must not feel threatened by the existence of the video camera or the later use of the videotaped elicitation sessions. The elicitation videotapes can be shared and replayed by the various participating parties. Figure 3.2 shows the techniques that can be used during the requirements elicitation process and the participants in this process. The exact combination of requirements elicitation techniques used depends on several factors, among which are the type and size of system being developed and the expertise of the requirements engineer. The key to a successful elicitation of requirement is that it is viewed as an engaging, trusting, and transparent partnership between the various participants in the requirements elicitation processes.

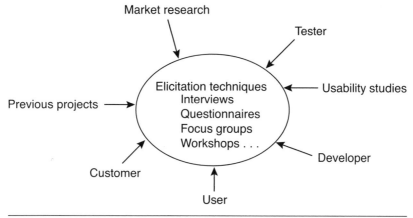

Figure 3.2 Requirements elicitation techniques

Use Case Modeling

Eliciting functional requirements can rely on the construction of a use case-based requirements model. The identification and documentation of the use case model is performed using various elicitation techniques. The elicitation of **actors**, **scenarios**, **use cases**, and their relationships is at the core of building the use case model and the functional requirements. Use case diagrams (UCDs) are introduced in unified modeling language (UML) as the primary diagram for building the use case model or viewing the system being developed. A UCD is composed of actors, use cases, and various interrelationships among actors and use cases. These interrelationships, which are detailed later, can exist among actors, among use cases, or between actors and use cases. Actors and use cases are related using the default **communicates** relationship. Actors can be related using the generalization relationship. Finally, use cases can be linked together using the **extend**, **include** and **generalization** relationships.

An actor represents someone or something that interacts with the system and expects some useful results. An actor is represented by a stickman with the unique actor name next to it. Actors are viewed as entities that are external to the system. Actors include people or other external systems. Different results are expected when interacting with different use cases of the system. A use case must primarily satisfy some functional requirements. The functional requirements are listed as the steps followed in the use case. Typically, five to seven steps, or functional requirements, are included in a use case. In addition, a use case might have to meet certain constraints and NFRs. A use case is represented by an oval with the use case name inside it. An actor, interacting with a use case, is linked with that use case. A line represents the fact that the actor and use case communicate. An optional directed line with an arrow pointing at the use case indicates that the actor initiates or triggers the communications with the use case. A plain line indicates a two-way communication between the actor and the use case. An actor initiates or triggers the communication with the use case to request a service through that

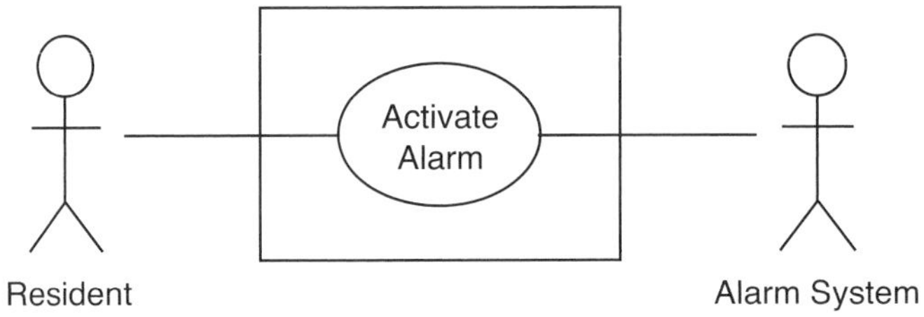

Figure 3.3 Actors Resident and Alarm System and use case Activate Alarm

use case. However, a use case communicates with an actor to prompt the actor for input or a decision, or to inform the actor of events or decisions made by the system. An actor can communicate with several use cases. Also, an actor can play various roles with different use cases. Furthermore, many actors can communicate with a single use case. However, one of the actors is frequently the initiator of the communication with the use case. To illustrate these concepts, Figure 3.3 shows the actors Resident and Alarm System and the use case Activate Alarm. Actor Resident is the primary actor triggering or initiating the communication with use case Activate System. Actor Alarm System is an external system and a secondary actor with which the use case Activate Alarm communicates.

Example 3.1

To illustrate the development of the use case model as part of the functional requirements, consider the following description of the Online Publisher Storefront (OPS). The OPS is a software system developed primarily to allow buyers to place book orders online. Buyers can be individual buyers or institutional buyers, for example, bookstore managers. Individual buyers have to supply payment information when they place their orders. Also, if registered, and after making purchases for more than $1000, they have special discounts and limited credit facility. However, institutional buyers must be pre-registered and must have a good credit standing. Buyers credit facilities and discounts are substantial. Once an order is placed, the credit of the buyer is checked by the finance department and the order becomes active if the credit is in good standing. The order is then sent to the order fulfillment department for processing. Once the order is placed, the buyer has 24 hours to cancel or modify the order. The order fulfillment department is informed accordingly. When the order is placed, modified, or cancelled, the buyer is notified by an e-mail that includes the order number in question. Once an order is fulfilled, it becomes a sale. Prior to placing an order, buyers normally browse the OPS catalogues to search for and select books and then place them in their electronic basket. The content of the electronic basket can be modified at any time prior to the user placing the order. Before confirming an item in the basket, the system checks for its availability in the warehouse. Buyers can enquire about their orders using the order number. Additionally, users can e-mail a complaint or complete a form to complain about the quality of the ser-

(continues)

Example 3.1   *(continued)*

vice or dissatisfaction with the books they have received. The complaints are saved and dealt with by the OPS management staff. Managers and staff of OPS are registered users with two sets of privileges. Managers can modify the book catalogues and create, delete, and modify the staff records. Managers can also generate monthly reports for online sales. Registered users can enquire about their orders, view their purchasing history, and change their personal information.

In Example 3.1, the actors are identified by considering the nouns or noun phrases that appear in the description. The list of nouns must be analyzed carefully and some of the nouns must be dropped if they do not meet the criteria of being actors. The list of nouns and noun phrases include:

OPS	limited credit facility	warehouse
software system	good credit standing	complaint
buyer	finance department	form
book order	order fulfillment department	quality of the service
individual buyers	e-mail, order number	management staff
institutional buyer	catalogue	sets of privileges
bookstore manager	book	staff records
payment information	electronic basket	monthly report
purchase	user	purchasing history
special discount	item	personal information

Many of the nouns and noun phrases are legitimate entity objects or their attributes, which is discussed in Chapter 4. However, only a few of the nouns qualify as actors.

OPS and software system both refer to the whole system being developed and, therefore, are not actors. The buyer is an actor with two specialized actors: the individual buyer and institutional buyer. The actors are related by the generalization relationship. A user is an actor who can be a bookstore manager, bookstore staff, or a buyer. The order fulfillment department, the finance department, and the warehouse are three actors representing external systems. The set of privileges is a descriptor of the actor user. Personal information is a descriptor of a buyer. Table 3.2 summarizes the list of actors in the OPS system.

Actors sharing common features and possessing other distinct features are structured using the generalization relationship. For example, in Table 3.2, actor Employee is linked using the generalization relationship with the two actors, Manager and Staff. We say that Employee is a generalization of Manager and Staff, and conversely, Manager and Staff are two specializations of the Employee actor. Figure 3.4 shows the generalization relationships among actors in the OPS.

Table 3.2 Identification of actors in the OPS system

Nouns	Remarks	Actors
OPS Software system	Refer to the whole system	None
Buyer Individual buyer Institutional buyer	Linked by generalization relationship	Buyer Individual buyer Institutional buyer
Employee Bookstore manager Staff	Linked by generalization relationship	Employee Manager Staff
Warehouse	External system	Warehouse
Finance department	External system	Finance
Order fulfillment department	External system	Order fulfillment

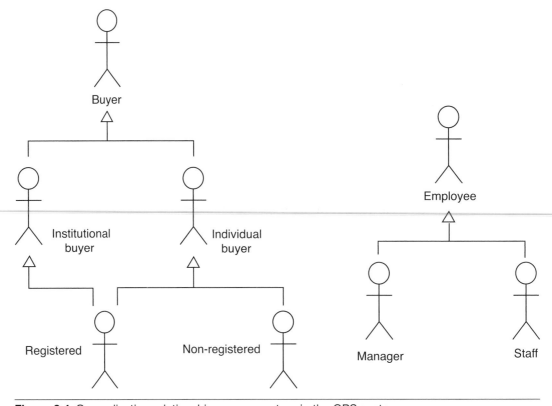

Figure 3.4 Generalization relationships among actors in the OPS system

Table 3.3 Identification of use cases in the OPS system

Use case	Triggering actor	Affected actors
Place order Modify order Cancel order Enquire about order	Buyer	Finance Warehouse
Enquire about order	Buyer	
Register	Buyer	
Browse catalogue	Buyer	Warehouse
E-mail buyer	System	Buyer
Check book availability	System	Warehouse
Provide payment information	System	Buyer
Check credit information	System	Finance
File complaint	Buyer	Manager
Check complaint	Manager	Buyer
Modify catalogue	Manager	Warehouse
Create, modify, or delete staff record	Manager	Staff
Generate monthly report	Manager	
View purchasing history	Registered buyer	
Change personal information	Registered buyer	

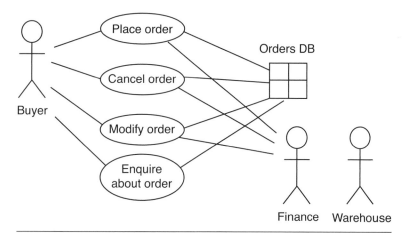

Figure 3.5 UCD including order-related use cases

The use cases of the OPS system are listed in Table 3.3. For each use case, the main triggering actors who are involved and the affected actors are shown.

To reduce the complexity of the use case-based requirements model, related use cases can be grouped together in one UCD. For example, Figure 3.5 shows the UCD that includes all order-related use cases.

Another approach to organizing UCDs is to group together use cases that are triggered by the same actor. In this case, we would probably group functionally unrelated use cases together.

Use Case Development

Many people are interested in the development of use cases because they will participate at various stages and they will play varying roles. The participants include customers paying for the system development, users, managers, requirements engineers, developers, including designers, programmers, testers, and finally, technical writers. To elicit the actors, the analyst has to identify the user types or groups that are supported by the system and benefit from its services. The services represent the main business functions provided by the system. In addition, actors performing administrative, maintenance, and support services need to be elicited. The actors include, among others, system administrators and security managers. Additionally, the external systems that are needed to interact with the system under development need to be identified and recognized as actors. A typical template for documenting a use case is shown in Table 3.4.

Other approaches to describe functional requirements include the specification of the services offered by the system and the specification of the user interfaces used to interact with the system. In this chapter, we concentrate on the use case-based approach.

To reduce the complexity of a use case, the requirements analyst breaks down a complex use case into smaller ones. One way of achieving this is to factor out some behavior from the original use case and then include that behavior in a new use case. The original use case and the newly-created one are then linked using the *include* relationship. This relationship is represented by a dashed arrow starting from the original use case and ending at the new use case.

Another way of reducing the complexity of a use case is to factor out all the behaviors that deal with either exceptional or abnormal conditions or optional behaviors. Exceptional or abnormal behaviors normally interrupt the progress of the original use case. Examples of such behaviors include timeout or failures occurring during the progress of the original use case (also called base use case) or cancelling the use case execution. Optional behaviors can be selected by one or more of the use case actors during the progress of the original use case. An example of an optional behavior is seeking help during the progress of the original use case. The behaviors can then be included in new use cases. The original use case and the newly-created ones, also called extended use cases, are then linked using the *extend* relationship. This relationship is represented by a dashed arrow starting from each newly-created use case to the original use case. We say that a use case UC1 extends another use case UC2 if during the flow of UC2 it is possible that the flow of UC1 is optionally needed or if there is a possibility that the progress of UC2 will be interrupted and the progress of UC1 is started. Once UC1 terminates, UC2 is either resumed or terminated according to the requirements specification. An advantage of recognizing the common behaviors and using them in include and extend relationships and including them in separate use cases is the possibility of reusing them in the same requirements or in future re-

Table 3.4 Template for the description of a use case

Identification	
Name	
Created by	
Date created	
Updated by	
Date of update	
Change history	
Stakeholders	

Actors involved
  Primary
  Secondary or triggering
  Affected	

Brief description	
Assumption(s)	
Precondition(s)	
Triggering event(s)	
Postcondition(s)	
Priority	
Frequency of use	
Normal flow of events (scenarios)	
Alternative or abnormal flow of events	
Used use cases (include)	
Interrupting use cases (extend)	
Non-functional requirements and constraints	
Attached sequence diagram(s)	
Attached activity diagram(s)	
Remarks and issues	

quirements specifications. Figure 3.6 shows the Place Order use case and its include and extend relationships that are listed in the complete use case description shown in Table 3.5.

When developing the details of a use case, the requirements analyst and other participants in the requirements elicitation process focus on discovering and producing potential scenarios for that use case. A use case is viewed as a collection of related scenarios. Inversely, a scenario is viewed as an identifiable instance or enactment of the use case behavior. Once an actor is identified, the tasks that the actor wants the system to perform and the information needed by the system or the actor are described using various scenarios. Some of the identified use case scenarios show the normal or optimistic alternative executions of the use case. Other scenarios show the abnormal or pessimistic executions. Abnormal scenarios include the executions that

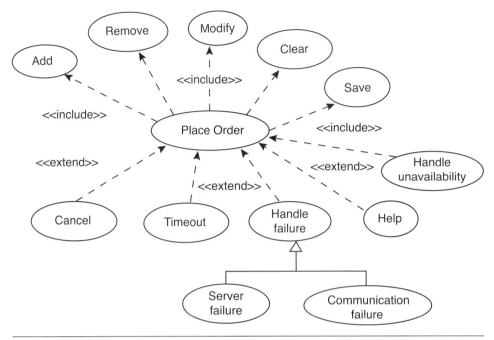

Figure 3.6 Use case Place Order with its include and extend relationships

are interrupted by other use cases using the extend relationships. The points at which the normal executions are interrupted are called extension points. Extension points can be explicitly shown in the use case description. The various scenarios related to the use case can be represented using sequence diagrams. The sequence diagrams can then be linked or referred to in the use case description. Sequence diagrams are discussed in detail in Chapter 4. More use cases are shown in the diagram in Figure 3.7.

After completing the use case-based requirements model, the use cases are reviewed during formal review meetings. The meetings are attended by the authors of the use cases as well as customer's, users', and developer's representatives. In addition, a recorder who is not technically involved in the discussions attends the review to record decisions and modifications to be made to the requirements model. A review moderator also attends to ensure the smooth progress of the discussions during the review. The requirements engineers, authors of the use cases, attend the review to clarify their decisions during the review if necessary and to keep the review on track. The clarity and completeness of the use case can be judged by the customer or user who will examine them to determine if they are understandable and reflect the desired behavior. On the other hand, a use case is clear and complete if, when passed to a designer and a tester, it can be used unambiguously as a good starting point to begin the design and to produce a test procedure that can determine if the use case implementation can be accepted.

Table 3.5 Place Order use case

Identification	UC x
Name	Place Order
Created by Date created Updated by Date of update	J. Smith, January 5, 2006
Actors involved	Triggering actor: Buyer Secondary (affected) actors: Finance and warehouse
Brief description	This use case is started by the buyer to construct electronic basket with books selected from the catalogue
Assumptions	Catalogue includes available books
Preconditions	Buyer could be a registered or unregistered individual user Buyer could be a registered institutional user Registered buyer has already logged on successfully
Postconditions	Electronic basket is created and closed prior to placing the order
Priority	High
Frequency of use	High (one hundred orders per day during the first year)

Flow of events (or steps)	1. Browse book catalogue
	2. Select books
	    2.1. Select a book and quantity
	    2.2. Confirm availability
	    2.3. Compute current total cost
	    2.4. Repeat 2.1 through 2.3 until desired books are purchased
	3. Confirm order
	4. Provide payment information and get confirmation of payment

Alternative flows	Use case can be interrupted at any point by the use cases E1 to E7. Use case is discontinued when interrupted by the use cases: E1 to E4. However, the use case continues after being interrupted by use cases E5 to E7.
Used use cases (include)	Add book to basket Remove book from basket Modify order Clear order Save order Send order Provide payment information Check credit information Check book availability
Interrupting or extending use cases (extend)	E1: Handle timeout E2: Handle communications failure E3: Handle server failure E4: Handle cancel E5: Handle invalid payment information E6: Handle book unavailability E7: Help place order
Non-functional requirements	See Section 3.5
Remarks and issues	

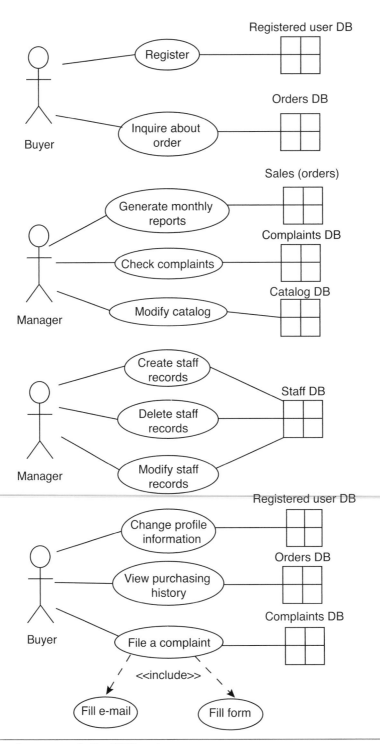

Figure 3.7 Additional use cases in the OPS system

3.5 ELICITATION OF NON-FUNCTIONAL REQUIREMENTS

NFRs are requirements that are related to the quality aspects of the system being developed or the functionalities provided by the system. The quality-based requirements cover both technical and non-technical aspects of the system and its functionalities. While eliciting the functional requirements using the use case modeling approach, the analyst must also elicit the NFRs that are associated with each use case. In addition to use case-specific NFRs, the analyst must also identify and elicit generic system-wide NFRs. Generic NFRs are use case independent and apply to the entire software system. For example, security requirements can be either use case-specific or generic. However, cultural, political, and standards conformity requirements are mainly generic requirements since they normally apply to the system as a whole. NFRs can be either technical or non-technical. Technical NFRs, such as performance requirements, are chiefly quantifiable and possibly automatically verifiable requirements. The types of requirements affect the whole software architecture and can impose or limit the possible design or architectural choices. Non-technical NFRs, such as standards conformity requirements, are mostly non-quantifiable and only verifiable using a non-automated review process. The proper elicitation of NFRs is critical. The types of requirements can conflict or affect each other; in addition, they can affect other functional requirements. For example, a security requirement can affect the performance of the software negatively, requiring, for example, the additional exchange of messages. Moreover, a security requirement can require additional functional requirements. NFRs can also be a main concern either to the users or to the developers. For example, testability is an NFR that affects the developer predominantly because it requires that the developer makes some additional effort to make the software system testable. However, making the software testable has a positive and indirect effect on the reliability of the software. Reliability is a technical NFR of particular interest to the users. On the other hand, performance is an NFR that mainly affects the user because response time delays and lack of memory are noticed by the user. However, the developer is also affected because meeting performance requirements must be dealt with at various phases of the software development process. This classification of NFRs is shown in Table 3.6.

Table 3.6 Types of non-functional requirements

	Mainly a user concern	**Mainly a developer concern**
Technical NFRs	Interoperability Performance Reliability Availability Robustness Security Safety Usability User friendliness	Implementation Installation Maintainability Operational Portability Reusability Scalability Testability Traceability
Non-technical NFRs	Business integrity Cultural Political	Legal Conformity to standards

Normally, non-technical NFRs are generic ones. However, technical NFRs can be either system-specific or use case-specific. For example, various performance requirements can be attached to multiple use cases, unlike, for example, standards conformity requirements that are system-wide requirements. Some of the NFRs can also be considered software quality attributes that are mainly of interest to the developer but can have a tangible impact on the users. NFRs must not attempt to prescribe or impose a technical solution. They are essentially technology-independent.

The types of NFRs that might be needed to constrain the software under development and its environment are introduced in this section.

Technical Non-Functional Requirements

To elicit the technical NFRs, the analyst, client, and user must consider each type of requirement thoroughly. Depending on the type of system being developed, it is determined whether the requirements are mostly system-wide or not. In the first case, the system-wide constraints and requirements must be considered first. Then, when considering each use case separately, it is decided whether to relax or modify the system-wide requirements.

In another approach, we first consider the types of requirements that are mostly system-wide requirements, such as usability and maintainability requirements. Then, we proceed to those requirements types that can be partly use case dependent, such as security and performance. In this way we attempt to minimize the rework of the requirements from generic to specific ones.

Interoperability

Interoperability requirements impose constraints on the types of systems with which the software has to interface. Software systems might have to interface and communicate with other software systems and hardware devices. An example of an interoperability requirement would state: *The system must be able to interface with all printers manufactured by company X.* This requirement imposes some dependability on the proper specification and implementation of the interface with the printers. Consequently, the requirements are indicative of some potential external risks to the development process.

Maintainability

Maintainability requirements impose constraints related to the ease with which the software can be fixed, adapted to new environments and technologies, or expanded. To meet the requirements, there can be various technical and non-technical measures that need to be taken. Technical measures can be related to the development environment and tools used as well as the development methodologies and models adopted. Non-technical measures include hiring decisions and appropriate developers training programs.

Operational

Operational requirements impose constraints on both the physical and logical environments in which the software under development will operate. The constraints can include the characteristics in which the servers are physically located, minimum speed of the network connections, the operating systems that are compatible, and the hardware devices with which the software interfaces.

Performance

Performance requirements impose some technical constraints on the response time delays, throughput of the system, and memory requirements. Response time delays can be either system-wide or use case specific. For example, putting an upper limit on the maximum response time delay for all system functions is a system-wide performance requirement. However, we can also require different upper limits, depending on the individual function or use case. Response time-related performance requirements can also be stated as throughput requirements, putting upper and lower bounds on the acceptable rate of completed transactions. A throughput-based use case-specific performance requirement might be: *The Update Salaries use case should process at least one million records in 10 seconds.*

Constraints on memory consumption are normally described by system-wide performance requirements. A memory-related performance requirement might be: *The maximum memory needed to run the system shall not exceed 1 MB of random access memory (RAM).*

Portability

Portability requirements impose some conditions related to the future deployment of the software system. Software portability is defined as the ease with which the software can be made to run on a different hardware platform or software environment. An example of a portability requirement might be: *The system should be able to run under Mac OS with the least development effort.* To meet this requirement, many constraints related to the development environment and the implementation programming language used have to be imposed.

Reliability and Availability

Reliability requirements impose some values related to the reliability of the software under development. Typical values include the mean time between failures or the maximum time allowed for failures over a period of time. Availability requirements can also be used to impose an upper limit on the downtime of the software system, indicating an acceptable level of failures. Availability requirements as part of the security requirements are discussed later.

Reusability

Reusability requirements impose constraints on the development of the system related to the degree of reuse. There are two types of reuse: development *with* reuse and development *for* reuse. Development with reuse aims at producing software faster by using existing software components. A development with reuse requirement helps the reliability of the overall system provided we are reusing good quality components. Development for reuse aims at producing highly maintainable software that is typically made of reusable components. The components can be reused in future projects by the same team or other development teams. A development for reuse requirement helps the maintainability of the software system and can impose specific decisions related to the software development methodologies used.

Robustness

Robustness requirements impose constraints related to the way the software handles abnormal and erroneous inputs and operational conditions. The requirements address the software behavior with respect to error recoverability and fault tolerance and can be system-wide or use case-specific requirements. An example of a system-wide robustness requirement is: *The system must recover from power failures and continue operating without any side effects on the currently executing transactions.* An example of a use case-specific requirement is: *Completing the Create Customer use case shall be guaranteed even in the case of a database server failure.* Robustness requirements should not state how to achieve software robustness or suggest a particular technological solution to do it.

Safety

Safety requirements are needed when the software being developed deals with safety-critical issues such as aviation software or power and chemical plants control software. The safety requirements must address and require the enforcement of safety standards that are known in the particular application domain. Eliciting safety requirements requires some expertise in the domain of the safety-critical application to avoid costly legal consequences should any of the requirements be omitted. For example, in chemical plant control software, a fail-safe safety requirement might state that: *In the case of software failure, a safety procedure XYZ must be activated immediately to ensure no chemical leakage takes place.*

Scalability

Scalability requirements impose constraints on how the software system should scale up to a high-input load at all interfaces. An example of a scalability requirement might be: *The system must be able to accommodate a maximum of 100 users logged on and performing all types of transactions.* This requirement can force specific architectural design choices on the development team. Ideally, scalability requirements are quantifiable and are normally verified during load testing (see Chapter 8).

Security

Security requirements are critical and need to be identified early in the software development process. A security requirement can be either a system-wide or use case-specific requirement.

Security requirements address four main security concerns: (1) confidentiality, (2) integrity, (3) availability, and (4) accountability. The concerns are dealt with by imposing and adhering to identification, authentication, authorization, integrity, immunity, privacy, non-repudiation, survivability, physical protection, and security standards conformity requirements.

Access control-related requirements, including identification, authentication, and authorization are used to address confidentiality concerns. Also, physical protection requirements can be useful in addressing confidentiality concerns at the physical level. Identification, authentication, and authorization requirements can be system-wide or use case specific. The client can require that certain functionalities are only accessible by identified, authenticated, and authorized users, and other functionalities can be publicly and unanimously accessible.

Integrity concerns are addressed using integrity, immunity, and privacy requirements. A privacy requirement might state, for example, that *the software shall allow a registered user to have control over its own private information.* An immunity requirement might state that *no files can be attached to a user profile without being disinfected by the software.* An integrity requirement can be system-wide or use case specific. An example of a system-wide integrity requirement might state that *all files saved by the software must be tamper proof so that any malicious and unauthorized modification of a file shall be detected.*

Availability issues are dealt with using the survivability and physical protection requirements. A survivability requirement can be applicable system-wide, such as *the system shall continue to provide its functions even if one node fails.* It can also be function- or use case-specific, for example, *the user validation shall always be performed regardless of some network nodes failures.* A physical protection requirement that addresses availability concerns might state that *the database servers shall be protected in fireproof data centers.*

Accountability concerns are dealt with using the non-repudiation and standards conformity requirements. An example of a non-repudiation requirement is *the software shall preserve a tamper-proof record of every privileged access to the system.* Accountability requirements can be either system-wide or applicable to specific functions or use cases of the system. However, standards conformity requirements are normally system-wide. An example of a standard conformity requirement could be *the software and the environment in which it operates shall conform to the ISO 17799 standard.*

Although security requirements are considered to be NFRs, some of them must be implemented by first identifying the appropriate security-related functional requirements. For example, identification, authentication, and authorization requirements are considered by introducing a logon use case as a functional requirement. These use cases are called security use cases. Other researchers have introduced the idea of a misuse case in which the involved actors are called misusers. A **misuse case** represents the abnormal behavior of an attacker or misuser and specifies the software reaction to the specified misuse.

Testability

Testability requirements impose constraints on the future testing of the developed software. Testability is defined as the ease with which testing can be performed. This requirement is somehow related to the maintainability requirements and the ease of software maintenance activities. The ease of maintenance is positively correlated with the ease of testing. Ideally, this requirement should be quantifiable. An example of a quantifiable testability requirement is *testing the software must be completed in 24 hours.* This requirement imposes some constraints on the test automation and the tools used for testing.

Traceability

Traceability requirements impose some constraints on the ease with which the software is traceable. This requirement can be related to the traceability of the different parts of the software development process deliverables or related to the traceability of the software during its execution. In the first type of traceability, the requirement refers to the ability to link every aspect of the software deliverables forward and backward. For example, each module in the software design can be traced backward to a requirement specification element, or forward to a particular piece of code or test cases, hence, enhancing the software maintainability and meeting the maintainability requirements. In the second type of traceability, traces collected during the execution of the software can be needed. Software execution traces are normally used for testing and debugging purposes, thus, enhancing the software testability to meet the software testability requirements. In addition, this aspect of traceability helps to meet the auditability and non-repudiation aspects of security requirements. Examples of the two types of traceability requirements are *all activities of an admin user session must be recorded by the system,* and *every functional requirement must be traced forward in the design, code, and testing documents.*

Usability

Usability requirements address the constraints imposed by the client in its representation of the user community. The objective for the constraints is to make the software easy to use by the various users interacting with it. The usability requirements are normally elicited by first knowing the intended users and their backgrounds and characteristics. This step would be the first to undertake in a usability engineering process. A system-wide usability requirement states *the software must be easy to use by 7- to 9-year-old children.* A use case-specific quantifiable usability requirement reads *eighty percent of students between ages 10 and 14 must be able to create a demo within one hour.*

User-Friendliness

User-friendliness requirements impose some constraints on the user experiences when interacting with the software. The constraints can have implications on the functional requirements and the graphical user interface design decisions. The availability of context-sensitive help versus generic help, a forgiving and courteous interface, and the ease of navigability are examples of user-friendliness requirements. Usability and user-friendliness requirements complement each other and are often seen as equivalent. A system can be easy to use but might not be friendly. Ideally, a highly-usable system is normally a user-friendly system. Issues related to graphical user interface design that address the user-friendliness requirements are presented in Chapter 5.

Non-Technical Non-Functional Requirements

The requirements are normally system-wide. However, it is possible to have a system with two types of users, admin users and normal users, with cultural requirements imposed only on normal users.

Cultural and Political

The **cultural** and **political requirements** address the cultural and political constraints that have to be considered when developing the software. The analyst and client must be aware of the cultural sensitivities of the countries in which the software will be deployed and used. These could include language use issues, use of symbols, and politically offensive contents, among others. Failure to properly elicit the requirements can affect its acceptability and market penetration. Should the requirements conflict in other countries or societies, several versions of the software might have to be developed and deployed.

Legal and Regulatory

Legal and **regulatory requirements** address the legal and regulatory issues related to the software. Adherence to local and international laws and regulations have to be observed by the software and the process by which it is developed. For example, for national security concerns, the development team must not include people that have resided in certain countries. Other requirements related to the software itself can require that the software is in line with copyright laws and regulations. If overlooked, the requirements can lead to lawsuits and criminal investigations affecting the economic feasibility and reputation of the development company.

Conformity to Standards

Standards conformity requirements indicate the standards that must be followed while developing the software system. There are different types and levels of standards. Internal standards that are developed by the software development company can include coding, testing, and documentation standards and templates. Specific country standards might have to be followed and the developer and client must be aware of them. Military standards exist and need to be followed if the military is one of the software stakeholders. Industry standards have to be considered. Specific standards exist for the health, finance, construction, and education sectors, among others. Professional standards can also be referred to in this type of requirements. An example of such standards is the IEEE standard for documenting the SRSs. Finally, international standards, such as those developed by the International Standardization Organization (ISO) and the International Telecommunications Union (ITU), can also be used as part of the standards conformity requirements. The software analyst representing the developer and the client representing the users must be aware of the standards related to the application domain of the software under development. Non-adherence to known and relevant standards and the failure to meet them can lead to unusable software or a delayed release of the software. Therefore, the requirements must be elicited carefully.

NFRs can be documented separately in the software requirement document if they are generic. However, if they are specific to a particular use case, they can be attached closer to the use case description. The constraints section of the use case can include specific NFRs applicable to that use case.

Example 3.2

Examples of generic system-wide NFRs for the OPS system are:

 a. Must be accessible from PCs, Sun Workstations, or Macintoshes using at least Internet Explorer and Netscape web browsers
 b. Must be modular software made of reusable components that are easily modifiable
 c. Must have speed of access to OPS and must be, as much as possible, location-transparent
 d. Must be portable to additional platforms with the least effort
 e. Must be highly available with only an average of one hour a week of downtime to allow for upgrades
 f. Must allow for 100 simultaneous user accesses during the first year of operations and 300 thereafter
 g. Must allow encryption for private user data and only users or programs with the right access control are allowed to decrypt this data
 h. Must log all critical transactions, including ordering, modifying order, or canceling order for future use
 i. Must be easy to use by novice computer users by providing contextual guidance throughout the interface
 j. Must allow language support, depending on the country from which it is accessed

---

Example 3.3

Examples of NFRs for the Place Order use case are:

a. Private data in the Place Order form must be encrypted in the order database
b. Timeout should occur if the Place Order form is not submitted within 20 minutes
c. Confirmation to the Place Order form, once submitted, must occur within 30 seconds
d. Cancellation and help should be available at any time during the ordering process

---

3.6 REQUIREMENTS VALIDATION

Requirements must be validated prior to refining them. The difficulty in the **validation** process is that it cannot be automated. The most effective way of validating requirements is by using good communication skills, both verbal and written, for eliciting and reviewing requirements. When writing requirements, the requirements engineer must make sure that the produced requirements possess good qualities. Requirements are not only to be used as the basis for obtaining a software design, they are also used as a basis for product acceptance testing. Ideally, requirements, and especially the NFRs, should be quantifiable as much as possible.

According to the IEEE standard for requirements specifications, desirable properties of software requirements include:

- correctness
- completeness
- clarity and comprehensibility
- non-ambiguity
- consistency
- feasibility
- modifiability and maintainability
- testability
- traceability
- verifiability
- reusability
- ranking for importance and criticality

A requirement is correct if, when implemented, it reflects the behavior expected by its users. A requirement is nonambiguous if it has a unique interpretation by all its stakeholders. Requirements are complete if they consider *all* functional and non-functional aspects of *all* tasks expected to be performed by *all* its users. Clarity and comprehensibility of requirements allow all stakeholders to understand them and, consequently, to pass an informed judgment on their correctness. Requirements are consistent with each other if one requirement does not impose some restrictions that conflict with other requirements and affect their validity. Often NFRs are in conflict with each other. For example, a usability requirement can be in conflict with a performance requirement. A requirement is technically feasible if it can be implemented using the available time and technology. It is also economically feasible if its automation or inclusion within the system can be financially rewarding. Requirements are modifiable if they are documented in a structured and well-presented manner. A requirement is traceable if it can be easily identified and referenced; in addition, its origins must be known. A requirement is verifiable if, once implemented in the system, checking whether the requirement is met can be feasibly verified either manually or automatically. A requirement is reusable if it is written or documented in a way that helps its reuse in future software projects. A requirement must be ranked for its importance for the success of the current version of the software under development. In addition, a requirement must also be ranked for its criticality with respect to the levels of risk that can hinder its fulfillment.

The validation of requirements can be accomplished using two approaches: synthetically or constructively during their development; or analytically after having been developed. In the synthetic approach, the process by which requirements have been obtained must be well-formed and structured in a way to ideally eliminate or minimize requirements errors. The use of industry-proven guidelines, templates and standards, and elicitation, formal specification, and prototyping techniques can help the development of good quality requirements. Although this approach involves some degree of automation, it still relies on human interactions. Analytic validation techniques must follow once the requirements are developed. The techniques are based principally on requirements inspection and walkthrough processes. The processes are used to ensure the various desirable properties of requirements, including correctness, completeness, nonambiguity, clarity, feasibility, modifiability, and verifiability. The efficiency and effectiveness of the processes rely on the traceability of the requirements and the comprehensiveness and thoroughness of the checklists used during the inspection and walkthrough process. Experience has shown that because of the human nature of the requirements development processes, both the synthetic and analytic approaches complement each other and there is a need to use both of them to ensure good quality requirements.

3.7 REQUIREMENTS MAINTENANCE

Requirements can be subject to varying types of maintenance activities. While in the specification and design phases, the developer might discover that the requirements are incomplete, ambiguous, or contradictory. The requirements errors must be dealt with before continuing the development activities. In fact, dealing with the errors sooner rather than later can save expensive maintenance costs rather than dealing with them after the release of the software. To deal with the errors, the developer has to coordinate with the originator of the requirements document, who in turn has to coordinate with the users' or client's representative. If the errors are extensive and have serious implications to the project plan, an intervention by upper management and the project leader must take place to avoid legal consequences or delays in the planned project deadlines.

After the software is released, many errors might be reported by the user population. Some of the errors might be caused by requirements and specifications errors that were not caught during software development. Moreover, new requirements can be requested by the client and users. Depending on the severity of the requirements changes, a software update or patch might have to be released prior to the scheduled release of a new version of the software.

Normally, requirements changes necessitate changes to the specification, design, and implementation of the software. Therefore, it is important to keep all subsequent deliverables up to date. Code should reflect the design and design should reflect the requirements and specifications.

In addition to changes to the requirements, sometimes the priority of requirements might be changed as a result of changes to the project scope. The change of priorities can have an implication to the software features and functionalities that will be available in the current and future releases of the software.

Because changes to the requirements can have serious implications to project scope and the deliverable deadlines, requests for requirements changes and their approvals should be made in a formal manner and must be considered an integral part of a change management plan normally included in a comprehensive software project plan.

3.8 SOFTWARE REQUIREMENTS SPECIFICATION DOCUMENT

The main deliverable of the software analysis phase is the SRS document. It contains the software requirements captured using the techniques described earlier in this chapter as well as the refinements specified using the techniques that are detailed in Chapter 4. The IEEE has recommended a standard practice for writing SRS. The IEEE standard 830 was first introduced in 1984 and was revised in 1993.

The recommended template for the SRS document contains three sections. The first section includes an introduction to the document. The second section contains an overall description of the software under analysis. The third section provides a description of the specific software functionalities, the NFRs, including performance, safety, security, and portability requirements, the external interfaces and interoperability requirements, and finally, the cultural, legal, regulatory, and political requirements.

The introduction in Section 1 of the SRS document describes the purpose of the SRS, its intended audience, its scope in terms of the overall use of the software produced, the definitions, acronyms, and abbreviations used in the rest of the document, references used in the document, and an overview of the organization and content of the rest of the document.

The overall description in Section 2 describes the context of the software that is being developed and the various types of its external interfaces, the user characteristics, the major functions that will be performed by the software, the general developmental constraints, and the assumptions and dependencies for the validity of the SRS.

The specific functional requirements in Section 3 contain the detailed description of the functional requirements. The functional requirements can be organized by system features, system modes, user classes, stimuli, responses, use cases, or objects. In addition, this section provides a further refinement of the requirements to complete the software analysis phase. Data-, behavioral- and object-oriented modeling techniques for describing data, functionalities and their relationships are used and their outcomes are documented. Chapter 4 discusses the analysis and modeling techniques that are needed to complete Section 3 of the SRS document.

Section 3 also includes the external interfaces and NFRs related to usability, user-friendliness, portability, and interoperability requirements. The interoperability requirements specify the communications interfaces with other external hardware and software systems. In addition, Section 3 of the recommended template includes other NFRs such as the performance, safety, security, standards conformance, legal, regulatory, and cultural requirements that the software must meet.

Table 3.7 shows the template used in the IEEE recommended practice for SRSs.

Table 3.7 Template used in the IEEE recommended practice for software requirements specifications

Title page
Change history
Preface
Table of contents
1. Introduction
    1.1 Purpose and intended audience
    1.2 Scope
    1.3 Definitions, acronyms, and abbreviations
    1.4 References
    1.5 Overview of the document
2. Overall description
    2.1 Product perspectives and context
        2.1.1 System interfaces
        2.1.2 User interfaces
        2.1.3 Hardware and software interfaces
        2.1.4 Communications interfaces
        2.1.5 Memory constraints
        2.1.6 Operational context
    2.2 Product functions
    2.3 User characteristics
    2.4 General developmental constraints
    2.5 Project assumptions and dependencies
3. Specific requirements
    3.1 External interfaces
    3.2 Functional requirements
    3.3 Performance requirements
    3.4 Database requirements
    3.5 Design constraints and standards compliance
    3.6 Software system attributes (Non-functional requirements)
4. Supporting information
    4.1 Appendices
    4.2 Index

SUMMARY

Software analysis is the first phase of a typical software development process model. It includes both the software requirements and specifications stages. In this chapter, we studied the software requirements stage of software analysis. The specification stage is studied in detail in Chapter 4.

Obtaining the proper software requirements is an important and crucial task in a software development project. Requirements are the foundation upon which a software architecture and design is developed. Along with a clear product vision and project scope document, a well-defined software requirement engineering process must be used to produce software requirements. A typical requirement engineering process starts with requirements elicitation. Requirements elicitation helps to capture, invent, and discover the software requirements. A requirements model based on the use case modeling approach can be developed and documented. Depending on the complexity of the target product to be developed, different elicitation techniques can be used.

There are two types of requirements, functional and non-functional. Functional requirements are related to the visible, user-interface-driven functions to be provided by the software product. NFRs, on the other hand, are mainly quality requirements related to the attributes of the offered functionalities. NFRs can be product-wide or function-specific requirements.

Once developed, software requirements must be reviewed and validated. Requirements prototyping is a useful method to obtain an approval on software requirements. Requirements management is also an important and often overlooked process that allows for the proper handling and maintenance of requirements. Once software requirements are obtained, they can be explained further using software specification techniques (see Chapter 4). The outcomes of the software analysis phase, including both requirements and specifications, can be documented using a recommended IEEE standard format for SRS.

KEY TERMS

access control	functional requirements	non-functional requirements
accountability	generalization relationship	operational
actor	group meeting	performance
availability	include relationship	political requirement
brainstorming sessions	integrity	portability
communicates relationship	interoperability	preliminary requirement
cultural requirement	interviewing	product vision
elicitation	legal requirement	project scope
ethnographic assessment	maintainability	prototype
extend relationship	misuse case	questionnaire

regulatory requirement	security	traceability
reliability	software analysis	usability
reusability	software requirements	use cases
robustness	specification	user-friendliness
safety	standards conformity	validation process
scalability	task analysis	workshop
scenario	testability	

REVIEW QUESTIONS

1. What are the main objectives of the product vision and project scope document? What are the main sections?
2. Who are the stakeholders in the requirements engineering process?
3. What are the components of a UCD?
4. What are the possible relationships among use cases?
5. What are the fields of a comprehensive use case template?
6. What are the types of NFRs?
7. What are the techniques for requirements elicitation?
8. Provide examples of types of security requirements.
9. What are the requirements review techniques?
10. What are the standards that can be referred to in NFRs?
11. What are the NFRs that are of principle concern to the development team?
12. What are the types of actors? Provide examples of each type.
13. Explain, using examples, how an NFR can affect a functional requirement.
14. What are the main parts of the SRS document recommended by IEEE?
15. What are the types of NFRs listed in Example 3.2?

EXERCISES

1. Produce a use case model (UCM) of the following problem. Your UCM should include UC diagrams and sequence diagrams: A Spell Checker System reads words from a text file. For each word in the file, the checker searches a Dictionary File. If the word is not found, the user is prompted whether they want to add the word to the dictionary. If the user answers positively, a new word is inserted in the Dictionary File, otherwise the Wrong Words file is updated accordingly.
2. For each of the NFRs below, state its type:
   a. Should include exciting colors and allow lots of interaction with children
   b. The software should be able to interface with blood pressure collectors

    c. Various types of users have different functionalities that are available only after proper authentication

    d. Should be easy for users who have minimal English language skills

    e. The software provides a reply within 10 seconds under any circumstances

    f. In a future release, the software should be ported to the Mac OS

    g. The product should provide all minimal guarantees that are set by the Ministry of Consumers

    h. The interface should be context-sensitive and not culturally offensive

    i. The product should be able to deal with ten thousand users, one hundred of which can be logged on at the same time

3. Given the following English specification for a web-based order processing system for a computer store: A new user can connect to the company's web page and create a new customer profile by providing personal information. This information is validated and saved in a customer information file on the company's server. The user is then provided with a user ID and password via an e-mail sent by the system. Using this password, the user can logon to the web again and place an order. The user can also delete or update an order within a day after placing the order. In all cases, the system verifies the transaction and reacts accordingly. If the transaction is not allowed (e.g., deleting after the deadline), the user is informed. Before accepting the transaction, the system checks the customer information file for a credit check as well as the inventory file for availability. If the ordered item is not available, the system asks the user whether to keep it in a backorder file or discard. If the product is available, the inventory and customer information files are updated accordingly. The ordered product is delivered along with a bill and the accounting file is updated. Once the payment is received, the accounting file and the customer information files are updated. From time to time, the system administrator sends e-mails to customers informing them of special deals. Identify the actors and use cases. Produce one or more UCDs. Provide sequence diagrams for two use cases of your choice.

4. Given the following English description: This system allows authors to submit their research work to a journal or conference for publication. An admin user assigns submitted papers to various reviewers by e-mailing them about the assignment. Reviewers logon and check the assigned papers, review them, and submit their evaluations. Once all evaluations of a submission are received, the admin makes the decision to accept or reject the paper and informs all reviewers and the author of that paper. The author should be able to check the status of the submitted work online. Identify the actors and use cases. Produce one or more UCDs. Identify possible security requirements for the system. Provide sequence diagrams for two use cases of your choice.

5. Given the following English specification of a web-based MovieActor application: The Cinema Employee can create, update, and delete movies from the Movie Database. In addition, the employee can create, update, and delete movie screenings from the Screening

Database. The MovieGoer can request the display of MovieActor details, and then, optionally, select a particular movie to display its screening details. A manager can request the display of summary reports on MovieActor information and Screening details. When creating or updating the movie screening information, some basic check for conflict and availability of a screening room is completed before committing to the change. Develop the use case model which should include one or more UCDs. Provide a detailed description of two use cases of your choice.

6. Produce data flow diagrams at various levels of refinement: A system is to be produced that holds details of deliveries of several brands of milk in a small town. As well as recording which households take which brand(s) of milk, this system also includes billing information and details of customer vacations when milk will not be delivered. The household phones the delivery company to change personal information, such as the address, to inform the company of vacation, and to change the milk order. For each delivery person, the system prints a daily list of which brands of milk are to be delivered to which households. The system should also be able to produce summary information showing how many liters of each type of milk are sold each day in the week. Customer bills are printed at the end of each month and delivered with the first delivery of the following month. The system should also produce error messages, confirmations, and warnings. Produce a use case model including one or more UCDs. Provide a detailed description of two use cases of your choice.

BIBLIOGRAPHY

Books

Alexander, I., and R. Stevens. *Writing Better Requirements*, Reading, MA: Addison-Wesley, 2002.

Aurum, A., and C. Wohlin, eds. *Engineering and Managing Software Requirements*, Berlin: Springer, 2005.

Bruegge, B., and A. Dutoit. *Object-Oriented Software Engineering*, 2d ed., Englewood Cliffs, NJ: Prentice Hall, 2004.

Bittner, K., and I. Spence. *Use Case Modeling*, Reading, MA: Addison-Wesley, 2002.

Chung, L., et al. *Non-Functional Requirements in Software Engineering*, Berlin: Springer, 1999.

Cockburn, A. *Writing Effective Use Cases*, Reading, MA: Addison-Wesley, 2000.

Davis, A. M. *Software Requirements: Objects, Functions and States*, Englewood Cliffs, NJ: Prentice Hall, 1993.

Horrocks, I. *Constructing the User Interface with Statecharts*, Reading, MA: Addison-Wesley, 1999.

Hull, E., et al. *Requirements Engineering*, 2d ed., Berlin: Springer, 2002.

Jackson, M. *Software Requirements and Specifications*, Reading, MA: Addison-Wesley, 1995.

Jacobson, I. *Object-Oriented Software Engineering: A Use Case Approach*, 2d ed., Reading, MA: Addison-Wesley, 2007.

Kohavi, Z. *Switching and Automata Theory*, 2d ed., New York: McGraw Hill, 1979.

Kotonya, G., and I. Sommerville. *Requirements Engineering: Processes and Techniques*, New York: John Wiley and Sons, 2000.

Kulak, D., and E. Guiney. *Use Cases: Requirements in Context*, 2d ed., Reading, MA: Addison-Wesley, 2003.

Lauesen, S. *Software Requirements: Styles and Techniques*, Reading, MA: Addison-Wesley, 2002.

Leffingwell, D., and D. Widrig. *Managing Software Requirements: A Use Case Approach*, 2d ed., Reading, MA: Addison-Wesley, 2003.

Loucopulos, P. and V. Karakostas. *Systems Requirements Engineering*, New York: McGraw-Hill, 1995.

Lutowski, R. *Software Requirements: Encapsulation, Quality and Reuse*, Boca Raton, FL: Auerbach Publications, 2005.

Reisig, W. *Petri Nets: An Introduction*, Berlin: Springer Verlag, 1985

Robertson, S., and J. Robertson. *Mastering the Requirements Process*, 2d ed., Reading, MA: Addison-Wesley, 2007.

Scott, K. *UML Explained*, Reading, MA: Addison-Wesley, 2001.

Shafer, L., and M. Christie. *Software Requirements: A Standard-Based Guide*, New York: Wiley-IEEE, 2005.

Sommerville, I., and P. Sawyer. *Requirements Engineering: A Good Practice Guide*, New York: John Wiley, 1997.

Thayer, R. H., and M. Dorfman, eds. *Software Requirements Engineering*, New York: IEEE Computer Society Press, 1997.

Wiegers, K. *Software Requirements*, 2d ed., Redmond, WA: Microsoft Press 2003.

Withall, S. *Software Requirements Patterns*, Redmond, WA: Microsoft Press, 2007.

You, R. R. *Effective Requirements Practices*, Reading, MA: Addison-Wesley, 2001.

Articles

Berry, D. "The importance of ignorance in requirements engineering," *Journal of Systems and Software*, 28(2):179–184, 1995.

Boehm, B. "Verifying and validating software requirements and design specifications," *IEEE Software*, 1(1):75–88, 1984.

Chung, L., and B. Nixon. "Dealing with non-functional requirements: Three experimental studies of a process-oriented approach," Seventeenth IEEE International Conference on Software Engineering, 1995.

Costello, R., and D. Liu. "Metrics for requirements engineering," *Journal of Systems and Software*, 29(1):39–63, 1995.

Davis, A. M. "A comparison of techniques for the specification of external system behaviour," *Communications of the ACM*, 31(9):1098–1115, 1988.

Easterbrook, S., and B. Nuseibeh. "Managing inconsistencies in an evolving specification," Second International Symposium on Requirements Engineering, 1995.

El-Emam, K., and N. Madhavji. "Requirements engineering practices in information systems development: A multiple case study," Second International Symposium on Requirements Engineering, 1995.

———."Measuring the success of requirements engineering processes," Second IEEE International Symposium on Requirements Engineering, 204–211, 1995.

Goldsack, S., and A. Finkelstein. "Requirements engineering for real-time systems," *Software Engineering Journal*, 6(3):101–115, 1991.

Gotel, O., and A. Finkelstein. "Extending requirements traceability: Lessons learned from an industrial case study," Fourth IEEE International Symposium on Requirements Engineering, 1997.

Holtzblatt, K., and H. Beyer. "Requirements gathering: The human factor," *Communications of the ACM*, 38(5):31–32, May 1995.

Hsia, P., et al. "Status report: Requirements engineering," *IEEE Software*, 10(6):75–79, 1993.

Hughes, K., et al. "A taxonomy for requirements analysis techniques," presented at IEEE International Conference on Requirements Engineering, 1994.

Kirner, T., and A. Davis. "Nonfunctional requirements for real-time systems," *Advances in Computers*, 1996.

Kosman, R. "A two-step methodology to reduce requirements defects," *Annals of Software Engineering*, vol. 3, 1997.

Leveson, N., et al. "Requirements specification for process-control systems," *IEEE Transactions on Software Engineering*, 20(9):684–707, September 1994.

Lutz, R. "Software engineering for safety: A roadmap," International Conference on Software Engineering, Limerick, Ireland, 213–226, 2000.

Mylopoulos, J., et al. "Representing and using non-functional requirements: A process-oriented approach," *IEEE Transactions on Software Engineering*, 18(6):483–497, 1992.

Nuseibeh, B., and S. Easterbrook. "Requirements engineering: a roadmap," Proceedings of International Conference on Software Engineering (ICSE-2000), Limerick, Ireland, ACM Press, 4–11 June 2000.

Roman, G. "A taxonomy of current issues in requirements engineering," *IEEE Computer*, 18(4):14–21, 1985.

Ryan, K. "The role of natural language in requirements engineering." *In* IEEE International Symposium on Requirements Engineering, 240–242, IEEE Computer Society Press, 1993.

Vaughan-Nichols, S. "Building better software with better tools," *IEEE Computer Magazine*, 36(9):12–14, September 2003.

Yeh, R. T., and P. Zave. "Specifying software requirements," *Proceedings of the IEEE*, 68(9):1077–1085, 1980.

Zave, P. "Classification of research efforts in requirements engineering," Second IEEE International Symposium on Requirements Engineering, IEEE Computer Society Press, 214–216, 1995.

Standards

IEEE Std 830, IEEE Recommended Practice for Software Requirements Specifications, 1998.

IEEE Std 1028, IEEE Standard for Software Reviews, 2002.

IEEE Std 1233, IEEE Guide for Developing System Requirements Specifications, 1998.

Web
Added
Value™

This book has free material available for download from the
Web Added Value™ resource center at *www.jrosspub.com*

Software Specification

Software specification is the second stage that is performed during the software analysis phase of the software development life cycle. The main purpose of the **software specification stage** is to use appropriate and relevant analysis techniques to bridge the gap between the user-centered software requirements specification (SRS) and the developer-centered software design. The deliverable of this stage is either a separate software specification document or a more refined SRS document such as the one discussed in Chapter 3. Software specification relies on the software requirements elicited from the users or clients and described in the software requirements document. Ideally, the software specification document allows for a better understanding of the software requirements by modeling the behavioral, data, and processing aspects needed to meet the requirements. Software analysis can be performed using either classical software analysis techniques or object-oriented analysis (OOA) techniques. The outcomes of the software analysis are used by software designers to produce an appropriate software design. Specification validation and verification is a critical activity aiming at discovering and removing specification errors as early as possible in the development process.

Learning Outcomes

In this chapter you will learn:
- Basic terminology in software specification
- Behavior specification techniques, how to use them, and how to validate them
- Data specification techniques, how to use them, and how to validate them
- Process specification techniques, how to use them, and how to validate them
- Object-oriented analysis (OOA) approach and how to use it

4.1 SOFTWARE MODELING

The requirements specification documents produced as a result of the first stage of the software analysis phase are user-centered. They are written by the development team in simple technical terms after a process of requirements elicitation involving the clients or users. This document is normally used as a legal contract between the developers and the client representing the users. It is also used to develop the software acceptance criteria described in the acceptance test plan. Before we proceed to software design, it is important to provide technical analysis of the software requirements that is more detailed and refined. The software specification process is mainly the process of refinement and elaboration on the user-centered requirements specifications to produce more technical details, thus allowing designers a more sound and formal idea about what the software under development is supposed to do.

Analyzed requirements enable designers to make better design choices and, more importantly, correct design decisions. It is evident that the more time spent in analyzing software requirements prior to the design phase, the more reliable the software produced will be. Moreover, errors in the understanding of what the software must do proliferate to errors in design, implementation, and production errors, which are the costliest to correct.

Requirements modeling techniques offer important tools for describing, visualizing, analyzing, and verifying the requirements before proceeding with design. Designers are able to start from more reliable requirements specifications. A good modeling technique is one that is easy to use, has a strong theoretical foundation, easily testable, easily automated, and has some automated tool support. Executable models are also useful for model checking and verification. Furthermore, they allow model simulation and a better understanding of the software requirements.

When modeling software for the purpose of analyzing it, it is important to capture all aspects of the software requirements. At a higher level of abstraction, a software application is a processor of data. It is used to accept incoming user inputs to trigger the execution of processing routines that will potentially use permanent or non-permanent data to produce outputs used by the issuing user. In a typical software system there are three important and complementary aspects to understand, refine, and analyze: (1) behavioral; (2) process; and (3) data. The behavioral and process aspects provide a dynamic view of the system. The behavioral aspect concentrates on describing the changes in internal and external states of the software system as a result of handling either internal or external inputs. The process aspect concentrates on the description of what the software processes do to the incoming internal or external data. The data aspect provides a static view of the system. It concentrates on the data requirements needed for the system to deliver its intended functions. Figure 4.1 illustrates the relationship between software requirements, specifications, and design.

The following three sections detail how to model each of the three system aspects.

4.2 BEHAVIOR MODELING

To model the behavioral aspects of software systems requirements, we look at the finite state machine (FSM) model and its extensions, the **Petri net** (PN) model and its extensions, and both the activity and **statechart diagrams** that are introduced in the Unified Modeling Language (UML). Each of these modeling techniques has its own expressive power and limitations. The software analyst can pick and choose the technique that seems relevant and appropriate to the software requirement to model.

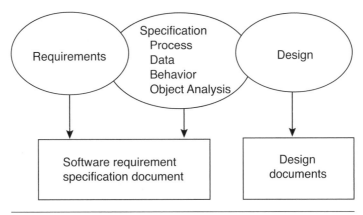

Figure 4.1 Relationships between software requirement, specification, and design

Finite State Machine

The **finite state machine** (FSM) is a modeling technique that can be used to describe the state-based behavior of a process within software systems. In addition, an FSM can be used to model the whole system as one process. This technique is used when the number of states the process can be in is small, and the next state of a process is determined by its current state and the inputs to the process. Typically, the process behavior is described by the next process state and by the output the process delivers after accepting an input.

Formally, an FSM modeling a process is described by a 6-tuple $M = (S, \Sigma_I, \Sigma_O, \Omega, T, s_0)$, where:

S = the set of states the process can be in
Σ_I = the set of inputs to the process
Σ_O = the set of outputs from the process
Ω = the partial output function (defined as: $\Omega: S \times \Sigma_I \rightarrow \Sigma_O$)
T = the partial state transition function (defined as: $T: S \times \Sigma_I \rightarrow S$)
S_0 = the initial state of the process and $S_0 \in S$.

This machine is also known as a Mealy machine in which the output is a partial function of the current state and the input applied at that state.

Graphical, Algebraic, and Tabular Representations

There are three alternative and equivalent representations of an FSM that can be represented graphically as follows: A circle represents a state. A directed edge between two states S_1 and S_2, also called a transition, represents a transition from S_1 and S_2. A label on the transition from S_1 to S_2, of the form i/o, indicates that when input $i \in \Sigma_I$ arrives while at state S_1, an output

$o \in \Sigma_O$ is generated and the process moves to state s2. It is also possible to have transitions occurring spontaneously or triggered after the elapse of time or the occurrence of a timeout. In this case, the input i is represented by Σ_I indicating that no input is needed for the transition to occur. Similarly, in a transition that does not produce any output, the output o in the label is represented by Σ_O indicating that no output is needed.

Example 4.1

Consider the graphical representation of an FSM M shown in Figure 4.2.

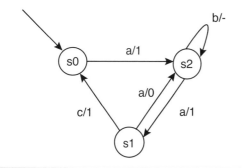

Figure 4.2 Graphical representation of FSM M

The FSM M in Example 4.1 corresponds to the following algebraic representation:

$M = (S = \{s0, s1, s2\}, \Sigma = \Sigma_I \cup \Sigma_O = \{a, b, c\}$
$\cup \{0, 1\}, \Omega = \{s0 \times a \to 1, s2 \times b \to \text{-},$
$s2 \times a \to 1, s1 \times c \to 1, s1 \times a \to 0\},$
$T = \{s0 \times a \to s2, s2 \times b \to s2, s2 \times a \to s1,$
$s1 \times c \to s0, s1 \times a \to s2\}, s0)$

Ω can be equivalently stated as:

$\{(s0, a,1), (s2, b, 1), (s2, a, 1), (s1, c, 1), (s1, a, 0)\}$

Similarly, T can be stated as:

$\{(s0, a, s2), (s2, b, s2), (s2, a, s1), (s1, c, s0), (s1, a, s2)\}$

Also, for simplicity, Ω and T can be merged together as follows:

$\{(s0, a/1, s2), (s2, b/1, s2), (s2, a/1, s1),$
$(s1, c/1, s0), (s1, a/0, s2)\}.$

An FSM can also be represented in tabular form. A two-dimensional table will have n rows and n columns, where n is the finite number of states in S, also called the cardinality of S. Each cell in the $n \times n$ table represents a transition from s_i to s_j denoted by (s_i, s_j). A table cell includes the label i/o for that transition. If no transition from s_i to s_j exists, the corresponding cell will include -. The tabular representation of the FSM in Example 4.1 is shown in Table 4.1.

Table 4.1 Tabular representation of the FSM M shown in Figure 4.2

$s_i \backslash s_j$	s0	s1	s2
s0	—	—	a/1
s1	c/1	—	a/0
s2	—	a/1	b/—

An alternative representation is to have an n $\times$ m table in which n is the number of states and m is the number of possible inputs. In this case, a cell shows the next state reached and the output generated. Table 4.2 illustrates the alternative table for the FSM representation in Example 4.1.

Table 4.2 Alternative tabular representation of the FSM M shown in Figure 4.2

S\Input	a	b	c	—
s0	s2,1	—	—	—
s1	—	—	s0,1	s2,0
s2	s1,1	s2,—	—	—

Properties of FSM-Based Models

In the following sections, some desirable properties of the FSM are introduced. Then, the implication of each of them on the FSM as a behavioral specification model are identified.

Completeness

An FSM is said to be complete or completely specified if, and only if, at each state there exists a transition for each input i $\in \Sigma_I$. In other words, the FSM should be able to react to every input at every state, and this reaction should be captured and specified in the model.

The FSM in Example 4.1 is not complete because at state S_0 it is not specified what to do if input b arrives while at this state.

A completely specified FSM should have at least n $\times$ m transitions, where n is the number of states and m is the number of input symbols (m is the cardinality of Σ_I). Also, an incompletely specified FSM can be clearly identified in tabular form if a cell includes - or Φ exists in the table.

Let us suppose that, at a given state, some inputs are valid and expected and the rest are invalid or unexpected. To produce a robust software system, it is desirable to specify what to do when both valid (good) and invalid (bad or unexpected) inputs are applied at each state of the system. Specification **completeness** allows the implementation of a robust process—a process capable of dealing with both correct and incorrect inputs.

Determinism

An FSM is said to be **deterministic** if, and only if, at any state, the reaction to an input is unique and unambiguously determined. Uniqueness means that for the same input, the FSM should move to the same next state and should deliver the same output any time it executes.

The FSM in Example 4.1 is deterministic because there are no distinct transitions with the same input at any given state.

It is extremely desirable that an FSM modeling software process be deterministic. A software implementation must be deterministic because a user, at the same state, would like to obtain the same result any time the same request (input) is present. This property is desirable also for any user-oriented systems (e.g., vending machine or telephone system). It is noted later that we may need to specify that it is possible to exhibit different behaviors for the same input and at the same state provided that other conditions result in different outcomes.

Strong connectedness

An FSM is said to be strongly connected if from any state we can reach any other state of the FSM immediately by executing one or more transitions. The FSM in Example 4.1 is strongly connected because any state is reachable from any other state in the FSM.

Normally, the **strong connectedness** feature is desirable for software processes. A state that is not reachable from any other state means that the process is somehow disconnected or discontinued. Therefore, one part of the process can be useless since it is unreachable. For example, normally in a user-driven interface any situation (state or screen) must be reached somehow at one point. Moreover, we should eventually be able to get out of that state or screen. However, there are situations in which we would like to specify the possibility of reaching a state out of which no transitions are possible. This state is referred to as a dead state.

Full connectedness

An FSM is said to be **fully connected** if from any state of the FSM we can reach each of the other states by executing one transition. This requirement is extremely restrictive and nonfeasible and is normally not desirable in software processes.

Minimality

An FSM is said to be minimal if there exists no other equivalent FSM with fewer numbers of states or transitions. Algorithms for reducing a given FSM can be found in Kohavi (1979).

The **minimality property** is desirable for both software and digital systems. Implementing a non-minimal FSM implies wasting development efforts on a nonreduced and somehow redundant specification. This definition of minimality assumes that all transitions are of equal complexity.

Limitations of the Basic FSM Model

The basic FSM model discussed is unable to describe certain process behavior requirements. Specifically, the basic model introduced so far cannot express timing and timeout specifications, conditional transitions, variable or data manipulations, and **concurrency specifications**. To increase the expressive power of the basic FSM model, we informally describe the extensions that need to be added.

Timing and timeout specification

Suppose that at a given state of the FSM we would like to specify that if no input is present within t time units, a transition should take place and an output should be delivered. This situation would occur in many real-time processes and in user-oriented interfaces and systems. The basic FSM model is not expressive enough to specify such timing and **timeout** constraints. We would like to have certain delayed transitions in which a time delay is specified instead of an input symbol. Therefore, for any given transition, the presence of an input symbol or time delay is mutually exclusive.

Conditional transitions

Suppose that at a given state of the FSM we would like to specify that in addition to the availability of an input symbol, certain predicate(s) should evaluate to true for the transition to take place. A predicate is a boolean function P: X → {True, False}, where X is an arbitrary set, and P is said to be a predicate on X. The basic FSM model is not capable of accommodating such conditional transitions. We would like to have certain predicated or **conditional transitions**. In addition to the availability of the correct input at the source state of a conditional transition, a predicate specified for this transition is evaluated. The transition would then take place only if the predicate evaluates to true.

The addition of a condition to a transition specification requires a change to the definition of determinism in the FSM model leading to the **extended FSM** (EFSM) model. An EFSM is said to be deterministic if at the same state, for the same input, and the same predicate, the same transition (next state and output) must always occur.

Variable manipulation

Suppose that a given state of the FSM, the reaction to the next input symbol, must change a certain variable value, which is critically needed in future transitions (for example in a predicate evaluation). Most often, these variables are also referred to as state variables. For example, in a user interface-driven process, at the logon state, the reaction to a bad login input can depend on the number of times a bad login input was performed earlier. Therefore, a variable holding a counter of the number of bad logins is needed.

Concurrency specification

Due to its inherently sequential nature, a basic FSM cannot model concurrent behaviors that can be needed to describe complex concurrent applications. However, extensions to this model were added in the UML statechart diagram to model concurrent execution by specifying concurrent substates.

Extended Finite State Machine Model

To overcome the first three limitations of the basic model described earlier, the following formal definition of the EFSM model is introduced.

An EFSM is formally described by an 8-tuple $M = (S, \Sigma_I, \Sigma_O, \Omega, V, T, s_0, v_0)$ where:

S = the set of states the process can be in
Σ_I = the set of inputs to the process
Σ_O = the set of outputs from the process
Ω = the partial output function (defined as: $\Omega: P \times S \times \Sigma_I \to \Omega$)
V = the set of model variables
T = the partial state transition function (defined as: $T: P \times S \times \Sigma_I \to S \times f(v)$)
    where P is the set of predicates and $f(v)$ is a function of v
s_0 = the initial state of the process and $s_0 \in S$
v_0 = the initial values assignments

In the EFSM model, the transition function determines for each transition:

- Predicate, if any is needed, that must be evaluated to true
- Time delay, if any, that must elapse before the transition takes place
- Changes to the variable values that must be performed when the transition occurs

However, if a time delay is specified for a transition, no input symbol should exist in the corresponding transition specification.

For example, the transition specifying the fact that at state s_i, if no input is available for 10 time-units, variable z should be incremented by 1, output error_1 should be delivered and we should move to state s_j, can be described by the following transition specification:

$$(-, \text{td} = 10, s_i, 1/\text{error\_1}, s_j, z = z + 1)$$

The first - means that no predicate exists and the second - means that no input is needed because a time delay is specified. However, suppose we want to specify the fact that when an input a $\in$ Σ_I arrives at state s_i before td elapses, predicate P evaluates to true and we want the process to move to state s_k, to output OK_msg, and to decrement z by 1. In this case, the following transition specification: $(P, -, s_i, a/\text{OK\_msg}, s_k, z = z - 1)$ is added.

As a result of the modification to the basic FSM model, a cell in the tabular representation of the EFSM can contain more than one entry. For example, from state s_i to s_j, as shown in Figure 4.3, we can have a delayed transition and one or more conditional or predicated transitions. Also, in an EFSM graphical representation, the time delay, the predicate, and $f(v)$ can be added to the label of the appropriate transition.

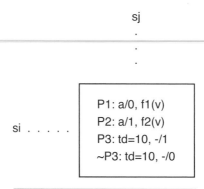

Figure 4.3 A cell in a tabular EFSM representation

Example 4.2

Consider the EFSM M′ shown in Figure 4.4.

The FSM M′ in Example 4.2 corresponds to the following algebraic representation:

$$M = (S = \{s_0, s_1, s_2\}, \Sigma = \Sigma_I \cup \Sigma_O = \{a, b, c\} \cup \{0, 1\}, \Omega = \{s_0 \times a \to 0, s_0 \times a \to 1, s_1 \times c \to 1,$$
$$s_1 \times c \to 1, s_2 \times - \to 0, s_2 \times a \to -, s_1 \times b \to 1, s_0 \times b \to 1, s_2 \times a \to 0\}, T = \{P_1 \times - \times s_0 \times a \to$$
$$s_1 \times -, \sim P_1 \times - \times s_0 \times a \to S_1 \times k = k + 1, P_3 \times - \times s_1 \times c \to s_1 \times k = 0, \sim P_3 \times - \times s_1 \times c \to s_1$$
$$\times k = 1, - \times td = 10 \times s_2 \times - \to s_2 \times k = k + 1, \sim P_2 \times - \times s_2 \times a \to s_1 \times -, - \times - \times s_1 \times b \to s_2$$
$$\times -, - \times - \times s_0 \times b \to s_2 \times -, P_2 \times - \times s_2 \times a \to s_0 \times 0\}, s_0, k = 0).$$

The transition and output tuples can be merged and listed as follows:

$$\Omega, T = \{(P_1, -, s_0, a/0, S_1, -), (\sim P1, -, s_0, a/1, s_1, k = k + 1), (P3, -, s_1, c/1, s_1, k = 0), (\sim P3, -, s_1,$$
$$c/1, s_1, k = 1), (-, 10, s_2, -/1, s_2, k = k + 1), (\sim P2, -, s_2, a/-, s_1, -), (-, -, s_1, b/1, s_2, -), (-, -, s_0, b/1,$$
$$s_2, -), (P2, -, s_2, a/0, s_0, -)\}$$

The tabular representation of M′ is shown in Table 4.3.

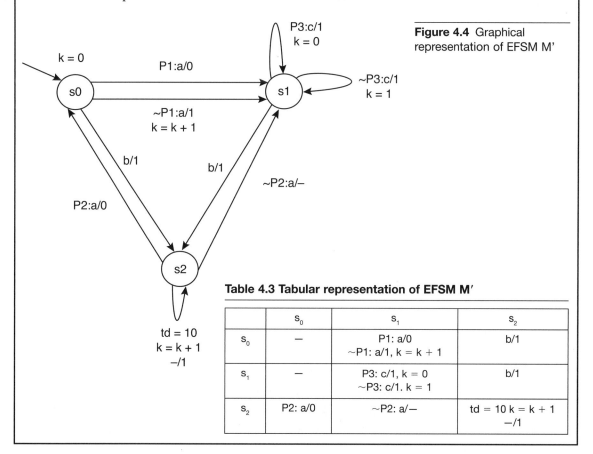

Figure 4.4 Graphical representation of EFSM M′

Table 4.3 Tabular representation of EFSM M′

	s_0	s_1	s_2
s_0	—	P1: a/0 ~P1: a/1, k = k + 1	b/1
s_1	—	P3: c/1, k = 0 ~P3: c/1. k = 1	b/1
s_2	P2: a/0	~P2: a/—	td = 10 k = k + 1 —/1

Example 4.3

Following is the description of the partial behavior of the ATM machine. First the user inserts the bank card in the ATM's card reader. Then, the ATM expects the user to enter the PIN within 20 seconds, otherwise the ATM will beep and eject the card. If the PIN is valid, the user is allowed to proceed with a choice of banking transactions. Otherwise if the PIN is invalid, the user can retry for a maximum of two more trials. After three unsuccessful attempts, the card is confiscated by the ATM and the user has to contact the main branch.

In the EFSM model, we assume that the ATM is initially at the idle state (s1). The states include:

Idle state (s1)
Wait-for-pin state (s2)
Start-selection state (s3)
Card-confiscated state (s4)

The inputs include:

Client's card (i1)
PIN code (i2)

The outputs include:

Screen getting the PIN (sc1)
Waiting for PIN timeout message (o1)
Invalid PIN error message (e1)
Card-confiscated message (e2)
Start transaction selection screen (sc2)

Predicate P1 evaluates to true if the number of trials did not exceed two and predicate P2 evaluates to true if the entered PIN code is valid. Only one variable to count the number of trials is needed ($v1$). Also, at the wait-for-pin state, if no input is available within 20 seconds, the ATM is reset to the idle state. Figure 4.5 shows the graphical representation of the EFSM model.

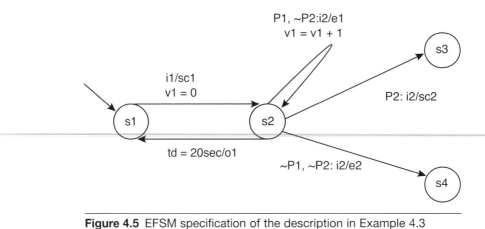

Figure 4.5 EFSM specification of the description in Example 4.3

Applications of the EFSM Model

The EFSM is a powerful model for describing many complex software systems. For example, it can be used for describing a graphical user interface, telephone system interactions, programming language parser, communications protocols, and many more types of software systems.

Graphical user interface specification

Consider the graphical user interface (GUI) as a process with a deterministic behavior. The set of states typically correspond to the set of screens. Inputs include all those possible to the screens at the interface. Outputs correspond to the distinct outcomes from the system, including voice messages, control signals, warning messages, error messages, help messages, and printed logs.

Communications protocol specification

A **communications protocol** is the backbone of any distributed system. A protocol describes the timely and orderly exchange of messages between two or more distributed protocol entities. A protocol also defines the structure that the messages must have and their meanings. Each protocol entity or participating machine can be described by an EFSM. For example, in a protocol involving three interacting protocol entities, M1, Mi, and Mj, a transition in machine M1 is denoted by Mi.msg1/Mj.msg2. This transition indicates that M1 receives a message msg1 from Mi and then sends message msg2 to Mj. Note that if only two entities are involved in the exchange, there is not a need to prefix the received or sent message with the entity name.

A global state of the distributed system is composed of the individual states of each FSM and the content of the communications channels between the communicating FSMs. The initial global state is when each FSM is at its initial state and all channels are empty. We assume that the channels handle messages on a first-in-first-out (FIFO) basis using a queue implementation.

Example 4.4

Consider the following informal requirement specification involving a distributed system of three communicating FSMs corresponding to three interacting processes in the system. The user process (UP) requests a data item from the server process (SP). The SP directs any request to the database process (DP) which returns either with a data item or an error message, indicating that the requested item is not available. Once the SP receives the data item (data), it increments a counter (c) of services requested by 1 and passes the data item to the UP. However, if the SP receives an 'item not available' (nav) message from the DP, it tries again after the elapse of two seconds. If, for the second time, it receives the 'item not available' (nav) message, it returns to the UP with the message 'item not available' (nav).

Figure 4.6 illustrates the EFSM specification of this requirement. The figure shows the three processes and their behaviors. Counter c is used to keep track of the number of successful requests resulting in returned data. Also, predicate Q is used by the DP to determine if the request can be satisfied by returning a data item.

(continues)

Example 4.4 *(continued)*

The outcome of Q is determined by DP. The label UP.req/DP.REQ in process SP specifies that message req is received from process UP, and, as a result, message REQ is sent to process DP.

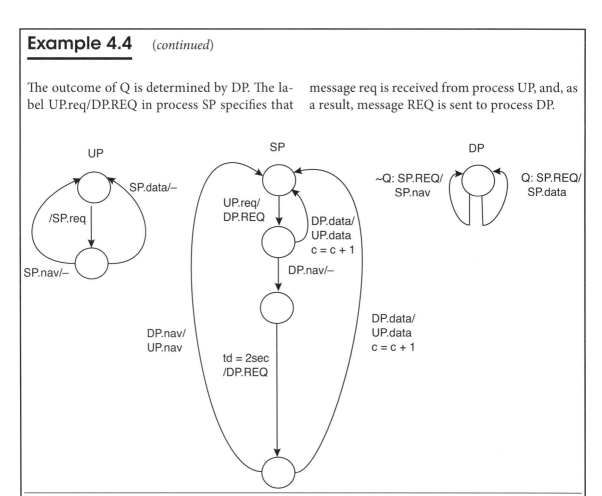

Figure 4.6 The EFSM specification for the system described in Example 4.4

Additional Properties of EFSM-Based Models

When modeling distributed systems and protocols using the EFSM, additional required properties of the model need to be checked when validating the model. Following, we describe some important and desirable features of communicating EFSM models.

Deadlock-free

A communicating EFSM model is deadlock-free if no global state can be reached at which all the communications channels are empty and each of the FSMs remains at a state waiting for a message to arrive. If such a global state is reached, it is said that the modeled system contains a **deadlock**. All machines will remain waiting indefinitely in the states they have reached.

Absence of unspecified receptions

A communicating EFSM model has an **unspecified reception** error if, at a given state, a machine M in the model specifies or expects the reception of a message; however, the incoming channel has an unexpected message at the head of the queue. This error leads to the non-progress or blocking of machine M.

Cyclicity

A communicating EFSM model is cyclic if the initial global state is reached after the exchange of messages. The initial global state is characterized by the fact that each FSM of the model is at its initial state and all the communications channels are empty. In some systems, **cyclicity** can be a desirable property that needs to be checked in a model.

Livelock-free

A communicating EFSM model has a livelock if the modeled system enters a loop involving message exchanges with no possibility of breaking out of the loop. The presence of a **livelock** in a model is a symptom of a bad model specification. The absence of livelocks must be checked in a communicating EFSM model.

Liveloop-free

A communicating EFSM model has a liveloop if the modeled system enters a loop involving message exchanges with the possibility of breaking out of the loop if certain conditions are satisfied. The presence of a **liveloop** in a model can be a symptom of poor model specification and needs to be investigated further. If needed, the absence of liveloops must be checked in a communicating EFSM model.

Petri Net Model

Petri nets (PNs) were first introduced by Carl Petri in 1963. A PN provides a powerful modeling technique with a strong mathematical foundation. Because of this foundation, the verification of the model properties is facilitated.

Mathematical and Graphical Representations

A basic PN is represented by a quintuple $PN(P, T, B, F, M_0)$ where:

> P = a non-empty set of places and the cardinality of P is P
> T = a non-empty set of transitions and the cardinality of T is T
> B = $P \times T \rightarrow N$, a backward incidence function that determines the number of arcs emanating from transitions to places in the net
> N = the set of natural numbers

$F = P \times T \rightarrow N$, a forward incidence function that determines the number of arcs emanating from places to transitions in the net

N = the set of natural numbers

M_0 = the initial marking of the net that specifies the initial distribution of tokens inside the p places of the net.

If we order the sets P and T, then the functions F and B can be represented by $p \times t$ matrices. n_1 arcs exist from transition t_i to place pk if, and only if, $B(pk, t_i) = n_1$. Also, n_2 arcs exist from place p_1 to transition t_j if, and only if, $F(p_1, t_j) = n_2$. Finally, M_0 is a $p \times 1$ vector, called initial marking of the PN, representing the initial mapping of tokens where $M_0(p) = n$ is represented by n tokens in place p. A marking M can be considered as one state of the net. Marking M_0 denotes the initial state of the net. The definition of B implies that if no arcs exist from t_i to p_j, $B[p_j, t_i]$ will be 0. Similarly, if no arcs exist from p_i to t_j, $F[p_i, t_j]$ will be 0.

A PN is represented graphically as follows:

1. A place is represented by a circle
2. A transition is represented by a horizontal bar
3. A forward (backward) transition is represented by an arc starting from a place (transition) and terminating at a transition (place)
4. A token is represented by a bold dot and i tokens exist inside a place P if $M_0(P) = i$.

The initial distribution of tokens, in M_0, among the many places of the net is a choice that depends on the initial state of the system we are modeling. In Figure 4.7, t1 and t2 are transitions and p1, p2 and p3 are places. Arc a is a forward arc and arc b is a backward arc. The initial marking M_0 is (1, 0, 1).

A transition is called a synchronization transition if it has two or more incoming arcs and one outgoing arc. Also, a transition is called a forking transition if it has one incoming arc and more than one outgoing arc. Firing a forking transition specifies the enabling of concurrent executions. A transition can be both a synchronizing and a forking transition.

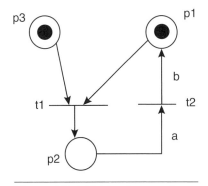

Figure 4.7 A Petri net example

Figure 4.8 shows the graphical representation of a net PN. In this PN, t1 is a forking transition and t3 is a synchronizing transition.

The mathematical representation of PN is: PN = (P = {p1, p2, p3, p4, p5}, T = {t1, t2, t3, t4}, B, F, M0 = (2, 0, 0, 0, 0)) The **backward matrix** (B) and **forward matrix** (F) are shown in Figure 4.9.

Given a PN and a transition t ∈ T, we define: (1) PRE(t) = {p ∈ P/F(p, t) ≠ 0} to be the set of input places of transition t, and (2) POST(t) = {p ∈ P/B(p, t) ≠ 0} to be the set of output places of transition t. The PN **incidence matrix** C is defined as:

$$C(p, t) = B(p, t) - F(p, t)$$

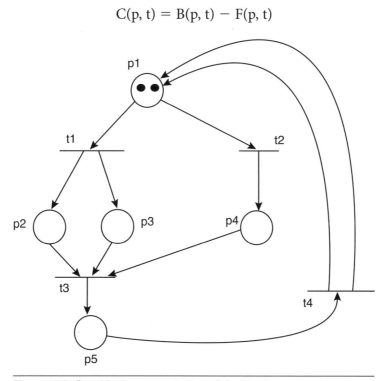

Figure 4.8 Graphical representation of the Petri net

		t1	t2	t3	t4			t1	t2	t3	t4
	p1	0	0	0	2		p1	1	1	0	0
	p2	1	0	0	0		p2	0	0	1	0
B =	p3	1	0	0	0	F =	p3	0	0	1	0
	p4	0	1	0	0		p4	0	0	1	0
	p5	0	0	1	0		p5	0	0	0	1

Figure 4.9 Backward and forward matrices for the Petri net in Figure 4.8

The formula defining the incidence matrix C implies that the new marking is the net result of the tokens that are gained minus the tokens that are lost as a result of the firings of certain fireable transitions.

Given a marking M, we say that a transition t of a PN is enabled or fireable if, and only if, for every $p \in PRE(t)$, $M(p) \geq F(p, t)$. Firing of a transition $t \in T$ is defined by the transformation of the enabling marking M into a new marking M' such that:

$$p \in P, M'(p) = M(p) + C(p, t)\,\sigma$$

The main advantage of the PN as a specification model lies in its verifiability. It is possible to verify the correctness of a PN-modeled system using some mathematical manipulations from linear algebra. In the following, we describe two distinct types of PN properties, namely, the liveness and safety properties and how we can verify them.

Properties of the Petri Net Model

Two types of properties can be verified in a PN model of a system: the safety and liveness properties. Safety properties are related to the semantics of the net and can be verified using static or structural analysis techniques. These techniques verify the existence of some predefined net invariant. Liveness properties are related to the syntactic correctness of the net and can be verified using dynamic or **enumerative analysis** techniques. These techniques verify the freeness from deadlocks, livelocks, and the identification of live loops and home states in the PN model.

Structural properties and invariant analysis

Verification of safety properties, using the so-called **structural** or **invariant analysis**, aims at proving the existence of desirable place and transition invariants in the net.

A **place invariant** is a subset of the places of the net in which the total number of tokens remains constant at any time during the execution of the net. A PN is said to be conservative if, and only if, the total number of tokens in the net remains constant. This means that the set of places P forms a place invariant. A **transition invariant** is a sequence of transition firings starting from M that will return the net to the same marking M.

Given a system to model, meanings are attached to places and transitions of the net model. Then the designer has to identify semantic properties related to the places and transitions. For example, in Figure 4.13, place p1 corresponds to a processor (resource), place p2 corresponds to the use of a processor, p3 corresponds to a request for processing, and a token is placed in p1 (p2) to represent the availability (use) of the processor. Transition t1 (t2) corresponds to the allocation (de-allocation) of the processor.

A semantic property 'Processor can only be used by one process at a time' can be formulated. This can be transformed to a place invariant stating that the total number of tokens in p1 and p2 is always 1. Therefore, {p1, p2} makes a place invariant. An example of a transition- or execution-related property is that when the processor is free, and a request for processing arrives, the processor becomes busy and eventually it is released. This requirement can be transformed to the transition invariant {t1, t2}.

Finding place invariants of a net can be achieved by solving the equation $\Phi\, C = 0$, where Φ is a vector of p values and p is the number of places in the net. Intuitively, a place invariant includes all places corresponding to rows of the incidence matrix C, such that, when added, a vector of p 0s is obtained. More than one place invariant can exist in a net.

A net is said to satisfy the place invariants if, and only if, all the semantic requirements formulated as place invariants are found in the solution of the equation $\Phi\, C = 0$.

Finding transition invariants of a net are achieved by solving the equation $C\, \sigma = 0$, where σ is a vector of t values and t is the number of transitions in the net. More than one solution can exist. A solution vector corresponds to a set of transitions that can be fired in a specific order to bring the net back to the starting marking. σ_1, the ith element of $\sigma_1, . , . , \sigma_i, \ldots \sigma_t$, is equal to 1 if t_i is part of the invariant.

A home state is a state that corresponds to a starting marking involved in a transition invariant.

A net is said to satisfy the transition invariants if, and only if, all the semantic requirements formulated as transition invariants are found in the solution of the equation $C\, \sigma = 0$.

For the PN in Figure 4.8, the incidence matrix C is shown in Figure 4.10, and the place and transition invariants are computed below.

	t1	t2	t3	t4
p1	-1	-1	0	2
p2	1	0	-1	0
C = p3	1	0	-1	0
p4	0	1	-1	0
p5	0	0	1	-1

Figure 4.10 Incidence matrix for the Petri net in Figure 4.8

Example 4.5

Find the transition and place invariants in the PN of Figure 4.8.

To find the transition invariants, we solve the equation $C\, \sigma = 0$, where $\sigma = (\sigma_1\ \sigma_2\ \sigma_3\ \sigma_4)$. We obtain the following equations:

$$\sigma_1 + \sigma_2 = 2\sigma_4$$
$$\sigma_1 = \sigma_3$$
$$\sigma_2 = \sigma_3$$
$$\sigma_4 = \sigma_3$$

The two possible transition invariants are: (1) the trivial invariant (0 0 0 0), involving no firings

(*continues*)

Example 4.5   (*continued*)

and (2) a nontrivial invariant (1 1 1 1). This only nontrivial transition invariant indicates that the initial marking can be reached by firing the four transitions in a certain order. This order may be either $t_2 t_1 t_3 t_4$ or $t_1 t_2 t_3 t_4$. Note that the solution invariant does not relate the order of firings.

To find the place invariants, we solve the equation $\Phi C = 0$, where $\Phi = (\Phi_1 \Phi_2 \Phi_3 \Phi_4 \Phi_5)$. We obtain the following equations:

$$\Phi_1 = \Phi_2 + \Phi_3$$
$$\Phi_1 = \Phi_4$$
$$\Phi_5 = \Phi_2 + \Phi_3 + \Phi_4$$
$$2\Phi_1 = \Phi_5$$

Since the only solution to the equations is the trivial one, where $\Phi_1 = \Phi_2 = \Phi_3 = \Phi_4 = \Phi_5 = 0$, we conclude that there are no place invariants. We can also confirm this result by inspecting the incidence matrix because no addition of any combination of rows results in (0 0 0 0).

Dynamic properties and enumerative analysis

Verification of liveness properties, using reachability or enumerative analysis, aims at proving the freeness of the model from deadlocks and livelocks. Such analysis is also used to identify liveloops or home states in the net. This analysis is based on the construction of the PN reachability graph. Safety features of the PN model will be revealed after analyzing the constructed graph.

Let σ be a sequence of transitions $t_1 t_2 \dots t_k$. σ is called a legal firing sequence starting from M if, and only if, there exists a sequence of markings M ... M* such that: $M \rightarrow M_1 \rightarrow \dots \rightarrow M_i$. $M \rightarrow M_1$ means that M_1 is reachable from M by firing transition t_1. Marking M* is said to be reachable from M by firing σ denoted by $M \overset{*}{\rightarrow} M_i$.

The PN reachability graph is a directed graph whose root is the initial marking or state of the net. Nodes of the graph correspond to the reachable markings. Nodes are linked by transitions. A transition exists from marking M_i (node$_i$) to marking M_j (node$_j$) if, and only if, M_j is reachable from M_i by firing a single transition.

A PN reaches a deadlock state if, and only if, during the construction of its reachability graph, a state (or node) is reached from which no transition is enabled or fireable in the entire PN, meaning that no transition can be extended at any leaf node of the tree.

A PN contains a livelock if, and only if, its reachability graph contains a cycle which, once entered, cannot be exited. This is a dynamic deadlock in which the net is not doing anything other than progressing (uselessly) inside this cycle. A PN contains a liveloop if, and only if, its reachability graph contains a cycle in which the system can cycle. Eventually, a transition that allows the net to exit the cycle is enabled and becomes fireable.

A PN is said to be bounded by k, if, and only if, $M(p) \leq k$, for any marking in the reachability tree of the net. A PN model is said to be safe if, and only if, it is free from deadlocks and livelocks and satisfies all of its required invariants.

The reachability graph of the model is shown in Figure 4.11.

The reachability graph shows that by firing the sequence of transitions t2 t1 t3 t4 or t1 t2 t3 t4, starting from M0, the model returns back to M0, hence, a cyclic model confirming the transition invariant found in the structural analysis discussed earlier.

Extensions to the Basic Petri Net Model

To enhance the expressive power of the basic PN model, various useful extensions were introduced. Some of these extensions are described briefly in the following sections.

Inhibitor arc Petri net

In this type of PN, a special type of arc called an inhibitor arc is added to model the requirement that the presence of a token in the source place disables the incident transition. In Figure 4.12, the presence of a token in place p2 disables transition t making it nonfireable.

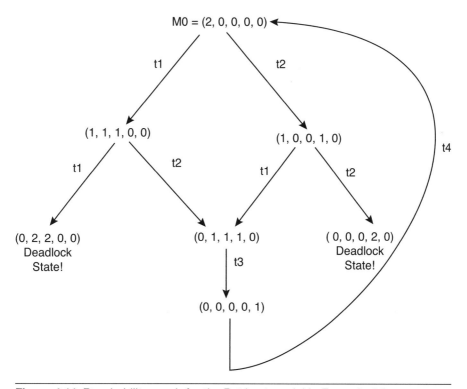

Figure 4.11 Reachability graph for the Petri net model in Example 4.8

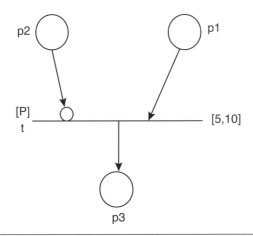

Figure 4.12 Petri net with inhibitor arc, predicate, and time specification

Predicate Petri net

In the basic PN, we stated that a transition is fireable when each of the incoming places carries the needed tokens to enable the transition. However, sometimes we need additional contextual or operational conditions satisfied to enable the transition. A **predicate** can be added to the transition specification. In Figure 4.12, transition t is fireable when one token exists in place p1 and when predicate P is true.

Timed Petri net

In addition to a predicate, we can add a time interval (t_{min}, t_{max}) to a transition specification. This interval indicates that once the conditions for **fireability** are satisfied, the transition must fire after a minimum of t_{min} time units and before t_{max} time units. If no time interval is specified, as in the basic model, the default time interval is (t_{min} = 0 and t_{max} = 0), meaning that if the conditions for fireability are met, the transition must be fired immediately. For example, in Figure 4.12, transition t must be executed after a minimum of 5 seconds and a maximum of 10 seconds from the time it became enabled. Note that no token should exist in place p2 for t1 to become enabled.

Other extensions of the basic PN model include, among others, Numeric, Object, Colored, Hierarchical, and Stochastic Petri nets. These extensions allow for the modeling of a wide range of complex systems. For more on PNs, the interested reader can refer to the bibliography section of this chapter.

Modeling Requirements

Starting from an informal requirement, the challenge is to define the PN elements that can best model the requirement. The places and their meanings must be defined and the predicates, and possibly the timing requirements, needed in the model must be identified.

Example 4.6

In a request handling system, the handler must immediately process an incoming request once it is received. The processing takes between 5 and 10 seconds to complete. Once a request is handled, the system must be able to handle new requests immediately. The system should keep track of the number of handled requests.

Figure 4.13 shows the PN model of this system. A token in place p1 indicates the arrival of a new request. A token in place p2 indicates that the handler is ready. A token in place p3 indicates that the handler is processing a request. Finally, the number of tokens in place p4 indicates how many

requests have been handled by the system thus far. Transition t1 is called a synchronization transition, whereas t2 is a concurrency transition. The time interval at transition t1 is $[0, 0]$, indicating that the firing is immediate once the transition becomes fireable, meaning that the handler is free and a new request has arrived. The time interval at transition t2 is [5 msec, 10 msec], indicating that the processing must terminate after at least 5 msec and at most 10 msec. The initial marking of the system is $M0 = (1, 1, 0, 0)$.

The backward (B), forward (F), and incidence (C) matrices of the PN in Figure 4.13 are shown in Figure 4.14.

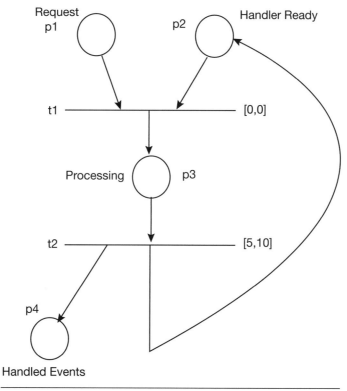

Figure 4.13 Petri net model of Example 4.6

(continues)

Example 4.6 *(continued)*

$$B = \begin{vmatrix} 0 & 0 \\ 0 & 1 \\ 1 & 0 \\ 0 & 1 \end{vmatrix} \qquad F = \begin{vmatrix} 1 & 0 \\ 1 & 0 \\ 0 & 1 \\ 0 & 0 \end{vmatrix} \qquad C = \begin{vmatrix} -1 & 0 \\ -1 & 1 \\ 1 & -1 \\ 0 & 1 \end{vmatrix}$$

Figure 4.14 The backward, forward, and incidence matrices for the model in Figure 4.13

In this model, there is one transition invariant other than the trivial one. This is true because the initial marking $(1, 1, 0, 0)$ can never be reached again. The model is cyclic because the sequence t1 t2 is fired infinitely as long as new requests are arriving. Also, the only place invariant is p2 p3, indicating that the number of tokens in places p2 and p3 remains constant at 1. This is true because the handler is either free, waiting for an incoming request, or busy processing a request. Also, using either reachability or structural analysis, we can prove that the number of firings of t1 is the same as the number of tokens in p4. We can then state that the PN model faithfully captures the given informal specification. Being visual and mathematical, and hence executable, the modeler can modify the model and validate it iteratively and interactively until a refined and satisfactory model is obtained.

Statechart Diagram

A statechart diagram is a UML diagram that is similar to the FSM model with some extensions related to expressing concurrent behaviors. In a statechart diagram, a state indicates a set of conditions at which a system or entity can be during its execution. Based on changes in these conditions or upon reception of an external or internal event, the system or entity can move to a new state. A statechart diagram shows the possible states at which the system or entity can be. It also shows the transitions between these states. Transitions needing no events to occur are called triggerless transitions. Typically, a transition is labeled by an incoming event and an action. If a guard condition is added to the transition, the event is discarded if the condition evaluates to false, and no action takes place. A statechart diagram includes one entry state and possibly one final state.

Actions can be associated with a state. There are four types of **actions** that can be triggered when reaching a state. They are *on entry*, *do*, *on event*, and *on exit* actions. If an action has to take place when a state is entered or exited, an on entry action or an on exit action is added inside the state symbol (rounded rectangle), respectively. Also, actions that must be executed while at this state are specified using do actions. Finally, actions that are executed when an event occurs while at this state are specified using on event actions.

States in a statechart can be composite. A **composite state**, also called a **superstate**, is a state that includes multiple-nested states or substates. Substates can describe both sequential and concurrent behaviors. A composite state that includes two or more concurrent substates is split accordingly into parallel flows. Each flow has its own initial and final states. Transitions can occur between composite and noncomposite states.

Basically, a statechart is similar to the EFSM model described earlier but can express complex state behavior, including concurrency.

Example 4.7

Consider the following requirements describing the life cycle of a bank account entity. A bank account is first created by a bank manager. The customer owning the account has to activate the account within one month, otherwise, this account is automatically cancelled. Once activated, the customer can use the account to perform bank transactions. The account becomes blocked for security reasons or if it is dormant for more than six months. In either case, the cus-

tomer is asked to contact the bank. After being blocked for two weeks, if the customer does not contact the bank, the account is cancelled. The customer can cancel the account at any time while it is active.

From the above informal description, we can identify the customer account as an entity that goes through different states. The states that are identified are: created, activated, blocked, and cancelled. Figure 4.15 shows the UML statechart diagram specifying the behavior of the account entity.

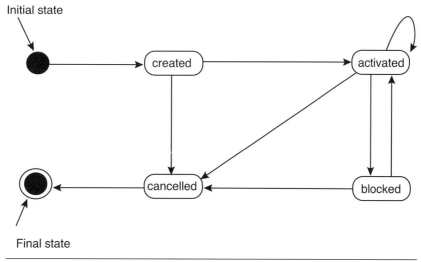

Figure 4.15 A statechart modeling the behavior of a bank account entity

Example 4.8

To demonstrate the use of complex superstates, we consider the following requirement. At the created state, the account card is printed and shipped to the customer. At the same time, logs are generated and the customer service and security departments are informed. Figure 4.16 shows the created superstate divided into two concurrent sequences of substate transitions also called **swimlanes**.

UML statecharts are useful for the modeling of some behavioral aspects of both the software requirements and the design specifications. At the requirements level, states are normally the overall states of the system. Inputs and outputs are normally external interactions occurring at the system interfaces. Specifying behaviors of user interfaces can be performed using statechart diagrams.

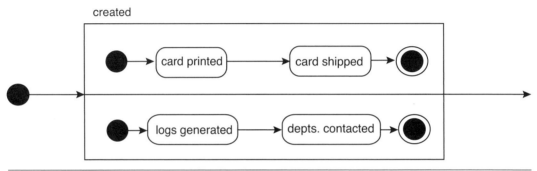

Figure 4.16 Superstate specification for Example 4.8

Activity Diagram

An **activity diagram** is a UML diagram that can be used to describe the **dynamic behavior** of a system. An activity diagram specifies both sequential and concurrent flows of activities. It is typically used to describe high-level requirements such as workflow models, business processes, and low level design specifications such as procedural logic. Similar to interaction diagrams, an activity diagram can be used to model the dynamic behavioral aspect of the use case view developed during the requirements stage of the analysis phase. In addition, it can model the dynamic aspect of the design view of the system. An activity diagram involves activities that usually span more than one use case (or functionality).

An activity diagram consists of **action states**, **activity states**, and transitions between them. It uses other symbols from PNs, flowcharts, and FSMs, such as a diamond for branching and merging alternative flows, join transition for synchronizing activities, and fork transition for spawning concurrent activities. Similar to a predicate in PNs, a guard condition can be used to label an edge out of a decision diamond. A guard condition is a Boolean expression that must be true for the labeled edge to be traversed. The activity diagram has one initial node and one final node typically. An activity state can be decomposed into other action and activities states. An activity is also nonatomic and hence interruptible. Action states are atomic and nondecomposable. We can view an activity as consisting of a block of statements that takes some time to execute, whereas, an action consists of a single statement and takes an insignificant amount of time to execute.

Actions and activities can be grouped according to the actor, object, or system that performs them. Vertical lines separate the obtained groups. A swimlane includes all the grouped action and activities between two vertical lines. Actions and activities are normally totally-ordered. However, activities and actions across swimlanes can be either totally- or partially-ordered due to the possibility of concurrent behavior modeling.

Example 4.9

Consider the flow of activities within a company that receives orders through the Internet. Once the order is received by the Customer Service department, the customer's credit is checked. If the customer has a bad credit rating, the order is rejected and closed. Otherwise, an invoice is prepared and sent to the Finance department for follow up and, at the same time, the order is sent to the Order Fulfillment department. The Finance department processes the payment once received and informs the Customer Service department. Also, the Order Fulfillment department checks to see if the ordered items are available. If available, the order is delivered to the customer, otherwise it is back ordered. In either case, the Customer Service department is informed to close the order.

Figure 4.17 shows the activity diagram specifying the above informal requirements. The diagram shows three swimlanes, each corresponding to one department. It also includes two decision diamonds, one related to the customer's credit and the other related to the item availability. In addition, there is one fork transition and one join transition. The various activities are shown inside the rounded rectangles. Finally, the initial and final nodes are shown in the customer service department swimlane.

(continues)

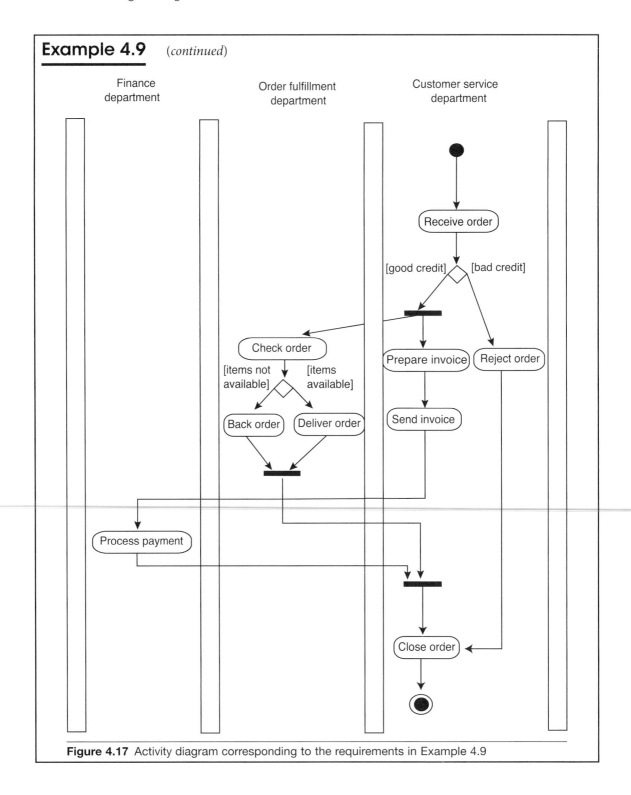

Example 4.9 (*continued*)

Finance department

Order fulfillment department

Customer service department

Receive order

[good credit] [bad credit]

Check order

[items not available] [items available]

Prepare invoice

Reject order

Back order

Deliver order

Send invoice

Process payment

Close order

Figure 4.17 Activity diagram corresponding to the requirements in Example 4.9

4.3 PROCESS MODELING

The traditional structured approach to software analysis is based on **process modeling**. The structured approach starts by modeling the software system as a high-level process. Then, using successive stepwise refinement and process **decomposition**, the system is transformed into a set of interrelated processes. When modeling a software system as a processor of information, **data flow diagrams** can be used. The system can be further refined into lower level processes until we reach processes that are simple, functional, and nondecomposable. Such functional processes can then be described using decision tables or decision trees if they are stateless. Otherwise, **behavioral modeling** techniques such as FSMs or PNs can be used.

Data Flow Diagrams

At a high-level of abstraction, a software system can be viewed as a processor of information. The entire software system is considered a process. This process takes input interactively from the types of **data sources** and produces outputs to the various types of data destinations. A data source or data destination can be a user of the software system, a file, another software system, or a hardware system or device. Files that are data sources or destinations are also called **data stores**. Data flows in and out of a process or from a data source or destination. A data flow can be composed of one or more data elements that are labeling an arrow depicting the flow of data and its direction. Figure 4.18 shows the four basic elements of a data flow diagram (DFD): the data source or destination, the flow of data, the process, and the data store.

A system level DFD, also called context level, can be refined in a top-down decomposition process. A lower level process must always be **consistent** with the higher level in terms of the internal interactions with other processes or external interactions with data stores and external data sources or destinations. For example, Figure 4.19 shows a possible decomposition of a high-level process P into four lower level processes while preserving the inputs and outputs consistency.

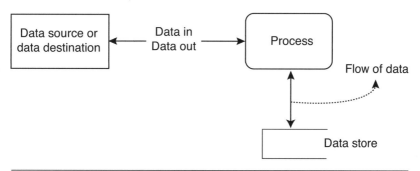

Figure 4.18 The four basic elements of a DFD

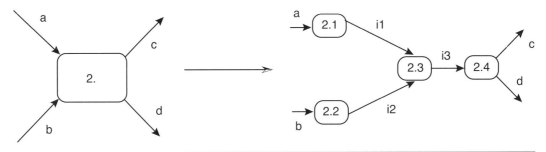

Figure 4.19 Decomposition of a process while preserving consistency

Example 4.10

Let us consider the following informal requirements. An online book ordering system accepts orders from buyers, which could be either human users or software agents. A book order is normally made after the buyer browses a book catalog. The system checks the availability of the ordered items in the store inventory and the status of the buyer in the customer file. If all items are available and the customer has a good record, the buyer is asked to provide credit card payment

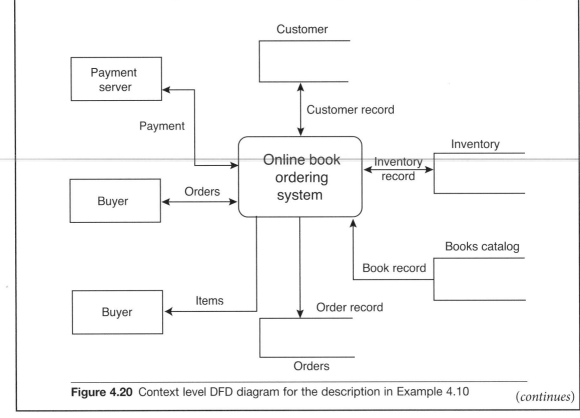

Figure 4.20 Context level DFD diagram for the description in Example 4.10

(*continues*)

Example 4.10 (*continued*)

and shipping information. The payment information is then passed to a payment server to verify their validity. If the payment information is valid, an online bill and payment confirmation is sent to the buyer. Otherwise, the buyer is informed of the rejection of the payment information and, consequently, the order. In the meantime, the inventory file, the customer information file, and the orders file are updated. In addition, customer information, including name and shipping address, is used to deliver the ordered items to the buyer. The context level DFD corresponding to the description is shown in Figure 4.20.

In a top-down decomposition process, the context-level process will be further refined and decomposed into other processes. The first top-down refinement of the context level is referred to as level 0 DFD. In this DFD, processes are numbered 1, 2, ..., then a refinement of process 1 at level 0 will include processes numbered 1.1, 1.2, 1.3, etc. As a guideline, no more than five to seven processes should be included at a particular level. Also, not all processes at a given level

should be refined. A process performing a simple function is not decomposable.

A decomposition of the context level process into level 0 processes is shown in Figure 4.21. Level 0 DFD contains five processes: (1) fill order; (2) validate order; (3) process payment; (4) update inventory; and (5) deliver item.

The process *validate order* can be further decomposed into three processes: 2.1. check status; 2.2. check availability; and 2.3. execute order. Figure 4.22 shows the decomposition of process validate order. The reply data flow from process validate order to the buyer is further refined into three data flows carrying messages provided to the buyer. To avoid cluttering the diagram, these three messages are fully described in the data dictionary. Msg1 indicates that an order is rejected because of a poor customer status, Msg2 indicates an order rejection because of the unavailability of the ordered items, and Msg3 indicates a confirmation of the validity of the order and the request to proceed to payment.

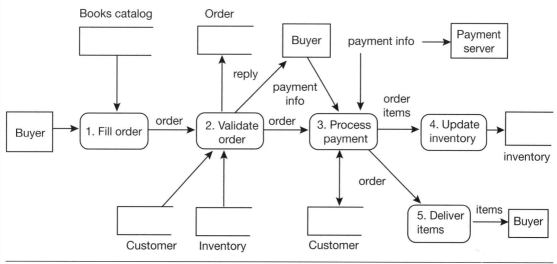

Figure 4.21 Level 0 DFD for the context level DFD in Figure 4.20

(*continues*)

Example 4.10   (*continued*)

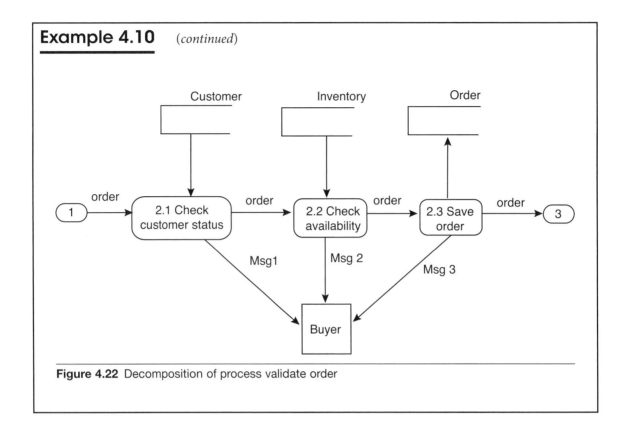

Figure 4.22 Decomposition of process validate order

Decision Table

A **decision table** is a useful tool for representing and illustrating the functional specification of a stateless (or memoryless) computational process. Rows in the table are of two types: condition rows and action rows. A column represents a combination of condition outcomes and the corresponding actions to take. A column is also referred to as a rule. A complete decision table specifies one rule for each combination of the condition outcomes. For example, if we have three independent binary conditions, the number of combinations or rules must be $2^3 = 8$. Also, a decision table contains redundancy if there exists two columns that are equivalent. Finally, a decision table is ambiguous or contradictory if, for the same combination of condition outcomes, the specified actions are different. A decision table is correct if it has no redundancies or contradictions.

Example 4.11

The structured English or pseudocode specification of the process take_speeding_decision is:

If the driver's age is below 21 then
    If there were a previous speeding ticket and the speed exceeds 120 then
        Penalty is $100 and deducts 2 points
    If there were a previous speeding ticket and the speed did not exceed 120 then
        Penalty is $75 and deducts 1 point
    If there were no previous speeding ticket then
        Penalty is $50
If the driver's age is 21 or more then
    If there were a previous speeding ticket then
        Penalty is $150 and deducts 3 points
    If there were no speeding ticket then
        Penalty is $125 and deducts 1 point

In the decision table, we have used the predicates shown in Table 4.4 whose outcomes are bi-

Table 4.4 Predicates used in Example 4.11

Predicate	Meaning
P1	Driver's age < 21
~P1	Driver's age ≥ 21
P2	Previous speeding ticket was issued
~P2	No previous ticket was issued
P3	Speed > 120
~P3	Speed ≤ 120

nary (true or false). Also, action rows are shaded in the table.

Table 4.5 shows the decision table specification of the process take_speeding_decision.

The decision table shown in Table 4.5 is complete and correct because it clearly specifies what actions to perform for every combination of condition outcomes. Note that since in rules 3 and 4, 5 and 6, and 7 and 8, the actions are the same regardless of the outcome of predicate P3, the table can be reduced to the one in Table 4.6.

Table 4.5 Decision table specifying the process take_speeding_decision

Condition/predicate	1	2	3	4	5	6	7	8
P1	Y	Y	Y	Y	N	N	N	N
P2	Y	Y	N	N	Y	Y	N	N
P3	Y	N	Y	N	Y	N	Y	N
Penalty	100	75	50	50	150	150	125	125
Points	−2	−1	0	0	−3	−3	−1	−1

Table 4.6 Modified decision table specifying the process take_speeding_decision

Condition/predicate	1	2	3/4	5/6	7/8
P1	Y	Y	Y	N	N
P2	Y	Y	N	Y	N
P3	Y	N	Y/N	Y/N	Y/N
Penalty	100	75	50	150	125
Points	−2	−1	0	−3	−1

Decision Tree

A **decision tree** is a tree in which a non-leaf node includes a condition to evaluate. The edges out of a non-leaf node represent the outcomes of decisions made at that node. A decision tree is a binary tree if all outcomes are binary, meaning that their outcome is either true or false. Like decision tables, decision trees are useful for specifying simple and stateless processes.

Example 4.12

A decision tree representing the pseudocode in Example 4.11 is shown in Figure 4.23. Notice that the tree is not necessarily a binary tree or a bal-anced tree. A non-leaf decision node in the decision tree can have any number of children nodes, depending on the number of possible outcomes at each decision node.

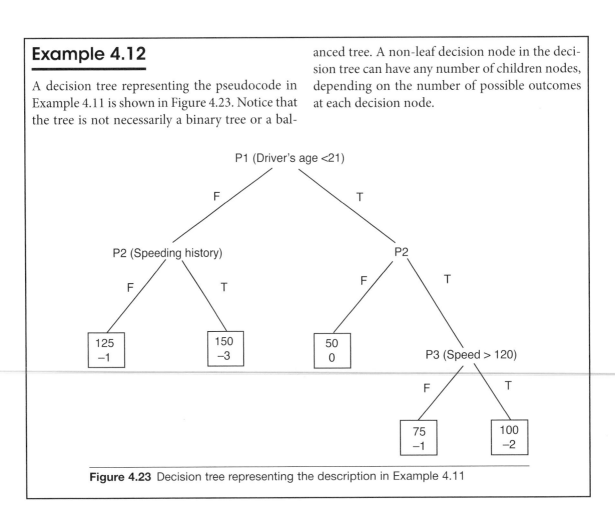

Figure 4.23 Decision tree representing the description in Example 4.11

4.4 DATA MODELING

Data modeling allows the specification of the data entities and the relationships that are needed to understand the software requirements. Of interest are the data that must be in permanent storage to support the specified software operations. Data modeling is the first step toward the design of a correct database. Trivially, any real-life software application requires a database in the back end. The most popular data modeling approach was introduced by Chen in 1976. Because the basic model consists of data entities and their relationships, it is known as the entity-relationship (ER) model. Its graphical representation is called the ER diagram (ERD).

Entity Relationship Model

In an **entity relationship model**, entities and relationships are connected in a way to explicitly describe their relevant and appropriate associations. The associations between entities and relationships reflect their semantics and their use in the context of the software system we are modeling.

An entity is graphically represented by a rectangle labeled with the entity name. An entity name is a noun describing the entity. An entity can be a physical or a logical entity. A physical entity can be a person, a place, or a device. A logical entity can be an event, an organizational unit, or an object.

A relationship is graphically represented by a diamond labeled with the relationship name. A relationship name is a verb describing the relationship. A relationship represents an association linking one, two, or more entities. A unary relationship links one entity to itself. For example, Course entity is linked to itself using the Has_Prerequisite relationship. A binary relationship links two entities and ternary relationship links three entities. For example, the three entities Project, Person, and Part are linked through the Use relationship. Figure 4.24 shows unary and ternary relationships.

An entity possesses attributes the values of which can distinguish among different instances of the entity. A set of one or more attributes is designated key attributes. At least one key must always exist to be able to distinguish among different entities. The values of key attributes are used to identify a specific instance. Similarly, relationships possess attributes the values of which can identify a specific instance of a relationship linking two specific instances of entities. Attributes of entities and relationships are determined based on the software requirements. Attributes are represented by ovals linked to the entity to which they are associated. Key attributes are underlined.

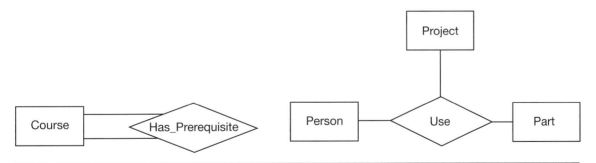

Figure 4.24 Unary and ternary relationships in an ER model

Example 4.13

A partial ERD showing the entities and relationships in the online book ordering system described in Example 4.10 is shown in Figure 4.25. The ERD includes entities Customer and Book, and the relationship Order. The Customer entity has three attributes: the customer name; customer number; and contact information. Customer number (Cnumber) is the key attribute. The Book entity has three attributes: the book ISBN number; book title; and book authors. The ISBN number is the key attribute for the Book entity. The relationship Order links both the Cus-

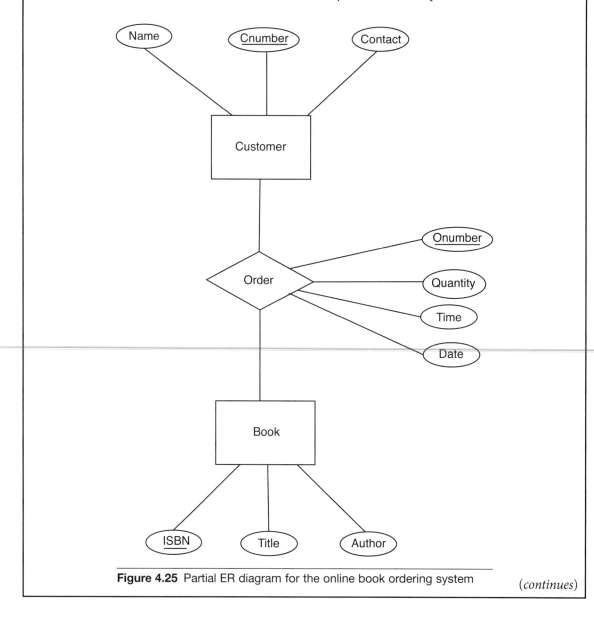

Figure 4.25 Partial ER diagram for the online book ordering system

(continues)

Example 4.13   (*continued*)

tomer entity and the Book entity. Useful attributes of the Order relationship include the order date, time, and quantity. In addition, the order number (Onumber) can be a generated sequence number used to identify an order.

The cardinality of a relationship is a constraint on the relationship between entities. Two types of cardinalities exist: minimum and maximum. They are denoted by min:max. For the previous ER diagram, because a customer can order one or more books, the cardinalities on the association between Customer and Order is 1:m. Similarly, because a book can be ordered by zero or many customers, the cardinalities on the association between Book and Order is 0:m. A strong entity is an entity in which an instance may or may not participate in any relationship with other instances. A weak entity is an entity whose instances may not exist on their own without participating in a particular association with other instances. In Example 4.13, both Customer and Book are weak entities. A max cardinality of 1 indicates that an instance of the entity can be associated with a maximum of one other instance. Figure 4.26 shows the cardinalities in the partial ER diagram of Figure 4.25.

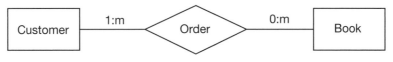

Figure 4.26 Cardinalities for the Customer-Order-Book relationships

Data Dictionary

A **data dictionary** is a document describing all the data items used in a software system. These data items can be parts of file record structures. For example, the order file record structure can be described as: order_file_record = order_number and buyer_name and buyer_id and ordered_items. Then each of these data items is defined in terms of their types, ranges, size, and possibly their default or initial values. Having a centralized data dictionary for a large information system helps reduce ambiguities, redundancies, and inconsistencies of data representation and manipulation. In addition, data dictionary items can be reused in the various parts of the system documentation to ensure consistencies across the software development processes and deliverables.

In addition, the data dictionary can include descriptions and elaborations of items that are used in the specification and possibly design documents. For example, messages, events, data flows, predicates, and other labels used in the diagrams can be described in more detail in the data dictionary.

The data flow reply shown in level 0 DFD of Figure 4.21 can be described by: reply = Msg1 or Msg2 or Msg3 in the data dictionary. Also, these three possibilities for reply can be described as: Msg1 = Unable to accept your order, Msg2 = Unavailable items, and Msg3 = Thank you for your order—Please proceed with payment.

4.5 FORMAL SPECIFICATION TECHNIQUES

The software specification literature is flooded with specification techniques. Many of these techniques have not been used in the real software world. They are either implementation-oriented or theoretical making them unusable by software analysts. A useful formal specification technique should be neither highly theoretical, making it unreadable, nor implementation-oriented, making it constrained and specific. A desirable formal specification model should be:

1. General and applicable to a wide range of software applications
2. Formal and have well-defined semantics
3. Expressive and allow the description of complex software behaviors
4. Readable and allow easy understandability and modifiability of the specification
5. Modular and allow the stepwise development of large and complex specification models
6. Adequately abstract and allow enough details to produce a good design
7. Executable and allow the simulation or prototyping of the specified model
8. Testable and traceable and facilitate the automatic checking and forward and backward traceability of the specification model.

A wide range of specification formalisms and techniques have been introduced in the literature. Each of these techniques satisfies some combinations of the features listed above. These formalisms and techniques can be classified under seven models:

1. Transition-based, which include FSM and PN
2. Programming language-based
3. Formal language-based
4. Temporal logic-based
5. Behavior-based, which include the communicating sequential processes (CSP) and the calculus of communicating systems (CCS)
6. Trace-based
7. Standard **formal description techniques**

Extended state transition language (ESTELLE), language of temporal ordering specification (LOTOS), and specification and description language (SDL) are three formal description techniques (FDTs) that have been standardized by ISO. They have been introduced mainly for the description of distributed systems. However, their main application is in the area of communication protocols and services. They enjoy strong support by researchers and practitioners in the telecommunications industry. They are also supported by a variety of tools for the editing, simulation, and validation of specifications, and the automatic generation of test suites.

FDTs are characterized by strict rules that allow the unambiguous description of distributed systems that enable the specifier to write unambiguous, clear, and concise specifications. They allow the analysis of specifications for correctness with respect to user requirements so that errors can be detected earlier in the design. Also, they make the derivation of system designs providing the functionality expressed in the specifications easier. Moreover, they facilitate the automated generation of partial implementations and allow the use of formal test generation and selection methods.

The Z specification language is a formal language for the description and modeling of software. It has a strong theoretical foundation based on the axiomatic set theory, lambda calculus, and first-order predicate logic. Z was standardized by ISO in 2002.

4.6 OBJECT-ORIENTED ANALYSIS

Object-oriented analysis (OOA) provides an alternative to the data and process-centered structured approach studied earlier in this chapter. OOA aims at modeling the software requirements by identifying problem-domain objects and their interrelationships. The problem is tackled by partitioning it into objects. Objects encapsulate data and operations or services. Modeling problems using problem-domain objects seem more natural and reflect real-life objects. In an object-oriented model, the interfaces and interrelationships among objects are well-defined, the state of an object is well-specified, and the specification of each object's operation is well-described. In a way, we can think of an object-oriented model as a hybrid model mixing data modeling, process modeling, and behavior modeling.

The main steps of an OOA include:

1. Identification of the model objects, their attributes, and their operations
2. Identification of the various types of relationships among objects
3. Identification of objects' states and the transitions among these states
4. Description of the interactions among objects

Problem-domain objects are identified by examining an informal requirements specification and then by performing a textual analysis of its nouns and verbs. Typically, nouns are potential objects and verbs are either use cases or operations carried out on objects. Objects that can be part of an object-oriented model are entities that:

- Have more than one attribute
- Need to be retained in permanent storage for future use
- Are external and produce information to be used or consumed by the system, or that consume information generated or produced by the system
- Are events or actions that occur during the system's operations
- Are roles played by people interacting with the system

- Are organizational units and places that are important in the problem domain such as flight crew teams or an airport
- Are logical items such as flight reports and documents
- Are composite physical items such as an airplane or a personal computer

External entities can be people, hardware devices and systems, or other software systems. An object with one attribute should not be considered on its own and can be reduced to an attribute of another object. Also, objects representing external entities are problem-domain objects but not necessarily solution-domain objects.

Identifying Objects

The objects in the analysis model consist of the concepts that are elicited during the requirements specification phase. To help obtain a complete list of objects, it is useful to consider three types of objects: entity, interface, and control.

Entity Objects

Entity objects need to be saved in permanent storage. Any object that must be tracked across different executions of the system can be classified as an entity object. An entity object can be saved in an object-oriented database or can be mapped to one or more rows in a relational database. Non-anonymous users of a software system and important events or messages can also be considered potential entity objects. Typically, entity objects are nouns that are used repeatedly in the use case descriptions. In addition to entities, activities and events that need to be tracked by the software system are legitimate entity objects. Finally, entities that generate or receive data are also considered entity objects.

Example 4.14

Let us analyze the following text that provides a partial description of the requirements for a Proposal Evaluation System (PES). PES allows different types of users to perform their functions. The three types of users are Evaluators, Administrators, and Proposal Submitters. Users must first logon successfully to the system to be able to work. Submitters will submit their proposals. An Administrator will perform a basic evaluation of the proposal before assigning it to an Evaluator. The basic evaluation checks whether the Submitter has already submitted another pending proposal. If so, the submission fails the check. In addition, the Submitter cannot have more than two accepted proposals to pass the basic check. If the proposal does not pass the basic check, the Submitter is informed and the refusal is logged in history. An Administrator sends an e-mail to the Evaluator once she/he is assigned to a proposal. The Evaluator will evaluate the proposal and will send his/her evaluation to the Administrator either by e-mail or

(continues)

> **Example 4.14** (*continued*)
>
> by filling out a form on the Internet. The Administrator will inform the Submitter of the result of the evaluation. At this point, the proposal evaluation process is considered complete.
>
> The nouns user, evaluator, administrator, proposal submitter, proposal, and proposal evaluation are potential entity objects. The system must track all of its users, submitted proposals, and the proposal evaluations. If the exchanged e-mails or the filled forms contents need to be tracked, then the e-mail or form content object are also classified as entity objects.

Interface Objects

Interface objects represent the input/output interactions between the actors and the software system. Examples of interactions include error messages, warning messages, input forms carrying user inputs to the system, output forms carrying system outputs to the user, reports generated, printed, or displayed on the user's monitor, and e-mails. Interface objects are typically transient objects that normally do not need to be saved in permanent storage. They are created and destroyed dynamically during the software operations. However, due to certain security requirements, some interface objects need to be tracked and traced back to their originators, then, in this case, these objects can be reclassified as entity objects. In the PES example, the form to be filled by the evaluator is an interface object whose content can be saved as an entity object. Also, notifications sent to the submitter about the state of the proposal can be considered interface objects.

Control Objects

Control objects encapsulate the control flow behavior needed to perform the use cases. Typically, for each use case, one control object is created, encoding the business logic of the use case. Additionally, one control object can be created for each actor involved in the use case. In this example, the actor-based control object contains the actor's behavior within the use case. Control objects are created and destroyed dynamically during the software execution. Normally, as a response to a user input that selects an interface option representing a particular function (or use case), a control object supervising the execution of the selected function is created. This object is destroyed upon termination of the selected function. Control objects can create or spawn other control objects. Also, control objects can create other interface objects during their executions. In the PES example, five control objects are needed: the Submit_Proposal; Check_Proposal; Evaluate_Proposal; Logon; and Send_Notification. Figure 4.27 shows the three types of objects that are identified in the PES.

Once objects are identified, the attributes and operations of each object, and their visibility requirements, must be specified. After a complete identification of the objects and their constituents, we can move forward to identify the relationships that exist among these objects.

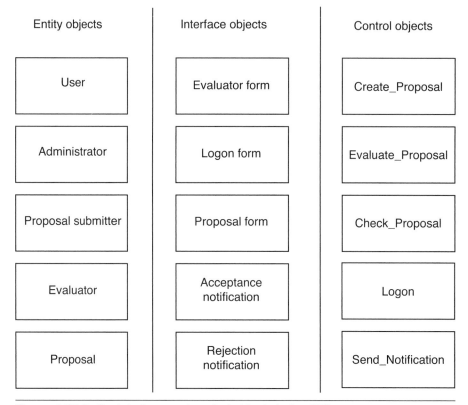

Figure 4.27 Entity, interface, and control objects in the PES

Objects Relationships

Objects are entities that have attributes and operations. Operations in one object that are accessible by operations in other objects are also called services. Typically, the values of the object attributes at a specific time represent the object's state. Attributes modifiability is determined by explicit visibility specifications. An object's attribute can be itself an object. Therefore, it can be said that an object is composed of other objects. Thus, objects can be linked by the *part-of* relationships. The *part-of* relationship is also known as an **aggregation relationship**.

Templates of objects sharing the same attributes and operations are called classes. Classes can form a hierarchy linking classes using the *is-a* relationships between a class and its subclasses. The *is-a* relationship is also called an **inheritance relationship** or **generalization-specialization relationship**. A subclass inherits all of the attributes and operations of its superclass. Operations inside an object can operate on the attributes of the object by reading or modifying its internal attributes. In addition, operations can communicate with other objects' operations. In this case, classes are linked among each other using the *communicates* relationships. Typically, the main operation in a control object is the run() operation that is executed once the control object is created or spawned. Figure 4.28 shows the *is-a* relationships between the User class and its three subclasses.

In Figure 4.29, assume that the User object is composed of one Profile object and other simple attributes. The number of objects inside the containing object is indicated by the multiplicity of the **composition relationship**. In the diagram, the multiplicity is 1:1 indicating that only one profile object is contained inside one User object.

Another type of relationship that exists between objects is called the association relationship. An association has a name, a role at each end, and a multiplicity at each end. Associations between entity objects are similar to the entity relationship links in an ERD model. However, associations between other types of objects provide more insight into the analysis model and help in understanding the requirements. For example, Figure 4.30 shows the proposes

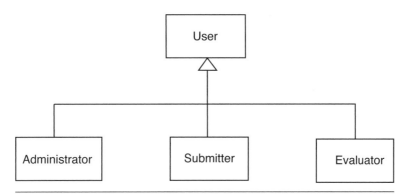

Figure 4.28 The *is-a* relationships between User class and its subclasses

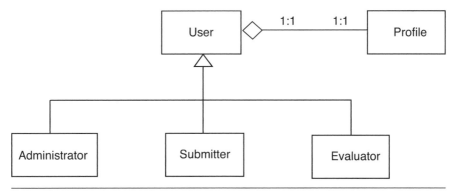

Figure 4.29 The *part-of* relationships between User and Profile classes

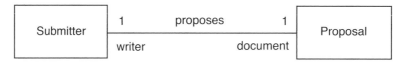

Figure 4.30 The association relationship between Submitter and Proposal objects

association between Submitter and Proposal in which the multiplicity is 1:1 since a Submitter cannot submit more than one Proposal, and a Proposal can be submitted by only one Submitter. The Submitter object plays the role of writer over the association, and the Proposal object plays the role of a document over the association.

Once all relationships between objects are understood and finalized, a class diagram can be drawn to visualize these relationships. Entity object structure or composition is not modified often. However, interface object structure changes more often as a result of changing the look and feel of the interface. Control objects are modified every time the business logic governing the execution of the underlying use case is modified. Class diagram relationships can be modified to ensure that the inheritance and composition relationships are used properly and that associations are simplified to avoid redundancies.

Unlike a structured analysis model, an OOA model is easily modifiable and maintainable. The addition and deletion of the three types of objects—entity, control, and interface—can be completed easily as can the modification of existing object structure or class involving the addition or deletion of attributes and operations.

Dynamic Object Behavior

Some of the identified objects in the analysis model can be described further using their state-based behavior. This behavior can be appropriately described using statechart diagrams. For example, the dynamic behavior of the Bank Account entity object was described earlier in Figure 4.15. In a typical state-based object, one or more attributes can be used to identify the state at which the entity object is. For example, the attribute account_status can be used to describe the account state. Another entity object that is state-based could be a student object in a student registration system. The attribute student_status can hold one of the following values: created, registered; onHold; suspended; or graduated. A statechart diagram can be used to describe the conditions under which a student object would move from one state to the other. Entity object states are saved in permanent storage. However, other types of objects, such as interface and control, can have internal states but are not usually saved permanently. Finally, in the Proposal Evaluation System example, the Proposal object can be in one of the following states: created; submitted; under evaluation; rejected; or accepted.

Objects Interactions

Objects interact among each other by exchanging messages. In UML, there are two types of interaction diagrams: sequence and communication. These two diagrams are semantically equivalent and can be used interchangeably. Given a sequence diagram, we can transform it into a collaboration diagram and vice versa. A sequence diagram shows explicitly the time ordering of messages exchanged among objects. However, in a communication diagram, the time ordering can be obtained by examining the order of the messages exchanged because a number depicting the order is attached to each message exchange.

Sequence Diagram

A **sequence diagram** is used to describe the interactions among objects during the execution of a use case. The interacting objects include entity, interface, and control objects that were identified earlier. A sequence diagram is also considered a visual representation of a scenario obtained earlier as part of the use case model. It helps in understanding and enhancing the object analysis model developed so far.

Objects participating in the use case interactions are placed on top of the diagram, each occupying a column. Normally, the left-most column is occupied by the actor or object that triggers the use case execution. Vertical lines representing timelines are drawn from each object downward. Objects interact by exchanging messages that are represented by horizontal arrows. These arrows are labeled with the message name and possible parameters. Message names are generally operation names in the message recipient objects. Sending a message from one object to another implies the execution of the corresponding operation in the receiving object. At a higher level, this exchange of messages is depicted by the communicates relationship in the class diagram.

Figure 4.31 shows a sequence diagram describing a scenario of the PES in which the proposal is submitted by the submitter and a basic check is performed. The diagram shows two control objects and one interface object that were created and terminated dynamically. As a result of the execution of this scenario, a proposal entity object is created and added to the Proposal permanent store.

Communication Diagram

A **communication diagram** describes the interactions among objects participating in a use case scenario. Prior to UML version 2.0, this diagram was called a collaboration diagram. Unlike a sequence diagram, no timeline is used to show the ordering of interactions and message exchanges. Instead, numbers are used to prefix the messages exchanged and to show the ordering. Figure 4.32 shows the communication diagram that is equivalent to the sequence diagram shown in Figure 4.31. Since both communication and sequence diagrams can be used to

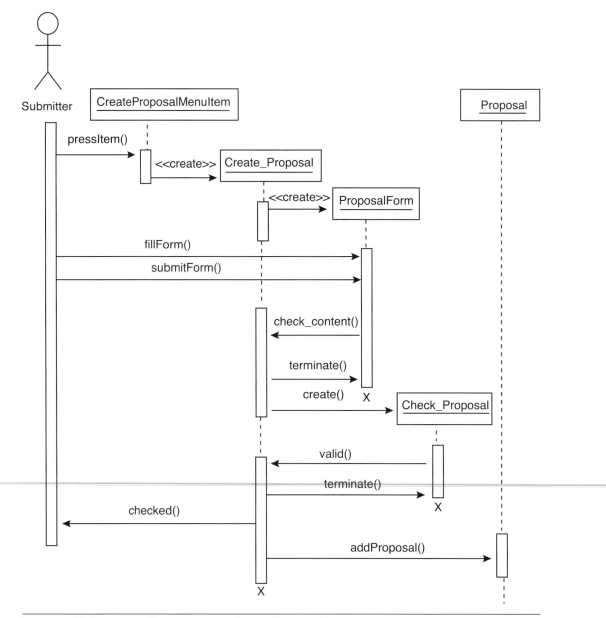

Figure 4.31 Sequence diagram for one Create_Proposal use case scenario

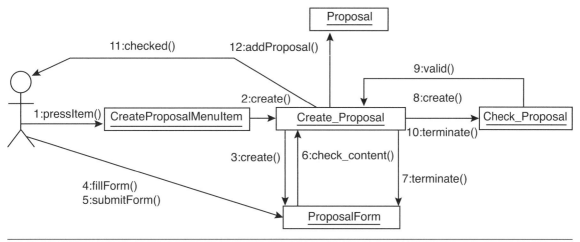

Figure 4.32 Communication diagram for one Create_Proposal use case scenario

show object interactions, either one of the two diagrams can be used to document interactions. The choice is dependent on the software analyst's preference.

4.7 VALIDATING SPECIFICATIONS AND TRACEABILITY

The software specification document is the main deliverable of the software analysis phase and is primarily used to start the design phase activities. After writing the software specifications, a thorough and formal review must be performed. This formal review is normally managed by the software quality assurance group using inspection and walkthrough techniques (see Chapter 8).

Specifications must be reviewed for completeness, consistency, and clarity with respect to the requirements elicited in the first stage of the software analysis phase. Overspecification and underspecification should be detected and dealt with prior to moving to the design phase. Mapping the different parts of the specifications to requirement use cases in the use case model ensures that specifications adequately cover those requirements. In addition, depending on the specification techniques that are used, various characteristics of the model can be checked. For example, as noted earlier, the FSM model can be checked for completeness, determinism, connectedness, and minimality. The communicating FSM model and the PN model can be checked for the absence of deadlocks and livelocks among other properties.

In addition to backward traceability, forward traceability can be used later to map the specification concepts to the various design concepts at different design levels (see Chapter 5).

3 Specific Requirements
3.1   External interfaces specifications
3.2   Use case model, including the use case diagrams and supporting sequence diagrams
       and activity diagrams (non-functional requirements can also be added here with
       each use case)
3.3   Entity relationship model
3.4   Data flow diagram (structured analysis)
or
3.4   Object model (object-oriented analysis): objects; attributes; operations;
       interrelationships; statecharts; sequence and communication diagrams
3.5   Data dictionary
3.6   Non-functional requirements

Figure 4.33 Possible content of Section 3 of the SRS

4.8 COMPLETING THE SOFTWARE REQUIREMENT SPECIFICATION DOCUMENT

After developing the software model by considering the behavior, data, process, and object models as necessary, the software requirements developers should update the SRS document. The third section of the IEEE recommended practice for writing an SRS document should include the details of the developed software analysis model. In addition to the specification of the non-functional requirements, the third section includes the following subsections:

- Subsection on external interfaces, which includes a detailed description of all inputs into and outputs from the system
- Functions subsection, which includes the use cases that are elicited as part of the use case model for functional requirements as introduced in Chapter 3
- Database requirements subsection, which includes the ER model
- Detailed requirements subsection, which includes either the structured analysis based techniques, including the DFD model, or the OOA of the software requirements. In this subsection, and as mentioned in the previous section, reference is made to the particular use cases of the use case model

Figure 4.33 shows the possible main subsections of Section 3 of the SRS document as recommended by the IEEE Standard 830.

SUMMARY

Software specification is the process of refining the software requirements to produce more elaborate and detailed requirements necessary to begin the design process. Detailed specifications make requirements more technically-oriented while still concentrating on what the software does. They explain the requirements from different perspectives: behavior, process, and data requirements, and object-oriented perspectives. Various specifications and modeling techniques were introduced to address each of these perspectives. These detailed specifications allow designers to make better design choices and a deeper understanding of the software.

To model the behavioral requirements of the software, FSMs, PNs, activity diagrams, and statecharts were introduced. To model the data requirements, the entity relationship model and data dictionaries were introduced. To model the process requirements, data flow diagrams were discussed. The composition-based data flow diagram technique is considered the main classical technique for the structured approach to software analysis. The OOA approach was presented as an alternative to the structured analysis approach. In this approach, various types of objects were introduced. Then, various types of relationships among objects were specified.

Specifications can be checked for consistency, completeness, correctness, unambiguity, and minimality. In addition, specifications must be traced back to requirements. They must also be mapped forward to the software design. Traceability allows easier software maintenance in the future.

KEY TERMS

actions
action states
activity diagram
activity states
aggregation relationship
backward matrix
behavioral modeling
communication diagram
communications protocol
completeness
composite state
composition relationship
concurrency specifications
conditional transitions
consistent
control objects
cyclicity
data dictionary
data flow diagrams
data modeling
data sources

data stores
deadlock
decision table
decision tree
decomposition
deterministic
dynamic behavior
entity objects
entity relationship model
enumerative analysis
extended FSM
finite state machine
fireability
formal description
    techniques
forward matrix
fully connected
generalization-specialization
    relationship
incidence matrix
inheritance relationship

interface objects
invariant analysis
livelock
liveloop
minimality property
object-oriented analysis
Petri net
place invariant
predicate
process modeling
sequence diagram
software specification stage
statechart diagrams
strong connectedness
structural analysis
superstate
swimlanes
timeout
transition invariant
unspecified reception

REVIEW QUESTIONS

1. What are the deliverables of the specification phase?
2. What is process modeling? Which techniques can be used in process modeling?
3. What is behavior modeling? Which techniques can be used in behavior modeling?
4. What is data modeling? Which techniques can be used in data modeling?
5. What is object-oriented modeling? What are objects?
6. What are the three types of objects?
7. What are the types of relationships among objects?
8. What is an activity diagram? a communication diagram? a statechart diagram? a sequence diagram?
9. What is the formal definition of an FSM model?
10. What is the formal definition of a basic PN model?
11. What are the extensions to the basic FSM model?
12. List the possible uses of the FSM model.

EXERCISES

1. Produce a decision table and a decision graph from the following: The power company will prepare a bill for each customer. For a regular customer, apply billing procedure A if the consumption is below 100 KWH, otherwise apply billing procedure A for the first 100 KWH and billing procedure B for the remaining consumption; in addition send the consumer a brochure on ways to save power. However, for a company customer, apply billing procedure B for any consumption below 200 KWH and apply billing procedure C if the consumption is equal to or above 200 KWH. Is this description complete? nonambiguous? nonredundant? Why?

2. A system of two processes is used to allow a user to logon to a user account. The User Process (UP) receives a user ID and password from the User that are then passed to a Validation Process (VP). The VP then checks in a local database and either returns OK or NOT OK. If the UP receives OK it moves to a logged state. However, if it receives NOT OK, it can retry after 5 seconds by resending a user ID and password to the VP. The UP can only try 3 times after which if a NOT OK is received, the UP will be blocked for 3 minutes before returning to the idle state waiting for another user ID and password from the User. HINT: the UP has the following states: IDLE; WAITING-FOR-VP-REPLY; LOGGED; BLOCKED-3MIN; BLOCKED-5SEC. Draw the state machine for both the UP and the VP. Draw three scenarios using three different sequence diagrams.

3. Describe the software development processes using a DFD at different levels.

4. Draw the EFSM modeling the following description. At the logon screen, if the user enters the incorrect identification, an error message is displayed and the user is invited to enter

the ID again. After 3 trials, the user is blocked and can only try to logon again after 5 minutes. Moreover, if the user stays idle for more than 3 minutes at the logon screen, a warning message is displayed. If the user does not enter an ID within 1 minute after the warning, the user is blocked for 10 minutes before given the chance to logon again.

5. Given the PN shown in Figure 4.34: Draw the reachability graph. Find the incidence matrix. Find all place invariants. Find all transition invariants. Is the net conservative? Why? Does it have a liveloop? a livelock?

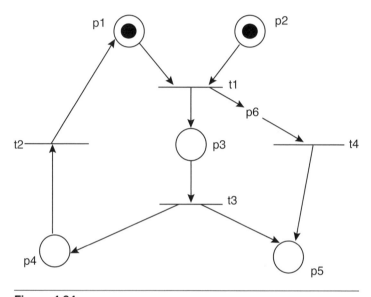

Figure 4.34

6. Given the following for a web-based order processing system for a computer store: A new user can connect to the company's web page and create a new customer profile by providing personal information. This information is validated and saved in a customer information file on the company's server. The user is then provided with a user ID and password via an e-mail sent by the system. Using the provided password, the user can then logon to the system and place an order. The user can also delete or update an order within a certain amount of time after placing the order. In all cases, the system verifies the transaction and acts accordingly. If the transaction is not allowed (e.g., deleting after the deadline), the user is informed. Before accepting the transaction, the system checks the customer information file for the credit check and the inventory file for availability. If the ordered item is not available, the system asks the user whether to keep the order in a back order file, if not, the order is discarded. If the product is available, the inventory and customer information files are updated accordingly. The ordered product is delivered along with a bill and the accounting file is updated. Once the payment is received, the accounting file

and the customer information files are updated accordingly. From time to time, the system administrator sends e-mails to customers informing them of special deals. Draw DFDs at all levels. Produce an OOA model.

7. The following is an informal description of a subsystem to compute employees' salaries: The subsystem is able to accept an employee key from an interactive user or from an employee record file that contains personal information and the employee's current salary. Based on the information recorded in a monthly file concerning the employee's work times, the system prints the salary for the month in question. Upon a request from the user, the subsystem also prints all the employees who did not work during the month. Produce DFDs at all levels.

8. Given the informal requirements for a Milk Delivery System: A system is to be produced that holds details of deliveries of different brands of milk in a small town. As well as recording which households take which brand(s) of milk, this system also includes billing details and details of customer vacations when milk will not be delivered. The household phones the delivery company to change the personal information, such as an address, to inform the company of a vacation, and to change an order. For each delivery person, the system prints a daily list of which brands of milk are to be delivered to which households. The system is able to produce summary information showing how many liters of each milk type were sold each day of the week. Bills for each customer are printed at the end of each month and left with the first delivery of the following month. The system also produces appropriate error messages, confirmation, and warnings. Produce DFDs at various levels of refinement. Produce an ER model. Produce an OOA.

9. Given the FSM shown in Figure 4.35: Describe the FSM in both the algebraic and tabular forms. Can you describe what this FSM specifies? Suppose that at any state (except the initial locked state) if we do not receive an input within 10 time units, we want the system to be blocked for 5 time units and then move to the locked state again. Add the necessary transitions and states to the FSM diagram. Is the FSM complete and deterministic? Why? If incomplete, can you suggest a modification to complete it?

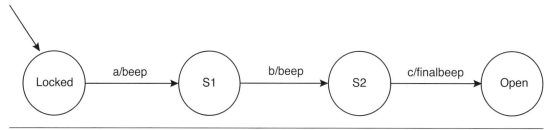

Figure 4.35

10. A distributed system is composed of three processes. We want to model each of them by an EFSM according to the following description. The Requestor process sends a request (REQ) to a Delegator process which, after communicating with the Executor process, sends either an OK or NOTOK message back to the Requestor. Upon receipt of the REQ from the Requestor, the Delegator process forwards the request to the Executor process that processes the request and replies back either with the message positive (POS) or negative (NEG). If the Delegator receives POS, it will forward OK to the Requestor, otherwise it tries again after 5 seconds, sending the same request to the Executor. Once a second NEG is received from the Executor, the Delegator forwards NOTOK to the Requestor. Draw the graphical representation of the EFSM specifications of the three processes. Show the tabular representation of the Delegator process.

11. Describe the following system using three communicating FSMs: A distributed system consists of three communicating processes. The user process (UP) requests a data item from the server process (SP). The SP directs any request to the database process (DP) that returns with a data item or returns item not available. Once the SP receives the data item, it increments a counter of service request by 1 and passes the data item to the UP. However, if the SP receives item not available, it tries again after 2 seconds. If it receives item not available again, it returns to the UP with the message item not available. Draw an activity diagram with three swimlanes corresponding to the above description.

12. Given the PN in Figure 4.36: What is its incidence matrix? List all place invariants. List all transitions invariants. Draw its reachability graph starting from the initial marking of the figure (i.e. (1 0 0 1 1)). Starting from the initial marking, what is the final marking after firing t3 100 times?

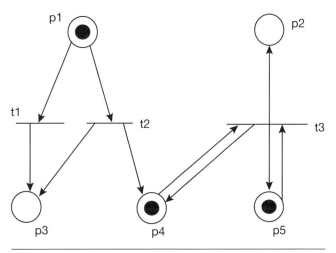

Figure 4.36

13. Given the EFSM model for Process M1 shown in Figure 4.37, provide the algebraic representation of M1. Provide both graphical and tabular representations of the EFSM model for Process M2, with which M1 can communicate (sends to and receives messages from). HINT: M2 has the same number of states as M1.

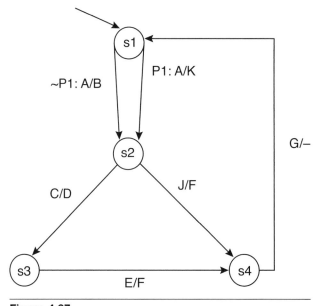

Figure 4.37

14. Complete the FSM description provided in Figure 4.15 by labeling the transitions with appropriate input and output messages.

BIBLIOGRAPHY

Books

Alexander, I., and R. Stevens. *Writing Better Requirements*, Reading, MA: Addison-Wesley, 2002.

Davis, A. M. *Software Requirements: Objects, Functions and States*, Englewood Cliffs, NJ: Prentice Hall, 1993.

Habrias, H., and M. Frappier. *Software Specification Methods*, London, UK: ISTE Publishing Company, 2006.

Horrocks, I. *Constructing the User Interface with Statecharts*, Reading, MA: Addison-Wesley, 1999.

Jackson, M. *Software Requirements and Specifications*, Reading, MA: Addison-Wesley, 1995.

Kohavi, Z. *Switching and Automata Theory*, 2d ed., New York: McGraw Hill, 1979.

Kotonya, G., and I. Sommerville. *Requirements Engineering: Processes and Techniques*, New York: John Wiley and Sons, 2000.

Reisig, W. *Petri Nets: An Introduction*, Berlin: Springer Verlag, 1985.

Robertson, S., and J. Robertson. *Mastering the Requirements Process*, 2d ed., Reading, MA: Addison-Wesley, 2007.

Scott, K. *UML Explained*, Reading, MA: Addison-Wesley, 2001.

Sommerville, I., and P. Sawyer. *Requirements Engineering: A Good Practice Guide*, New York: John Wiley, 1997.

Thayer, R. H., and M. Dorfman, eds. *Software Requirements Engineering*, New York: IEEE Computer Society Press, 1997.

Wiegers, K. *Software Requirements*, 2d ed., Redmond, MA: Microsoft Press, 2003.

Articles

Ardis, M. "Formal methods for telecommunication system requirements: A survey of standardized languages," *Annals of Software Engineering*, vol. 3, 1997.

Chen, P. "The entity-relationship model—toward a unified view of data," *ACM Transactions on Database Systems (TODS)*, 1(1): 9-36, March 1976.

Desharnais, J., M. Frappier, and A. Mili. "State transition diagrams," *Handbook on Architectures of Information Systems*, P. Bernus, K. Mertins, and G. Schmidt, eds., Springer-Verlag, 1998.

Murata, T. "Petri nets: Properties, analysis and applications," *Proceedings of the IEEE*, 77(4): 541-580. April 1989.

Probert, R., K. Saleh, and H. Yu. "Validation-directed specification of communications protocols", *Journal of Information and Software Technology*, 37(8): 403-410, August 1995.

Yeh, R. T., and P. Zave. "Specifying Software Requirements", *Proceedings of the IEEE*, 68(9):1077-1085, 1980.

Standards

IEEE 830, IEEE Recommended Practice for Software Requirements Specifications, IEEE, 1998.

ISO 8807, LOTOS: A Formal Description Technique Based on the Temporal Ordering of Observational Behavior, Geneva, September 1988.

ISO 9074, ESTELLE: A Formal Description Technique Based on an Extended State Transition Model. Geneva, September 1988.

ISO 10167, Guidelines for the application of Estelle, LOTOS and SDL, 1991.

ISO 13568, Z Formal Specification Notation – Syntax, Type System and Semantics, 2002

Z.100, Specification and Description Language (SDL). ITU-T Recommendation, Geneva, 1992.

Software Design

Software design encompasses various activities that are started once the specification of the software is completed and approved by the various stakeholders. Following the software definition stage, design is the first stage in the implementation of a generic software development life cycle model. Whereas the outcomes of the definition stage detail *what* the software is supposed to do, the outcomes of the design activities lead to a deeper understanding of *how* the software should be implemented by programmers. High-level abstractions of the definition phases are further refined in the design phase and details on software implementation are provided. Design activities lead to two main outcomes. A high-level or architectural design includes the building blocks of the software to be developed and their interrelationships. A detailed design describes the internal steps of the identified building blocks and the needed data structures. A graphical user interface design and a database design are also developed during this phase.

Learning Outcomes

In this chapter you will learn:
- Basic terminology
- Recurring concepts in software design
- Producing highly-cohesive and lightly-coupled modules
- Assessing and enhancing intramodule cohesiveness and intermodule coupling
- Transforming specifications into design using a top-down refinement process
- Documenting a software design
- Reviewing and validating a design
- Designing usable and user-friendly graphical user interfaces

5.1 MAPPING SPECIFICATION TO DESIGN

The software design process begins once the deliverables of the specification phase are completed and approved by the appropriate stakeholders. The software requirements specification (SRS) document is the main input to the design process. Design is supposed to provide a further

Table 5.1 Mapping of specification outcomes to design outcomes

Specification outcomes	Design outcomes
Data model	Database design
Process model and use case model	High-level design/object-oriented design Graphical user interface design
Behavioral model	Detailed design
Non-functional requirements	High-level and detailed design

refinement of the specifications needed to bring the abstraction down to a level allowing the proper and unambiguous implementation of the software. Whereas the specification concentrates on what the software is supposed to do, the design concentrates on how the specification can be implemented. All the elements of the specification document should be mapped to or addressed by elements or outcomes of the software design deliverables. The outcomes of the software design process include all the artifacts needed to begin the implementation or construction of the software (see Table 5.1).

The mapping of SRSs into an appropriate software design considers both functional and non-functional requirements (NFRs). The classical **structured design** approach using top-down refinement and the **data flow analysis** (DFA) techniques deals mainly with functional requirements.

The data model of the specification document is mapped to a **database design** in both high-level and detailed design documents. The process model of the specification document is mapped to a **design hierarchy** included in the high-level design document. The behavioral model of the specification document is mapped to the various module designs and their algorithms and data structures included in the **detailed design** document.

NFRs are dealt with in both the high-level architectural design and the detailed design. For example, performance issues and scalability requirements can be addressed by multithreading as part of the detailed design of the relevant modules in the design hierarchy. Availability requirements are addressed by the data and software distribution and replication as part of the high-level architectural design of the software. Security and fault tolerance are addressed at both the architectural design and detailed design levels.

5.2 RECURRING CONCEPTS AND DESIGN PROPERTIES

Important **recurring concepts** are those driving concepts and principles that are needed to manage and deal with the development of complex software systems regardless of the techniques and methods used. These concepts are valid throughout all of the stages of software development and maintenance. However, they are mainly relevant during the design phase when one design choice is selected among possible design alternatives. The recurring concepts should define a framework or way of thinking along which main decisions are made. Mastering these principles should begin during the first computer software course and continue throughout the professional life of a practicing software engineer. The proper use of these concepts at the design level leads to desirable design properties.

Recurring Concepts

The recurring concepts that are most relevant at the software design level are the concepts of abstraction, top-down refinement, separation of concern, modularity, encapsulation, information hiding, software interfaces, **concurrency**, and divide and conquer.

Abstraction

Abstraction is related to the hiding of details for the purpose of simplifying and managing the design of complex software. A software module, as a black box, is an abstraction of the control and data flow that can exist inside it. Similarly, we can also view the specification as an abstraction of the design and the design as an abstraction of the implementation; in this case, reducing the level of abstraction means moving toward a more concrete realization of the current level.

Top-down Decomposition

Top-down decomposition or stepwise refinement is a software analysis and design procedure by which a process or an abstraction at a high-level is broken into two or more lower-level abstractions. The decomposition procedure continues until a process or an abstraction is reached that cannot be decomposed further. Top-down decomposition is used to refine the context-level data flow diagrams (DFDs) until a set of low-level diagrams is obtained in which all processes in the diagram are not decomposable.

Information Hiding

Information hiding or **encapsulation** is related to the hiding of internal design decisions relative to the selected algorithm and data structures of a module in the outside world. The encapsulation reduces the **side effects** of future maintenance or modification of the design options, therefore minimizing the effect on the other modules in the design. Modularity, information hiding, and encapsulation aids in achieving the concept of separation of concerns.

Separation of Concerns

Separation of concerns is related to the partitioning of complex software into separate modules that are lightly-related or coupled. Modules can then be created by several designers with minimal interfacing.

Interfaces

Interfaces are the points of access through which modules or systems communicate. Each abstraction should possess a well-defined interface that clearly describes the expected inputs to and outputs from the abstraction.

Modularity

Modularity in design refers to the splitting of a large software system into smaller connected modules. Modules are interconnected through their interfaces. The interconnection should be simple to avoid side effects and costly maintenance. Two modules are directly connected if one module can call the other module and they can be indirectly connected if they share common files or global data structures.

Divide and Conquer

Divide and conquer is a concept used in developing a detailed design or an algorithm for a module. It is based on breaking the problem into smaller subproblems and then solving them. Joining the subproblems solutions provides a solution to the original problem. Solving problems recursively uses the divide and conquer approach in which backtracking will occur when the lowest unbreakable subproblems reached are solved.

Desirable Design Properties

A good design must possess numerous desirable properties. The design process should use techniques, concepts, and principles enabling the embedding of these properties within the design itself. Addressing these properties later in the development process leads to ad hoc implementations that can include undesirable side effects, requiring costly maintenance. For example, thinking about performance and security during the coding phase rather than the design phase definitely leads to poorly-secured and low-performance software. A short list of desirable design properties includes: adaptability and extendibility; fault-tolerance and error-recoverability; maintainability; portability; reusability; scalability; security; and testability.

Testability

A testable design is composed of testable modules with the least coupling possible among composing modules. A testable module is an easily-tested module that facilitates both the **observability** and the **controllability** of the module. Typical observable modules include a code for logging important steps so that a tester can easily trace and resolve errors. The special logging statements can be toggled off when the module is included in the production software build. A typical controllable module is a single entry and exit module, containing steps whose execution can be controlled from a caller module or a test driver. Special hidden interface parameters can be used for the purpose of enhancing module controllability. These interfaces can also be used for online real-time maintenance and are not declared public as part of the library application programming interface. Similar concepts of controllability and observability exist in hardware integrated circuits design, facilitating hardware **testability**.

Maintainability

The **maintainability** of a design is related to the ease with which the maintenance of an implementation of the design can be performed. Maintenance activities include enhancing the performance of certain algorithms in the design, fixing errors in some modules of the design, adapting to new operating environments, or dealing with new or revised requirements. A highly maintainable design is a modular design with high intramodule cohesion and low intermodule coupling.

Adaptability and Extendibility

The **adaptability and extendibility** of a design refer to the ease with which the design can be altered and expanded. These abilities are related to the maintainability of the design. An adaptable and extendible design is characterized by an open-ended design in which the modules are not strongly coupled. Intermodule coupling is discussed later in this chapter.

Diagnosability

A design is diagnosable if the occurrence of an error can be repeated easily and can be linked or traced back to a specific module in the design. **Diagnosability** helps reduce software maintenance cost and facilitates effectively dealing with a software defect, thereby improving the maintainability of the software. Typically, a diagnosable design is constructed from functionally cohesive modules that are not strongly coupled. The nature of the error can be attributed easily to a specific functional module. Diagnosability of a software design facilitates testability and testability contributes positively to maintainability.

Reusability

The **reusability** of a module refers to the ease with which a module can be reused as part of another software design. Typically, a highly reusable module is a functionally cohesive module whose interfaces are well-defined and whose dependence on other modules is kept at a minimum, in other words, the coupling with other modules is minimal. Modules that are low in the design hierarchy are normally highly reusable modules. On the other hand, top level modules are interface-driven and application-specific, therefore, they are less reusable. When designing a module, the designer should consider two facets of reusability: designing *for* reuse and designing *with* reuse. Designing for reuse implies that the designer must expend a maximum effort to design a module that is highly reusable in future software application designs. This can be achieved by designing highly cohesive modules with low intermodule coupling. (Both coupling and cohesion are presented in detail later in this chapter.) On the other hand, **design with reuse** implies that the designer should aim first at finding existing modules to be used and, also, to make use of proven design patterns (see Chapter 6). **Design for reuse** requires more effort in the short term, but in the long term it leads to lower cost software due to the high reusability of existing software modules. In addition, the reuse of already-proven modules leads to software with greater reliability, reducing the maintenance cost in the long term.

Portability

A design that provides **portability** is a modular design that can be easily modified to interface or integrate with a new operating environment, including an operating system or hardware platform. A portable design includes mostly hardware-independent modules. The modules that are machine-dependent are isolated and are typically low-level modules in the design hierarchy.

Security

A software design is secure if it deals with confidentiality, integrity, and availability concerns according to the security requirements defined earlier in the SRSs document. Availability refers to the ability of the software to deliver the requested services whenever needed. Designing for **security** is becoming an increasingly important topic for researchers and practitioners. Incorporating security design choices seamlessly as an integral part of the software design is essential to avoid the ad hoc addition of security controls during or after the implementation phase. Software security issues are studied in Chapter 7.

Scalability

A software design is scalable if it is capable of dealing with an increased load on the system without requiring any software modifications and without affecting the required minimum system performance. Typically, a scalable design would require the addition of hardware resources that are used by the scalable software implementation. Capacity planning deals with what resources are needed and when. For example, in a real-time system in which a thread is created for every user logging on to the system, with the increase of the number of simultaneous users, additional central processing units and memory is needed when a certain threshold is reached. Multi-threading and load balancing and distribution are two concepts that can be used to enhance the scalability of a software design. **Scalability** contributes positively to the availability and, therefore, the security of the software.

Reliability

The **reliability** of a software design refers to the ability of the software to deliver its specified functions or services under stated conditions and over a specified period of time. A dependable software design is highly available, reliable, and maintainable. The concepts of dependability, resiliency, and survivability of a software design are related. Reliable software is also highly-available and a more secure software.

Error Recoverability and Fault Tolerance

A software design is **fault tolerant** if it allows the software system to continue to operate even in the case of an error. Fault tolerance can be achieved by recovering from the error and continuing execution using either a backward or forward recovery approach. Checkpointing, event logging, redundancy and distribution, and exception handling are among common techniques used to achieve error recoverability and fault tolerance. Fault tolerance contributes positively to the availability and reliability and hence the dependability of the software.

Trustworthiness

A trustworthy software design is a secure, reliable, and privacy-preserving design. The **trustworthiness** property is becoming increasingly important because of the urgent need for developing more secure and reliable software systems; therefore, built-in security and fault tolerance are emerging concepts in software design.

Figure 5.1 shows the *contributes* relationships among the different software design properties. Note the importance of the trustworthiness design properties depicted in the figure.

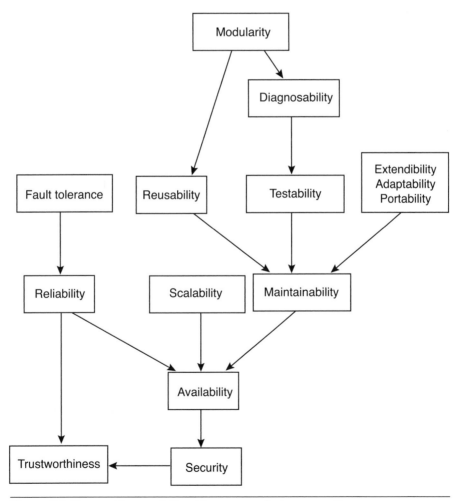

Figure 5.1 The *contributes* relationships among design properties

5.3 HIGH-LEVEL ARCHITECTURAL DESIGN

The **high-level design** (HLD), also called **architectural design**, transforms the process-oriented specification model, such as the DFDs, or the use case model (UCM) of the object-oriented approach (OOA) into a module hierarchy. The module hierarchy includes all the software modules needed to meet the specifications. In addition, the hierarchy shows the interrelationships, also called caller-called relationships, among these modules and describes their respective interfaces. Typically, low-level modules in the hierarchy are utility modules that are most likely to be reused from or in other software designs. High-level modules are typically user interface-driven control modules that are more application-specific and therefore they are low reusability modules.

A high-level design hierarchy can be assessed based on the intermodule relationships through direct and indirect interfaces and on some static characteristics of the hierarchy. In addition, an HLD possesses some attributes such as height, depth, width, and module fan in and fan out. The height or depth of the design hierarchy is the number of modules along the longest path from the top level module down to the lowest module in the hierarchy. The height of the hierarchy must not be excessive. In stack-oriented programming languages like C and Java, the height of the hierarchy points to the number of activation records that may exist in the run-time stack in addition to activation records of recursive modules along the longest path. Excessive height can lead to a run-time stack overflow error. The width of the design hierarchy is the largest number of modules existing at a given level of the hierarchy. The number of direct interfaces among modules is the number of links connecting modules in the hierarchy. The fan in of a module Mi in the hierarchy is the number of other modules that call Mi. The fan out of a module Mj in the hierarchy is the number of other modules called by Mj. A module Mi with a high fan in is typically a utility module called from many other modules in the hierarchy. High fan-in modules are also more likely to be reused in other software design hierarchies. A high fan-out module is a module that delegates most of its work by calling other modules in the hierarchy. An excessively large fan out of a module can be an indication of over modularization of the design. The width of the design can also be an indication of over modularization, depending on the level in the hierarchy at which the largest number of modules exists.

Example 5.1

Given the high-level design hierarchy in Figure 5.2, the height of the design is 4 and its width is 5. The number of interfaces is 12. Interface i2 is between modules M1 and M2. The module with the largest fan in is module M8 whose fan in is 3.

The module with the largest fan out is module M3 whose fan out is 4.

When developing the high-level design, two important features must be considered: the intermodule coupling and the intramodule cohesion. Coupling is discussed in the next section and cohesion is studied later in this chapter.

(continues)

Example 5.1 (*continued*)

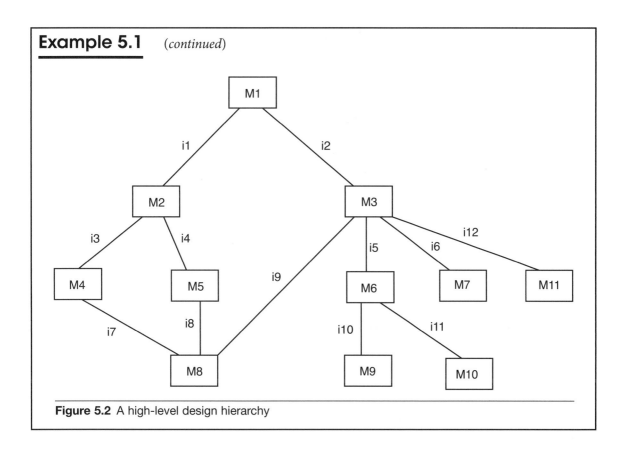

Figure 5.2 A high-level design hierarchy

5.4 INTERMODULE COUPLING

Coupling is a feature describing the interrelationship between two modules in a high-level software design hierarchy. Coupling is considered when developing the high-level design. Coupling between two modules can be assessed once the modules caller-called hierarchy, the interfaces, and the data and control flows are known in the hierarchy. A software designer must aim at the lowest possible coupling among modules to minimize side effects and the propagation of errors. Furthermore, the efforts needed for maintenance and regression testing, should the design be expanded or modified, are also reduced. The level of coupling between two modules varies from lowest to highest: no coupling, data, stamp, control, common, and content coupling.

Two modules are not coupled if there is no direct call or invocation from one module to the other. Also there is no indirect relationship between a pair of modules through the sharing of common variables or external data sources. Moreover, no step in one module has an effect on the steps of the other module.

Two modules M1 and M2 are **data-coupled** if they communicate (i.e., M1 calls M2) by parameter passing and the passed input parameters are the least necessary to achieve the work of the called module M2. Also, the returned value or output parameters must be the least necessary by the caller module M1. The interface between two data-coupled modules is called a *thin* interface. The coupling is also data coupling if no input parameters are passed from caller to called module and, further, either no value or a value is returned by the called module.

Two modules M1 and M2 are **stamp-coupled** if the caller module passes more information than needed to the called module when they communicate. An example is when a complete record or data structure is passed and the called module only needs a subset of record fields to perform its steps. Exposing more data than necessary defeats the principle of least privilege and can lead to undesirable side effects. The interface between stamp-coupled modules is called a thick interface.

Two modules M1 and M2 are **control-coupled** if the caller module, say M1, passes a control flag or variable among the input parameters passed to M2. Then, M2 uses the received flag to select and execute the appropriate steps. We say that module M1 is controlling the execution of module M2. Module M2 would then be logically cohesive.

Two modules are **common-coupled** if they are indirectly related due to the sharing of a common global data variable or structure, or data file. Common coupling is sometimes unavoidable because modules might need to refer to common data stores to perform their functions. However, the designer must make an effort to reduce it to a minimum. Common coupling leads to potential side effects and, therefore, hidden errors and lower maintainability and testability.

Two modules are **content-coupled** if one module includes a statement to jump and execute inside the other module or when one module changes the content of a variable or structure inside another module. Content coupling cannot exist in software modules that are developed using modern programming languages because it is not possible to jump directly into a label in another module.

Table 5.2 summarizes the levels of intermodule coupling.

Table 5.2 Summary of the levels of intermodule coupling

Level	Coupling	Brief description
0	No coupling	Module is called but does not share any data directly or indirectly with any other module
1	Data	Module is passing only the necessary data to another module
2	Stamp	Module is passing more data than needed to another module
3	Control	Module is passing a flag to control the flow of control in another module
4	Common	Modules are sharing common global data and data files
5	Content	Module branching out to a label in the other module

0 = Best   5 = Worst

Example 5.2

The structured chart representing the high-level design hierarchy of the following pseudocode is shown in Figure 5.3.

M1(boolean flag) { if (flag==true)call
    M6(studentRec); }
M2(int studentNum) { read studentRec from
    file A; call M1(studentRec.status); call
    M3(studentRec.studentName); }
M3(string stringToPrint) { print stringToPrint; }
M4(Record studentRec) { modify studentRec;
    update File A; call M3("record updated"); }
M5() { call M2(studentNum); call
    M4(studentRec); }
M6(studentRec) { sendEmailTo studentRec.
    studentName; }

The coupling among the modules in the design hierarchy is summarized in Table 5.3. An empty cell in row Mi to column Mj in the table indicates that no direct or indirect coupling exists between modules Mi and Mj. The coupling between modules M1 and M2 is a control coupling. Because control coupling is the highest level of stamp coupling due to the passing of the complete student record due to the passing of the control flag. The coupling between modules M1 and M6 can be reduced to data coupling if, instead of passing the complete student record, only the student name is passed. However, the coupling between M2 and M1 will still be control coupling (i.e., the highest level of data and control coupling).

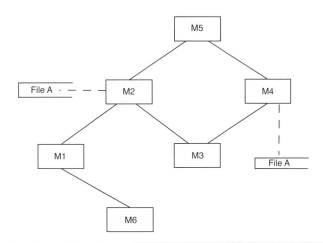

Figure 5.3 Design hierarchy corresponding to the pseudocode in Example 5.2

Table 5.3 Coupling among modules of the design in Figure 5.3

	M1	**M2**	**M3**	**M4**	**M5**	**M6**
M1						Stamp
M2	Control		Data	Common		
M3						
M4		Common	Data			
M5		Data		Data		
M6						

5.5 STRUCTURED DESIGN

The structured design process is based on the top-down refinement of the software modules. High-level modules, usually with low cohesiveness, is refined further until higher-level cohesiveness modules are obtained. A structured design can also be obtained by transforming the data flow model developed in the SRS document into a high-level design hierarchy. This transformation process is also called data flow analysis (DFA). Recall from Chapter 4 that lower-level data flow processes are obtained by refining processes at higher levels. A process is not refined further if it performs a simple cohesive function. These low-level processes map to functionally cohesive modules in the high-level design. Figure 5.4 shows the transformation of a process in a DFD into a module in a high-level design hierarchy.

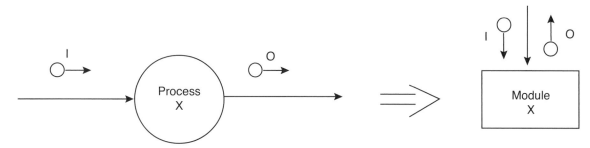

Figure 5.4 Transforming a process in a DFD into a module

5.6 DETAILED DESIGN

Once the high-level design is complete and has been reviewed, the detailed design process can begin. When completed and the design document is reviewed and approved, a unit test plan is developed for each module in the design hierarchy. In addition, the integration test plan is developed. The early development of these test plans guarantees an unbiased testing. Testing would then be based on the design and is independent from the coding. The approved detailed design document is also the main input to the implementation or coding phase of the development process.

A detailed design must be well-documented so that programmers are able to develop the source code by mapping the design to an implementation language. The documented design must be clear, unambiguous, and complete to avoid errors in the mapping from design to code. There are several ways to document the design of a module.

Pseudocode is a textual technique that is commonly used to represent the steps of the design. Pseudocode statements must be language-independent and close to English. A programmer must be able to unambiguously map pseudocode steps into statements in a high-level pro-

Example 5.3

The DFDs obtained in the refinements of Example 4.10 map into the high-level design hierarchy shown in Figure 5.5.

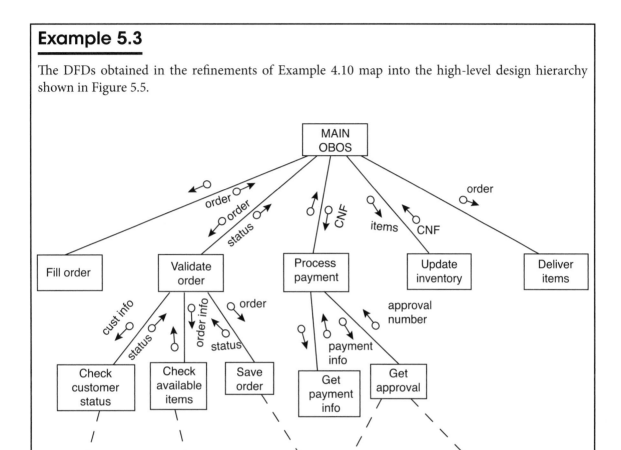

Figure 5.5 High-level design hierarchy corresponding to the DFDs in Example 4.10

gramming language. The pseudocode of a module must include the specification of the module input and output parameters and the value returned by the module in addition to the steps included in the body of the module once it is invoked. Pseudocode is also referred to as structured English. Other textual representations of a design have been proposed such as the program design language (PDL).

There are many methods for the graphical representation of a design, including the flowchart, Nassi-Shneiderman diagram, and UML diagrams such as the activity diagram and state diagrams described in Chapter 4. Figure 5.6 depicts a pseudocode and its equivalent flowchart and Nassi-Shneiderman diagram.

Pseudocode:

```
int counter = 0
if (n equals 0) return 0
repeat while n is not equal 0
        n = n / 10
        increment counter by 1
return counter
```

Flowchart:

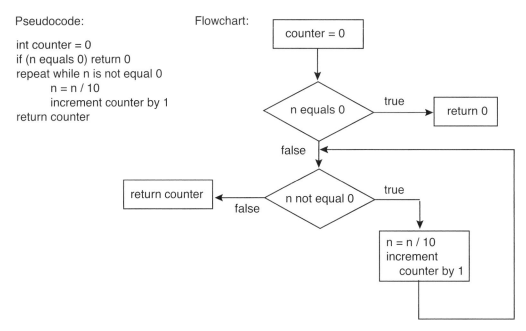

Nassi-Shneiderman Diagram:

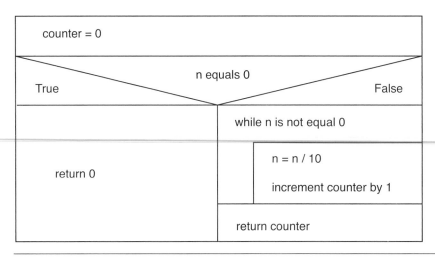

Figure 5.6 Alternative ways for describing an algorithm for a detailed design

The detailed design of a module must include both module header design and module body design. The module header design includes the module name and the input and output parameters, and their types, in addition to a brief description of the main function of the module. The module body design mainly includes the algorithms or steps that are to be performed once the module is invoked or activated. In addition, the data variables and structures used by the module steps need to be identified. The choice of the data structures and algorithms is clearly a main task performed by the software designer and must not be left to the programmer. Moreover, for the purpose of **completeness**, the detailed design of a module can also include the alternative design decisions that were considered by the designer—their merits as well as the reasons for not selecting them.

Table 5.4 illustrates a template that can be used to document a detailed design of a module. Tables 5.5 and 5.6 show the detailed design for modules ValidateOrder and CheckCustomer Status, respectively. These modules are shown in the high-level design hierarchy of Figure 5.4.

Table 5.4 Module-detailed design template

Module Name:	
Author:	Created:
Revision history:	
Module description:	
Module interfaces:	
Module returned value(s):	
Called by module(s):	
Calls module(s):	
File(s) accessed:	
External system(s) accessed:	
Data structures and global data used:	
Algorithm in pseudocode:	

Table 5.5 Detailed design for module ValidateOrder

Module Name: ValidateOrder
Author: Kassem Saleh   Created: January 12, 2006
Revision history: Revised by same on March 12, 2006
Module description: This module receives order information and checks whether the order can be filled. The returned value indicates the type of problem with the order, if any.
Module interfaces: Input: Order record
Module returned value(s): 0—Valid order   1—Bad customer standing   2—Item(s) not available   3—Cannot save order
Called by module(s): MAIN
Calls module(s): CheckCustomerStatus( ), CheckAvailableItems( ), and SaveOrder()
File(s) accessed: None
External system(s) accessed: None
Data structures and global data used: Order data structure filled by user

Algorithm in pseudocode:
  code = CheckCustomerStatus(customerInfo);
  if code != 0 return code
  code = CheckAvailableItems(orderItems);
  if code != 0 return code
  return SaveOrder(order);

Table 5.6 Detailed design for module CheckCustomerStatus

Module Name: CheckCustomerStatus
Author: Kassem Saleh   Created: January 13, 2006
Revision history: none
Module description: This module receives customer information and checks in the customer file to establish if the customer is in good standing
Module interfaces: Input: Customer information (part of the order information)
Module returned value(s):   0—Good standing   1—Bad standing
Called by module(s): ValidateOrder
Calls module(s): None
File(s) accessed: Customer file
External system(s) accessed: None
Data structures and global data used: customerInfo structure

Algorithm in pseudocode:
   Open file Customer for read only
   Query file for customerInfo.customerNumber
   If customerNumber does not exist return 0; —no record for new customer
   return foundCustomerRecord.status;

5.7 INTRAMODULE COHESION

Cohesion is an internal feature of a module in a given software design and must be considered during the design process. A designer should aim at highly-cohesive modules whose steps are strongly-related. Cohesiveness can only be assessed and measured once the high-level design is complete. A design whose modules are at their highest possible levels of cohesiveness is easily manageable and maintainable. Highly-cohesive modules are also easily reused and tested.

- A module is coincidentally cohesive if the steps performed by the module are not related. Normally, a symptom of **coincidental cohesiveness** is that it is hard to give a short or meaningful name for such modules. Also this module tends to be longer. For example, a module that gets input, performs searching, then sorting, and finally produces output, is clearly a coincidentally cohesive module. These modules are hardly reusable and maintainable. There are many ways to improve the cohesiveness of such modules. Related steps can be clustered together and the module can be split into two or more modules, each of higher cohesiveness levels. The level of cohesiveness of the modules obtained depends on the cohesiveness of their respective steps.

- A module is **logically cohesive** if the steps included in the module are clustered in two or more groups whose execution is mutually exclusive. The group of steps executed is determined by a discrete or logical value passed as a parameter from the outside of the module or by a global variable shared with other modules. To increase the reusability, maintainability, and modularity of this module, the cohesiveness level can be enhanced by splitting it into two or more modules each, including the steps of a mutually-exclusive group. The level of cohesiveness of the modules obtained depends on the cohesiveness of their respective steps.

- A module has a **temporal cohesiveness** if the steps included in the module are related in time. For example, once the software application is started or terminated, an initialization or termination procedure is executed. The initialization steps of a temporally cohesive module may include opening files, logging, playing music, and opening communication lines. The only relationship among these steps is that they must occur at the same time. Similarly, a termination or cleanup module is a temporally cohesive module that can include steps to close files and communication lines, free memory, stop playing music, and stop recording logs. To enhance the cohesiveness of such modules, the designer has to take into consideration the number of groups of closely-related temporal steps. If the number of groups is large, $n > 7$, splitting this module into n modules leads to over modularization. Again, if this module is small and is performing many temporally-related steps, it may be a good idea to keep it at the same temporal cohesiveness level. A temporally cohesive module is minimally reusable since startup and termination procedures are usually application-specific. However, such modules are highly-maintainable and can be adapted for use in other similar applications.

- A module is **procedurally cohesive** if the steps included in the module perform various activities that are sequential. These sequential activities implement a specific business process or transaction flow. If the module is large and its steps can be clustered into two or more cohesive groups of steps, the module can then be divided into two or more modules of higher cohesiveness. A typical procedurally cohesive module is a control module that calls other modules in the order prescribed by the business procedures. Such a module is normally of low reusability but can be easily maintained.

- A module is of **communicational cohesiveness** if the steps included in the module perform various activities that refer to the same input or output. Each activity includes related steps. The cohesiveness can be enhanced by splitting the module into two or more modules each including the related steps of an activity. The shared input or output variables and structures can be made available to the newly-created modules. Clearly, by doing so, we are creating common coupling among these modules. A tradeoff has to be made between increasing cohesiveness, increasing coupling, and over modularization. A typical module of communicational cohesiveness can be found in compiler software in which many activities refer to the symbol table data structure.

- A module is **sequentially cohesive** if the steps included in the module can be clustered into sequential groups of steps. The outputs or actions of the first group are needed to perform the steps of the second group, and so on. The cohesiveness of the module can be enhanced by including each group of related steps in a separate module. The cohesiveness of a new module depends on its enclosed steps.

- A module is **functionally cohesive** if the steps included in the module are related and aim to perform a single function. Naming functionally cohesive modules is easy because the

Table 5.7 Summary of the levels of intramodule cohesiveness

Level	Cohesion	Brief description
0	Coincidental	Module performs unrelated activities that are included in the module by coincidence
1	Logical	Module performs one activity exclusively among many similar activities based on a control variable passed to the module
2	Temporal	Module includes unrelated steps that must be performed at the same time
3	Procedural	Module performs an unrelated set of activities in a specific order according to a business process or procedure
4	Communicational	Module performs many unrelated activities sharing the same input and output
5	Sequential	Module contains a sequence of activities—the output of one activity is the input needed to perform the successor activity in the sequence
6	Functional	Module contains strongly-related steps or statements that perform a single function

0 = Worst   6 = Best

module name reflects the single function it performs. These types of modules are easily maintainable and most probably highly reusable.

Table 5.7 summarizes the levels of intramodule cohesiveness.

5.8 DATABASE DESIGN

Given the data model specified in the SRS document using the entity relationship (ER) diagram, the database design consists of mapping the model into a table or database schema design. In the relational database model, a database schema design can be produced by either using a normalization or synthesis process, or using a transformation or mapping process. The normalization process starts with the universe of atomic attributes in the data model and the functional dependencies among these attributes. The universe of attributes or database schema is iteratively decomposed into relational schemas until all schemas reach at least the third normal form.

The transformation or mapping approach starts with the ER model and uses the appropriate transformation rules to obtain the various relation schemas needed to meet the data model requirements. A relationship with a one-to-one cardinality linking two entities is normally mapped into one relational schema, a one-to-many cardinality is mapped into two relational schemas, and a relationship with a many-to-many cardinality is mapped into three relational schemas. The details and the rationale for these mapping rules can be found in a database textbook. In Example 5.3, we apply the transformation approach to a given ER model.

Example 5.4

In Figure 4.25, the relationship Order is a many-to-many relationship linking the entities Customer and Book. This simple ER model is mapped to the following three relational schemas: two representing the Customer and the Book entities, and the Book Order representing the Order relationship between the two entities. The Customer schema includes the CustomerNumber, Name, and Contact, where CustomerNumber is the key attribute. The Book schema includes the ISBN, Title, and Author, where the primary key is the ISBN. Finally, the Book Order schema includes the OrderNumber, CustomerName, ISBN Quantity and Time, where the OrderNumber is the key attribute and the alternate key is the combination of the two attributes CustomerName and ISBN. The complete relational schema design for the Customer, Book, and BookOrder schemas is shown in Figure 5.7.

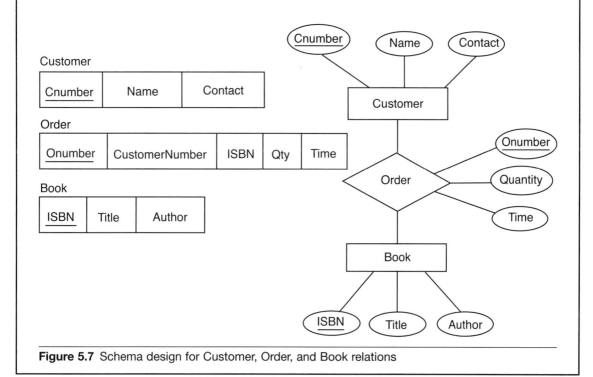

Figure 5.7 Schema design for Customer, Order, and Book relations

5.9 GRAPHICAL USER INTERFACE DESIGN

Most software systems and applications are driven by **graphical user interfaces** (GUIs) supporting various types of users. The design of the GUI strongly affects the **usability** and acceptance of the software, hence affecting the economic bottom line for profitability and productivity. A careful design of the GUI must be performed.

For a large application, a dedicated GUI development team can be solely responsible for the analysis, design, implementation, and testing of the GUI. A GUI team manager is responsible for the coordination with the other software development teams and for the integration of the GUI components with the other software components.

The design of the GUI must consider some guidelines that enhance the usability of the interface. The GUI design must be preceded by the specification of the needed interactions at the various interfaces. While the interface specifications identify all the necessary GUI artifacts needed to support the functional software specifications, GUI design provides details on how these artifacts look as well as their sequencing and interrelationships. The GUI design guidelines are centered around certain desirable properties.

Consistency

One of the most important criteria for the success of a GUI is **consistency** of the interface within the same application and across similar applications. Examples of consistency within the same GUI design include the use of:

- Similar font sizes and styles in the screens, dialogs, and forms
- Same function keys and control keys to perform the same actions on screens of the design; such as using F6 to get contextual help in various screens
- Same format to display error messages
- Same icons to mean the same thing such as using the error, warning, and information icons

Also, issues must be dealt with similarly; for example, opening any file by double clicking on the file icon regardless of the file type.

Reusability

When designing a new interface, the designer should aim at reusing GUI artifacts and elements from existing and proven graphical interfaces. Reuse allows consistency of the GUI across various applications thereby enhancing the usability and the user familiarity with the new interface and reducing the need for future changes to the interface. For example, the menu bar in existing editing applications includes menus and menu items in an order with which the users are familiar. Unless there is a proven benefit or compelling reason to deviate from familiar interface design, new GUI design should reuse the same GUI layout.

Flexibility and Efficiency

The interface should be flexible and allow novice and expert users to use different paths to navigate the interface. Expert and frequent users can use shortcuts to improve the efficiency of the navigation. Default settings can be used by novice users and should be easily modified if the user wishes to do so. In addition, the interface must be easily navigated by users.

Forgiveness and Tolerance

The GUI design should allow the user to confirm or undo critical actions. In addition, the interface should correct trivial user input errors and continue operating normally thereafter. Forgiveness and tolerance contribute to the user-friendliness of the system.

Readability, Simplicity, and Clarity

The GUI design must include simple GUI artifacts, such as simple screens with clear, uncrowded messages. For example, the use of appropriate colors, font sizes, and styles that is convenient for the target users of the software. A usability questionnaire should be developed prior to the GUI design to understand the type of audience and their preferences. For example, if 90 percent of the users are novice users and their ages are above 50, the interaction style must be based mainly on pointing devices and the font size used in text must be selected accordingly. Also, colors must be carefully selected to deal with color-blind users. Displayed error, help, and warning messages must be clear, concise, and as elementary as possible to assist the user in properly choosing the next action to be performed. Also, the inclusion of a user preferences section is desirable to allow changes, for example, the user increasing the font size.

User-Friendliness

The GUI design must be **user-friendly**, providing helpful, courteous, and non-offending messages. For example, an error message displayed by the system should spell out exactly what the error is and how it can be avoided. Displaying a system error number without any additional information could offend the user's intellect. Help messages must be concise and contextual by providing only the needed and requested help. Also, adapting the user interface to different languages and cultures is crucial in today's global context. Whereas user-friendliness is important, the modern, secure application must avoid messages that reveal data that an attacker could exploit.

Visibility

The GUI should not include any hidden artifacts. GUI components that should be conditionally available for particular user types should be disabled. The existence of nonvisible interface components can be harmful in terms of security and must be dealt with carefully during code reviews. On the other hand, there can be some design decisions related to GUI usability metrics included in the GUI design. These decisions do not involve the addition of hidden GUI components, but are reflected later in additional GUI-related code, including counter and probes to collect statistics used in the future enhancement of the software GUI.

A GUI design **inspection checklist** can be developed to cover the design principles we have discussed. Assessment of existing checklists can also be performed based on these principles. Moreover, GUI test plans can be developed around the checklist that include all design principles.

5.10 THE SOFTWARE DESIGN DOCUMENT

A standard for documenting a software design was recommended by the IEEE. IEEE standard 1016 includes the recommended practice for software design descriptions. The standard recommends a structure for a design document. The software design document describes how a software system can be implemented starting from the SRS document. The design document can then be used as a basis for implementation and for the development of unit and integration test plans. A complete design document must cover all aspects of the SRSs.

A requirement is reflected in one or more design entities. The standard defines a design entity as system, subsystem, module, program, data file, and processes. These design entities result from a top-down decomposition of the software requirements. Each entity must have a name, type, purpose, and function; composing subentities or subordinates; interface; dependencies; needed resources; internal data; and the processing rules used by the entity to perform its function. Subordinates show the hierarchical structure of the entity. Dependencies can be shown using DFDs and structure charts depicting a high-level design hierarchy. Resources are elements that are already designed as part of other systems and are needed by the identified design entity.

The recommended design document contains four design views of the software:

1. Decomposition: Shows the partitioning of the system into design entities. This view can be expressed using a hierarchical diagram, perhaps a class diagram, of components and their composite subcomponents.
2. Dependency: Shows the relationships among design entities, using **structured charts** and data dependency diagrams.
3, Interface: Includes the description of all design entity interfaces allowing their proper use through interface files and parameter lists.
4. Detailed: Includes the internal detailed structure of a design entity, using flowcharts, pseudocode, Nassi-Shneiderman diagrams, or detailed schema description.

A recommended table of contents is structured around these four views. The recommended design document contains six sections. Section 1, an introduction, includes the purpose and scope of the document and a list of definitions and acronyms. Section 2 contains the references used in the design document. The remaining four sections include the decomposition, dependency, interface, and detailed design view descriptions. The decomposition view in Section 3 identifies and describes all modules and data entities. The dependency view in Section 4 identifies and describes all intermodule and data dependencies. The interface view in Section 5 identifies and describes the interfaces needed to access each module. Finally, the detailed design view in Section 6 provides the detailed data structures and processing description for each module listed earlier. In addition, the detailed description of each data entity used is provided.

Clearly, a different structuring of the design document including the same design information can be adopted. Table 5.8 shows an alternative table of contents for a design document.

Table 5.8 An alternative design document template

1. Introduction
        Purpose, scope, assumptions, and references
2. High-level design
        Transforming the data flow diagram into a structured chart or object-oriented design
        Detailed description of each module or method interface
3. Database design
         Mapping the entity relationship model into a database schema design
        Detailed description of the relational schema structure
4. Graphical user interface design
        Screen design and ordering of screen sequences
5. Detailed design
        Detailed description of each module or method listed in the high-level design section using
        a unified template

5.11 DESIGN VALIDATION AND REVIEW

Before proceeding to the software implementation or coding phase, the deliverables of the design phase must be validated for conformance to the software specifications. The design deliverables must be reviewed by the various design stakeholders. These stakeholders include representatives from the various teams, including specification, design, software quality assurance, and implementation. In addition, the design activities and the remaining project plan activities should be reviewed by the management team and the design stakeholders.

As detailed in Chapter 2, and according to the IEEE standard 1028 on software reviews, five types of software **design reviews** should be conducted:

1. A **management review** is used to evaluate and assess the metrics collected during the design phase and to document the lessons learned during this phase. Deviations from and modifications of the project management plan are also documented.

2. A **technical review** of the design deliverables concentrates on the suitability of these deliverables and their readiness for use in the implementation phase. Also, conformance to the design guidelines and standards are checked.

3. A **design inspection** is one type of review aimed at the detection and identification of software design anomalies. The design is inspected for conformance with the various standards and the specification document. In addition, the design inspection verifies whether various desirable design attributes are satisfied. Design inspection checklists should be developed and used to inspect the high-level design, detailed design, user-interface design, and database design. Inspection checklists can be used to check the quality of work prior to submitting the design to a formal inspection review.

4. A **design walkthrough** is one type of review in which the designer first presents the main ideas and driving principles of the design. Then the designer walks through the

various design deliverables and discusses, in detail, the design options and the rationale for the selected design option. Suggested changes are recorded and a design review report is generated. Depending on the severity of the review concerns, a follow-up review or a redesign might be considered. Ideally, a walkthrough is conducted after a design inspection review.

5. An **audit** is a type of review that provides an unbiased assessment of the conformance of the design document to the various applicable standards, guidelines, and regulations. The software quality assurance group is normally the prime entity responsible for initiating and conducting an audit and might need the services of an external audit organization.

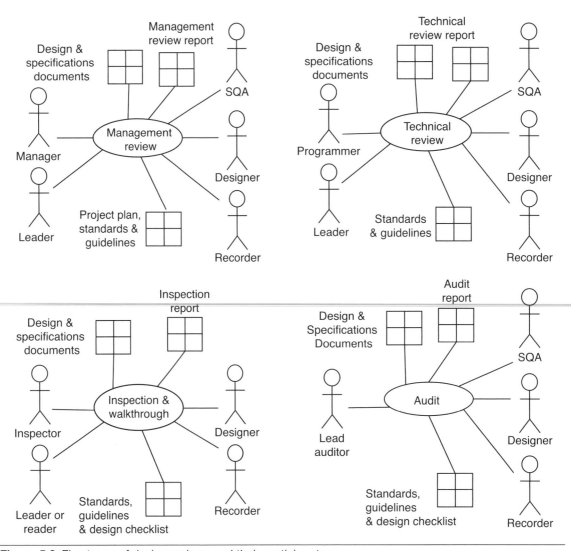

Figure 5.8 Five types of design reviews and their participants

Figure 5.8 shows the various participants in each type of design review.

Inspection checklists should include items for checking the completeness, consistency, non-ambiguity, **modifiability**, **robustness**, **traceability**, and testability of the various design deliverables. Table 5.9 lists typical inspection questions that can be used to address each of the design features.

Table 5.9 Inspection questions addressing some desirable design features

Completeness • Is each module in the design hierarchy described in detail using a uniform template? • Are all functionalities covered by the design? • Are all data files described in detail? • Are all user functionalities covered by the graphical user interface design? • Are all module interfaces completely specified in terms of type and size? • Have all non-functional requirements been covered in the design?
Consistency • Are module interfaces consistent with respect to type compatibility? • Are the user interface artifacts consistent in size, color, format, and so on? • Are all modules described consistently using a common template? • Are all data consistently declared and defined?
Correctness • Is the algorithm described for each module correct? Is the logic correct? • Are the sequences of interactions in the user interface design correct according to the requirements specifications? • Is the design hierarchy correct? Does it have the appropriate levels of coupling and cohesion? • Is the database design correct? Are all relation schemas in the appropriate normal forms? • Are all data variables, data structures, and files properly initialized? • Have all non-functional requirements in the design been dealt with properly?
Non-ambiguity and readability • Is the logic of each module clear and simple? Does it lead to a single interpretation by the programmer? • Is the user interface clear and simple?
Modifiability and changeability • Is it easy to modify the high-level design hierarchy if new functionalities are added? Is the software to be ported to a different platform? • Is it easy to modify the database design to meet new data requirements? • Is it easy to modify the user interface design to deal with new or changed functionalities?
Robustness and fault tolerance • How is a module algorithm dealing with an exception of abnormal input values if applicable? • How is the user interface dealing with illegal inputs at different contexts?
Traceability • Are all requirements specifications covered in the design documents? • Can each module be referred to in order to address some elements of the requirements specifications?
Testability • Is each module easy to test on its own? • Can the modules be integrated easily and then tested? • Does critical code include probes to help in testing and diagnosing errors?

It is also possible to develop separate checklists, one dealing with the functional requirements and GUI and the other dealing with the NFRs. Moreover, depending on the criticality of the NFR in question, a dedicated checklist can be used. For example, a checklist can be developed to address the types of security requirements needed for the system.

Automated software design validation tools can also be used. For example, the behavioral aspects of a communications protocol design described in an executable description language such as one of the formal description techniques (FDTs) introduced by ISO can be validated using FDT-based tools. An example of such languages is ESTELLE, a description technique based on the finite state machine (FSM) model. Completeness, consistency, and **correctness** of the protocol design can be validated automatically using tools developed in industry and academic institutions.

SUMMARY

Software design is the process of refining the software specifications to obtain a basis for describing how the software can be implemented. The deliverables of the software design phase include the high-level architectural design, the detailed design, the database design, and the GUI design. The high-level design is obtained by transforming the data flow process specification of the SRSs or by a top-down decomposition process. The high-level design can be described by a module hierarchy linking the various modules of the design and using clearly-defined interfaces. The cohesion of each module in the design must be as functional as possible. The coupling among modules should be at the lowest level possible. These two desirable levels of coupling and cohesion contribute to the production of high-quality software with a low maintenance cost. Recurring design principles, including modularity, abstraction, and information hiding, lead toward desirable design properties. Important desirable design properties include reusability, maintainability, testability, security, availability, fault tolerance, and trustworthiness. The detailed design consists of describing the data structures and algorithms that are used in each module in the high-level design hierarchy. The database design process consists of transforming the ER model of the specification into a database schema design in which each relation is guaranteed to be in a desirable, normal form avoiding redundancy and integrity problems in the database implementation. Design principles for desirable and usable GUIs were presented. Various design review techniques were discussed as well as potential organizations of a design document.

KEY TERMS

abstraction	coincidental cohesiveness	concurrency
adaptability and extendability	common coupled	consistency
architectural design	communicational	content coupled
audit	cohesiveness	control coupled
cohesion	completeness	controllability

correctness
coupling
database design
data coupled
data flow analysis
design for reuse
design inspection
design hierarchy
design reviews
design walkthrough
design with reuse
detailed design
diagnosability
divide and conquer
encapsulation
fault tolerant
functionally cohesive

graphical user interfaces
high-level design
information hiding
inspection checklist
interfaces
logically cohesive
maintainability
management review
modifiability
modularity
observability
portability
procedurally cohesive
recurring concepts
refinement
reliability
reusability

robustness
scalability
security
separation of concerns
sequentially cohesive
side effects
stamp coupled
structured charts
structured design
technical review
temporal cohesiveness
testability
top-down decomposition
traceability
trustworthiness
usability
user-friendly

REVIEW QUESTIONS

1. List and explain the levels of intramodule cohesiveness.
2. List and explain the levels of intermodule coupling.
3. Briefly describe the main deliverables of the software design process.
4. Assess the impact of high coupling on each of the desirable design properties.
5. Which of the recurring design concepts are related to coupling and why?
6. Which of the recurring design concepts are related to cohesion and why?
7. List the features of a good GUI design.
8. List the three methods used for documenting an algorithm. Which one do you prefer and why?
9. Can you use an FSM diagram to describe an algorithm? Provide an example.
10. Provide a detailed design description, using the template, for modules GetApproval() and ProcessPayment() in the design of Figure 5.4.
11. Discuss how maintainability of software design can contribute to the trustworthiness of the design.

EXERCISES

1. Produce a high-level design from the DFD obtained in Exercise 4.6.
2. Produce a high-level design from the DFD obtained in Exercise 4.7.

3. Produce a high-level design from the DFD obtained in Exercise 4.8.
4. Produce a detailed design for the high-level design obtained in the previous exercise.
5. Produce a database design from the ER model obtained in Exercise 6.8.
6. Given the following java code, produce an HLD hierarchy and assess the coupling and cohesion in the design. Suggest possible enhancements to the design.

```java
import javax.swing.*;
import java.io.*;
import java.util.*;
class SPC
{    static String word;
     // files for input and output
     static PrintWriter wwf;
     static BufferedReader tf;
     static BufferedReader df;
     static StringTokenizer words;
     static String line = "";
     static String dict [] = new String[10000];
     static int index = 0;

     public static void main(String args[]) throws IOException
     {    String line= "";
          boolean flag1, flag2;
          init();
          while ((word = getWord()) != null)
          {    flag1 = validate(word);
               if (flag1 == false)
               {    flag2 = checkWithUser(word);
                    if (flag2 == true)
                        addToDict(word);
                    else addToWWF(word);
               }
          }
          finalizer();
     }
     static String getWord() throws IOException
     { if (words.hasMoreTokens()== false)
          {    line = tf.readLine();
               if (line != null)
                   words = new StringTokenizer(line);
               else return null;
```

```
            return words.nextToken();
        }
    else return words.nextToken();
    }
    static void init() throws IOException
    {   wwf = new PrintWriter(new FileWriter("wwf.out"));
        tf = new BufferedReader(new FileReader("tf.in"));
        df = new BufferedReader(new FileReader("df.in"));
        line = tf.readLine();
        words = new StringTokenizer(line);
        String line1 = "";
        while ((line1=df.readLine() ) != null)
            dict[index++] = line1;
    }
    static void finalizer()throws IOException
    {   df.close();
        PrintWriter df = new PrintWriter(new FileWriter("df.in"));
        Arrays.sort(dict,0,index);
        // load array back in dictionary file
        for (int c=0;c < index;c++) df.println(dict[c]);
        System.out.println("DONE");
        df.close(); wwf.close();
    }
    static boolean validate(String w)
    {   for (int i=0; i < index; i++) if (dict[i].equals(w)) return true;
        return false;
    }
    static boolean checkWithUser(String w)
    {   String answer = JOptionPane.showInputDialog
("Is the word " + w + " valid ? Enter T or F ?");;
        if (answer.equals("T")) return true;
        else return false;
    }
    static void addToDict(String word)
    {   dict[index++] = word;
    }
    static void addToWWF(String word)
    { wwf.println(word);    }
}
```

7. Given the following pseudocode:

M1 () { write into file B; }
M2(int x) { ...; print x; ...; }
M3() { write into file A }
M4(Record StudentRecord) { print Student Number; call M1(); }
M5() { int i = 0; call M2(i); }
M6() { call M1(); }
M7() { call M4(CompleteStudentRecord); call M5(); go to L1;}
M8(Boolean x) { if (x == true) call M9() ; else call M6();
call M11(); write into file B; }
M9() { call M3() ; call M1(); }
M10() { call M8(Boolean flag); call M7(); }
M11() { ...L1: write to file C; }

Produce a structured chart representing the high-level design hierarchy obtained from the given pseudocode. What is the coupling level between the various modules of the design hierarchy? What is the cohesion level of each module in the design?

8. Obtain a reasonably-size software design document from the Web. Does it contain all the design information recommended in IEEE 1016?

9. Obtain a software design inspection checklist from the Web. Can you comment on its completeness? Can you use it to inspect the design document from Exercise 8?

10. Obtain a GUI design document from the Web. Provide an inspection report using an inspection checklist of your choice.

11. Obtain a GUI design checklist from the Web. Assess it according to the design principles and guidelines of this chapter.

BIBLIOGRAPHY

Books

Bass, L., P. Clements, and R. Kazman. *Software Architecture in Practice*, 2d ed., Reading, MA: Addison-Wesley, 2003.

Booch, G., J. Rumbaugh, and I. Jacobson. *The Unified Modeling Language User Guide*, Reading, MA: Addison-Wesley, 1999.

Budgen, D. *Software Design*, 2d ed., Reading, MA: Addison-Wesley, 2004.

Cross, N. *Developments in Design Methodology*, New York: John Wiley & Sons, 1984.

Dorfman M., and R. H. Thayer, eds. *Software Engineering*, New York: IEEE Computer Society Press, 2002.

D'Souza, D. F., and A. C. Wills. *Objects, Components, and Frameworks with UML—The Catalysis, Approach*. Reading, MA: Addison-Wesley, 1999.

Fowler, M. *Refactoring: Improving the Design of Existing Code*, Reading, MA: Addison-Wesley, 1999.

Jayaswal, B., and P. Patton. *Design for Trustworthy Software: Tools, Techniques and Methodology for Developing Robust Software*, Englewood Cliffs, NJ: Prentice Hall, 2006.

McConnell, S. *Code Complete: A Practical Handbook of Software Construction*, Redmond, WA: Microsoft Press, 2004.

Mili, A. *An Introduction to Program Fault Tolerance*, Englewood Cliffs, NJ: Prentice Hall, 1990.

Papers

Aizenbud-Reshef, N., B. Nolan, J. Rubin, and Y. Shaham-Gafni. "Model traceability." *IBM Systems Journal*, 45(3): 515–526, 2006.

Avizienis, A., J. C. Laprie, and B. Randell. "Fundamental concepts of dependability." *University of Newcastle Upon Tyne, Technical Report Series,* 2001.

DeMarco, T. The Paradox of Software Architecture and Design. *Stevens Prize Lecture*, August 1999.

Dick, J. "Design traceability." *IEEE Software*, 14–16, November 2005.

Laprie, J. C. "Dependable computing and fault tolerance: Concepts and terminology." *Proc. 15th IEEE Intern. Symposium on Fault-Tolerant Computing*, 1995.

Mundie, C. et al. "Trustworthy computing." Microsoft White Paper, 2002.

Torres-Pomales, W. Software Fault Tolerance: A Tutorial, NASA, Virginia, October 2000.

Wirfs-Brock, R. "Towards design simplicity." *IEEE Software*, 9–11, March 2007.

Standards

IEEE Std 1016, *IEEE Recommended Practice for Software Design Descriptions*. IEEE, 1998.

IEEE Std 1028, *IEEE Standard for Software Reviews*. IEEE, 1997.

IEEE Std 1471, *IEEE Recommended Practice for Architectural Descriptions of Software-Intensive Systems*. Architecture Working Group of the Software Engineering Standards Committee, 2000.

ISO Std 9074, ISO OSI, ESTELLE—A Formal Description Technique Based on the Extended State Transition Model, 1988.

Object-Oriented Design

Object-oriented design (OOD) originates with the object analysis model built during the object-oriented analysis (OOA) phase. Whereas the analysis model concentrates on the **problem domain** objects and classes and what the system does, the OOD concentrates on the **solution domain** objects and classes and how the system can be implemented. Solution domain classes refine the already identified problem domain classes. In addition, new and modified classes are identified at the design level mainly to deal with non-functional requirements (NFRs) such as performance, security, scalability, and fault tolerance requirements. When refining the design model, the designer can benefit from past design experiences by reusing known design patterns and software architectural styles.

Learning Outcomes

In this chapter you will learn:
- How to produce an object-oriented design
- Design patterns and their uses
- Software architectural styles and their uses
- Documenting object-oriented design

6.1 FROM ANALYSIS TO DESIGN

As discussed in Chapter 5, an analysis model is produced during the OOA phases. The analysis model includes a problem domain object model that contains objects that are elicited to reflect the external users' point of view. The initial list of attributes and operations included in each object are identified. In addition, the various relationships among objects are identified, including composition, association, and communication relationships. In addition, the analysis model includes the use case model consisting of the use case diagrams (UCDs) and related sequence diagrams. The analysis level sequence diagrams show the ordering of interactions between the various actors and entities that are outside the system. Outcomes of the analysis model are used to reach an agreement between the developer and the client.

The OOD extends the analysis model obtained in several ways. The design provides more details and refinements of the analysis model. The use case model is extended by considering additional use cases dealing with NFRs such as fault tolerance and security. In addition, special use cases dealing with functionalities related to startup, cleanup, or shutdown procedures are added. Also, use cases dealing with abnormal and exceptional situations are defined and are linked to existing analysis model use cases using the *extend* relationship. These use cases are also called solution domain use cases. The object model is refined by examining the analysis objects and their relationships. In addition, solution domain objects are added taking into consideration high-level and architectural issues. Finally, the detailed design of each object is developed.

The detailed design includes a detailed description of the operations or methods in each class of the solution domain. For each method, the preconditions and postconditions can be specified. In addition, the data structures and algorithms used can be documented using various description techniques as described in Section 5.6 in Chapter 5. A method template similar to the module detailed design template introduced in Table 5.4 can be used. Unified modeling language (UML) state diagrams are utilized to describe internal state changes of permanent objects. Activity diagrams can be used to describe the concurrent or multithreaded activities within a method. Activity diagrams describe activities across multiple objects in the design, whereas sequence diagrams are used to describe interobject communications. Figure 6.1 depicts the inputs and outputs of the OOD phase.

The deliverables of the object-oriented process should be reviewed during formal design review meetings. Participants in these meetings include one or more representatives from each of the design and analysis teams, a representative from the quality assurance team and the testing team, and a meeting moderator. Design walkthrough and inspection techniques similar to the

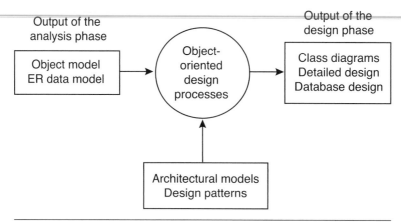

Figure 6.1 Inputs and outputs of the OOD phase

ones used in the traditional design review process can be used. The design review must ensure that all of the functional requirements described in the OOA model are met in the design. In addition, NFRs must be verified to ensure that the design meets them. Implementation independent and design-based test plans can be developed by the designers to be executed later by the testers or implementers of the design.

6.2 OBJECT-ORIENTED HIGH-LEVEL ARCHITECTURAL DESIGN

The high-level **object-oriented design** (OOD) first examines the existing object analysis model. For each object, the attributes and their types are confirmed. In addition, the access visibility to each of the attributes is defined. Private attributes are accessed by methods within the same object, whereas public ones are accessed by external methods. The operations or methods of each object are checked and their signatures and return types are defined. Similarly, access visibility of each method is defined. Private methods can only be invoked from within the same object, whereas public ones are accessible by external methods.

The methods included in each object must be closely related if dealing with the same object. Each method must have a well-defined functional description. A highly cohesive object contains related methods and each method is itself functionally cohesive. The communication between methods of objects must be minimal. The communication relationship among the objects of the analysis model must be examined and refined to ensure the lowest coupling possible between objects of the design model. It is obvious that objects need to communicate to perform specific functions in a collaborative manner. However, the number of communication links and the type and amount of data exchanged during the communication must be kept to a minimum.

The analysis model should also be reviewed to refine both the inheritance and composition relationships among objects. Inheritance relationships lead to more optimal implementations and higher reusability. All possibilities of inheritance among objects must be explored and clearly identified at the design level. In addition, identifying objects that can be parts of other objects lead to higher reusability and, therefore, lower implementation and maintenance costs.

To deal with the complexity of the design process, the principle of design reuse should be explored. There are numerous common aspects and features in the applications we develop. Lessons learned in the design of software systems must be exploited so that previous errors are avoided and new systems can be designed faster. The software research and industrial communities have documented experiences in the design process. Software architectural styles and design patterns include high-level and architectural design concepts and experiences that can be reused across applications. To make use of these patterns the designer has to understand the requirements and issues at hand and select the best architectural style(s) and design patterns that can be used in their current design. The documented architectural styles are mainly programming language- or implementation-independent. However, design patterns are based mainly on the object-oriented concepts and are limited to object-oriented programming languages. In the following sections, the most popular architectural styles and design patterns are described briefly.

6.3 ARCHITECTURAL PATTERNS

Software architecture provides a high-level view of the system being developed. An architecture identifies the software components or subsystems needed as well as the way that they interact and communicate among themselves. In addition, the interactions with external subsystems are defined. The deliverable of the software architecture is an architectural model that describes the elements of the architecture. The package, component, and deployment diagrams can be used to graphically describe the software architecture.

The architectural model can be built using one or more of the well-known architectural patterns or architectural styles for software systems. An **architectural pattern** is a documented industry-proven approach used to describe the software subsystems and their interactions. The choice of the pattern depends on the application context and the non-functional software requirements. Specifically, NFRs issues related to modifiability and maintainability, robustness and fault tolerance, reusability, traceability, and testability are addressed by the selection of the proper architectural style.

Layered

To deal with the complex software design, the layered software architecture leads to the distribution of the software modules onto separate layers with well-defined interfaces among them. A low layer is said to provide services to the layer just above it. Moreover, modules in one layer interact with both the modules at the layer below and above. The number of messages crossing between layers should be kept at a minimum to reduce the coupling between layers and their enclosed modules. Application programming interfaces are defined and used for interlayer communication. A typical **layered architecture** exists in communications software. The communication protocol stack such as the Transmission Control Protocol/Internet Protocol (TCP/IP) and the Open System Interconnection Reference Model (OSI-RM) is typically designed along a layered architecture. The layered communication architecture leads to highly-testable and -maintainable software. Moreover, the modules at each layer provide closely related services. Figure 6.2 illustrates modules in a layered architecture and Figure 6.3 shows the layered architecture of the OSI-RM communication model. In this figure, the transport layer provides transport-related services to the session layer after it receives services from the network layer modules.

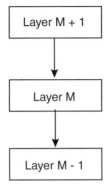

Figure 6.2 Layered architecture model

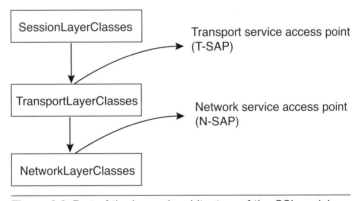

Figure 6.3 Part of the layered architecture of the OSI model

Client/Server

In the **client/server architecture**, modules are divided into client modules and server modules. Typically, these modules are geographically distributed. Client requests are normally sent across the network. The server handles the request and sends its reply to the client module. In a client/server architecture, the server side includes the database server hosting the server information in addition to the server hardware and software. A strong coupling between the processing modules and the database exist. The coupling is reduced in three-tier and multi-tier architectures. The client modules deal with the preprocessing of the user request utilizing a user-friendly interface. After a simple prevalidation of the request, the request is channeled to the server. The server processes the request and consults the local database if necessary. Figure 6.4 is an example of a client/server architectural model.

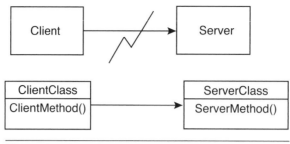

Figure 6.4 Client/server architectural model

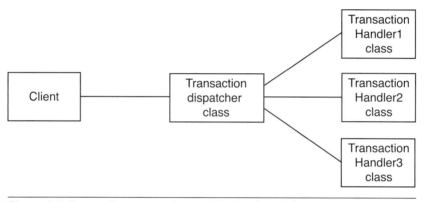

Figure 6.5 Transaction processing architectural model

Transaction Processing

In a **transaction processing** architecture, a transaction is received first from a user and validated for completeness and correctness. A transaction dispatcher is responsible for dispatching or directing the transaction to the appropriate transaction handler. The handler is also responsible for servicing the transaction. This architecture allows for the decoupling between the dispatcher and its handlers as well as the maintainability and extendibility of the architecture. The transaction processing architecture can be blended with the client/server architecture in which both the dispatcher and the appropriate handler correspond to the server. Moreover, the dispatcher and the handler can be located on two distributed servers, bringing the model closer to three-tier architecture. One concern related to this architecture is the bottleneck introduced at the dispatcher that can affect the overall performance and availability of the system. Figure 6.5 depicts a transaction processing architectural model.

Peer-to-Peer

In a **peer-to-peer architecture**, a module M1 may need the services of another module M2. Similarly, M2 might also need the services of M1. M1 and M2 act as both client and server modules. Hence, there is no client/server or master/slave relationship between them. M1 and M2 are peers (equal). M1 can either request services from M2 or can provide services to M2. Peer-to-peer architecture is typically used in communications systems in which distributed entities can require similar services from each other. A file transfer request can originate from M1 and go to M2. Similarly, M2 can initiate a file transfer request to M1. Hence, M1 and M2 are peer entities. Moreover, peer-to-peer architecture can be considered together with the layered architecture. In fact, the OSI-RM mentioned earlier is based on both layered and peer-to-peer architecture models. Figure 6.6 shows the peer-to-peer architectural model.

Three-Tier

In **three-tier architecture**, the client modules preprocess the client request before sending the request to the server. The server modules analyze the request and consult one or more local or remote database servers to provide an answer to the client request. Once the server receives all necessary data, it aggregates them and sends them to the client. The Java programming model provides the facilities for a typical three-tier architecture. A downloaded Java applet running inside the Web browser represents the client or the interface tier. The applet preprocesses the user input and then passes it back to the Web server. The Web server includes the application or business logic tier. The Java program at the server receives the request and executes it. Using Java database connectivity, the server software can connect to many database systems and query them. The third tier includes the consulted databases. These database systems return to the server with query results. The server packages the answer and sends it back to the client. See Figure 6.7 for an example of the three-tier architecture using the Java model.

Multi-Tier

In a **multi-tier architecture**, more than one server might be needed in a chain or a hierarchy to process the client request. Moreover, each server in turn might need to connect to one or more database systems. Therefore, a multi-tier architecture can require many message exchanges

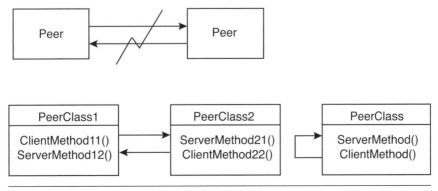

Figure 6.6 Peer-to-peer architectural model

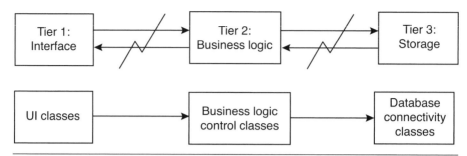

Figure 6.7 Three-tier architectural model

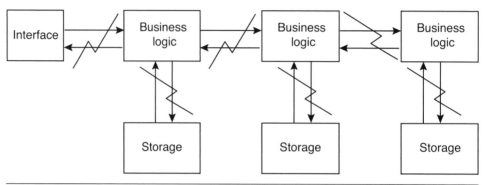

Figure 6.8 Multi-tier architectural model

across the network to service a client request. Location transparency can be a concern that needs to be addressed when selecting this type of architecture. Figure 6.8 is an example of a multi-tier architecture.

Pipe-and-Filter

In the **pipe-and-filter architecture**, the input stream is channeled through a pipeline consisting of a series of transformational processes. Each process in the series performs a well-defined operation transforming, refining, or filtering the input to the process to produce an output useable to the next process in the series. This model allows high reusability, maintainability, customizability, and extendibility of the architecture. Processes can be removed from or inserted into the pipeline. Moreover, processes can be reused in other pipelines and can be maintained or modified easily. For example, one filter in the pipeline can be responsible for the encryption of the input. Figure 6.9 is an example of a pipe-and-filter architectural model.

Distributed Object

In the **distributed object architecture**, software objects residing at distant locations in the network communicate and provide services to each other. Using a middleware like CORBA,

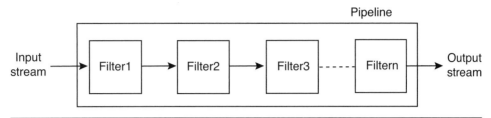

Figure 6.9 Pipe-and-filter architectural model

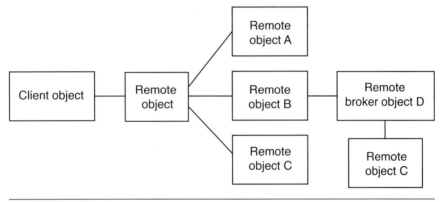

Figure 6.10 Distributed object architectural model

published and registered distributed objects communicate transparently by calling each other methods. Objects written in different programming languages are able to exchange messages through well-defined interfaces. The distributed object computing architecture and its underlying middleware allow for the integration of modern software written in Java with legacy software written in COBOL. Also, Java objects can communicate using the Java Remote Method Invocation package without requiring a middleware like CORBA that enables objects written in different programming languages to communicate among each other. The client/server and three-tier architectures can also be realized using distributed objects. Client objects embed the graphical-user interfaces and their validation logic. Server objects embed the business logic for processing client requests. Server objects can communicate with more than one database query and objects to retrieve the needed information. In addition to the decoupling of the various objects, the main advantage of this architecture is the design and development of lightweight objects that are highly-reusable and -maintainable. Figure 6.10 shows objects in a distributed object architecture model with or without the use of broker-based remote object invocation.

Mobile Object

The **mobile object architecture** is a variation of the distributed object architecture. In addition to being distributed, interacting objects can be mobile. A mobile object is able to move from one server to the other carrying its internal data and methods and encoding its processing logic. A mobile object is a lightweight software agent capable of moving across the network. The main idea of mobile objects is to bring computation to data rather than moving data to the stationary client objects. In mobile agent-based architectures, a mobile agent is created and launched at an initial server site. Then, the agent moves along a static or a dynamic route in the network. At each server along this route, the mobile agent interacts with stationary objects, processes the data obtained, and carries it along to the next server in the route. At each server, a mobile agent platform must be installed. The platform is needed to receive a visiting mobile agent and it is responsible for then re-launching the agent to the next server platform. Once the object finishes its journey, it returns to the originating server platform to report its findings. Another variation of this scenario is to have the mobile agent return its partial findings immediately to the originating platform, allowing for a more secure handling of collected information as well as having a lighter mobile object. The main advantage of using mobile objects is reduced network traffic. Moreover, in some applications, the use of mobile objects can be a natural and intuitive design choice. However, there are many security concerns that have to be dealt with in mobile agent-based systems. These concerns are related to the protection of the mobile agent while it is moving and processing at a server site. In addition, the receiving server could receive an object carrying infected code or performing illegal operations at the site. There are also security concerns related to possible hostile interactions among visiting agents at the same hosting platform. Mobile gaming and mobile bartering applications were developed based on the mobile object architecture. A mobile object is created by the client platform. The created mobile object moves from one platform to the next in the chain before it returns to the client platform. Figure 6.11 illustrates the mobile object architectural model.

Service-Oriented

In the **service-oriented architecture** (SOA), business processes are created, packaged, and offered as services that are located in the network. Services can be owned by various orga-

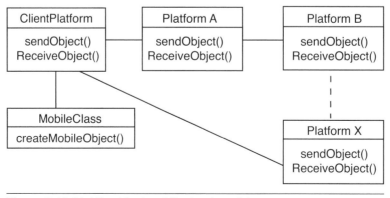

Figure 6.11 Mobile object architectural model

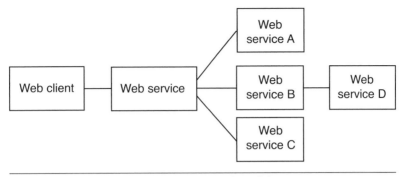

Figure 6.12 Service-oriented architectural model

nizations. A client discovers and locates the needed service and then sends a request. The client is only concerned with the provided service and not with how the service request is being processed. In an SOA, a complete business application corresponding to a workflow can be constructed or synthesized using existing services. Interoperability between services is important in an SOA because it allows services to interact with each other. Web services provide one approach to implement an SOA and use the Internet and its protocols as a vehicle to deliver services either to clients or other Web services. A service invokes another service by using specific protocols instead of including code for direct invocation of the other service. This allows better reusability of the services by decoupling them from each other. Workflows can use the same services but in a different order. The synthesis of a new business workflow from existing services in an SOA is called **orchestration**. Figure 6.12 shows a Web client requesting a service from a Web service. In this model, the Web service interacts with three other Web services to handle the client request, which in turn can interact with other Web services. Web services allow for software reusability, maintainability, and extendibility. They are also highly cohesive in the sense that they provide functionally-focused services.

6.4 DESIGN PATTERNS

Experiences in object-oriented software design have been documented by researchers and practitioners as design patterns. A **design pattern** is a reusable part of an OOD that can be used in similar contexts in another design. The use of a design pattern requires the proper identification of a similar problem that can be solved using the same pattern. Design patterns can be categorized based on their purpose in the design and include: fundamental; creational; structural; and behavioral design patterns. Other types of patterns that are not design-related have also been identified, including security patterns, testing patterns, and coding patterns.

Fundamental

Fundamental patterns are used in nearly every OOD. They can be included in other design patterns also. These patterns include:

Composite: Allows the construction of complex objects by recursively constructing similar objects in a tree-like structure. All constructed objects in the tree are handled using the same methods because they all should have the same superclass. See Figure 6.13.

Delegation: Allows the extension of the behavior of one class—the Delegator class—by making it invoke one or more methods of another class—the Delegate class. This pattern allows the reuse of the Delegate class by the Delegator class. Delegation is typically used when inheritance is not possible for reuse and when the two classes cannot be semantically- or logically-related by the generalization-specialization inheritance relationship. Clearly, the delegation pattern is a subpattern of other design patterns such as builder and **adapter patterns**. It is important at this point to distinguish between the communication and inheritance associations that can exist among objects. While inheritance provides better reuse opportunities, communication provides the possibility of delegating work of one object to other objects. This delegation of functionalities makes the design more flexible and possibly more cohesive. See Figure 6.14.

Immutable: Ensures that once an object of an immutable class is created that the object's state cannot be modified. This can be achieved by providing read-only methods, in addition to

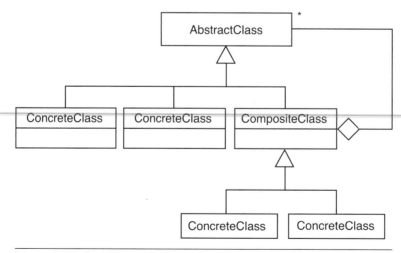

Figure 6.13 Component design pattern

Figure 6.14 Delegation design pattern

the constructor method. The constructor method is the only method that can change the values of the attributes defining the original and fixed state of the immutable object. See Figure 6.15.

Interface: Allows the decoupling between a Client class and a Service class by requiring an indirection using an abstract interface to the Service class. The Service class implements the abstract interface. The interface pattern is used when the client object needs only a few of the methods of the service object. The interface pattern is used in several other design patterns. See Figure 6.16.

Singleton: Ensures that a class has only one object or instance created from it. All other objects refer to the same singleton instance. Consequently, a controlled access to this single instance is needed. See Figure 6.17.

Creational

Creational patterns are concerned with the creation of objects in an object-oriented application. Creational patterns include the abstract factory, builder, factory method, and prototype designs. In addition to being fundamental patterns, the immutable and singleton design patterns can be considered creational design patterns.

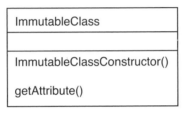

Figure 6.15 Immutable design pattern

Figure 6.16 Interface design pattern

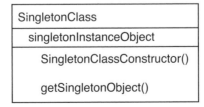

Figure 6.17 Singleton design pattern

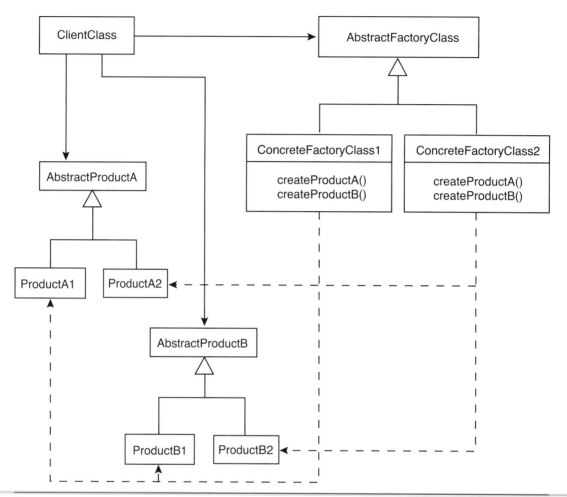

Figure 6.18 Abstract factory design pattern

Abstract factory: Allows the creation of instances of related or dependent objects from a corresponding set of concrete subclasses. The client class requests services from abstract classes without any knowledge of its concrete subclasses. The client object is isolated from the details of how product objects are created. See Figure 6.18.

Builder: Allows a client object to request a complex object from a director object by specifying the contents of that object. The client object is decoupled from the details of how the requested object is constructed by the director object. A builder object is then asked by the director object to construct the requested complex object. Once the object is constructed, the client object can obtain it. See Figure 6.19.

Factory Method: Requires the definition of an interface for creating objects of different types or classes in a Factory class. The requestor object requests the creation of a product object through the factory object. The factory object includes a method to create objects of the Product class. Consequently, the Requestor and Product classes are decoupled and new Product classes can be added later without any implications on the Requestor class. See Figure 6.20.

Prototype: Allows a client object to create other objects without knowing their classes or how these objects are constructed. The client object includes a method that can be called to add a prototype object to the collection of objects owned by the client. A prototype builder class is used to provide prototype objects to be used by the client object. Prototype objects implement the prototype interface allowing the provision of known methods that can be invoked by the client object. The prototype objects are then cloned by the client objects. See Figure 6.21.

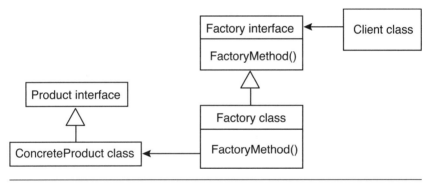

Figure 6.19 Builder design pattern

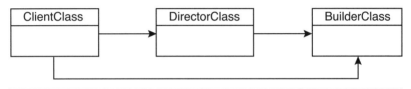

Figure 6.20 Factory method design pattern

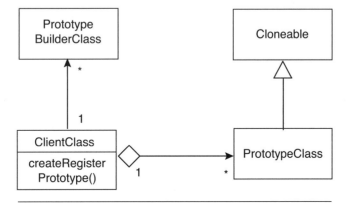

Figure 6.21 Prototype design pattern

Structural

Structural patterns are concerned with the class structure and relationships in an OOD. Structural patterns include the adapter, bridge, façade, and proxy designs. In addition to being a fundamental pattern, the composite design pattern is considered a structural design pattern also.

Adapter: Allows incompatible classes, client, and adaptee classes to work with each other. An adapter class implements an interface of one class known to one or more client classes. The implemented interface converts the method calls to a call to a different method in the adaptee class. This pattern introduces an intermediate class, whereas the client and adaptee classes remain decoupled. See Figure 6.22.

Bridge: Based on the decoupling between an abstract class from its implementation. The implementation class can then be the superclass of any number of subclasses that can override the implemented interfaces. The bridge pattern allows the decoupling of the interface used by a client object from the actual implementation of that interface. This leads to simpler maintenance in the future. See Figure 6.23.

Façade: Provides a common higher-level interface to a set of interfaces in a subsystem. The façade receives client requests and delegates them to the appropriate subsystem objects. Subsystems can also access each other through their façade interface. The façade pattern is useful to reduce the coupling between subsystem objects and external objects. It also allows for simpler client classes because the details of the workflow inside the servicing classes are shielded by the façade class. See Figure 6.24.

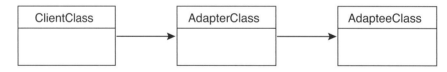

Figure 6.22 Adapter design pattern

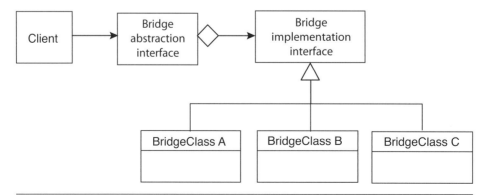

Figure 6.23 Bridge design pattern

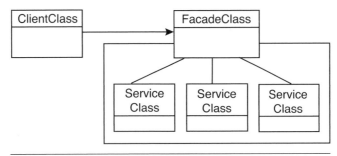

Figure 6.24 Façade design pattern

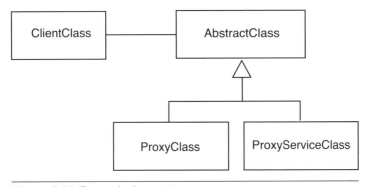

Figure 6.25 Proxy design pattern

Proxy: Requires method calls to a service object through the use of a proxy object and occurs in several other design patterns. When receiving a call, the proxy object delegates the call to the real service object. The proxy object shields the service object and can be used to enforce access control, priority management, and other control mechanisms to the service object. Both the service and proxy classes share the same abstract superclass. Ideally, a client object is not aware of the indirection caused by the presence of the proxy. See Figure 6.25.

Behavioral

Behavioral patterns are concerned with the class structure and class relationships in an OOD. Behavioral patterns include the chain of responsibility, command, iterator, mediator, memento, observer, state, strategy, template method, and visitor design patterns.

Chain of responsibility: Allows a client object to send a command to a chain of objects without knowing exactly which object is going to receive and handle the command. Hence, the client and server objects are decoupled. The pattern allows easy modification of the order of command handlers in the chain without affecting the client object. See Figure 6.26.

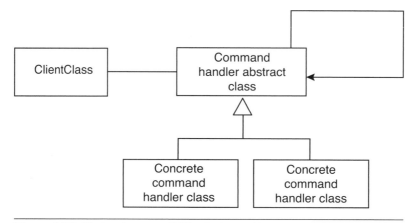

Figure 6.26 Chain of responsibility design pattern

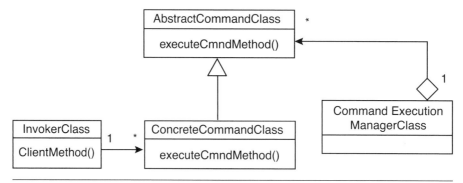

Figure 6.27 Command design pattern

Command: Encapsulates a request in a client object. Different request types can be included in a client object. The client object invoking the command object and the object executing the command are decoupled. A command object can be modified or processed at any time. For example, a command object can be queued for processing later and can be withdrawn if not executed within a certain amount of time. This pattern allows the separation and decoupling between the object creating or invoking the command and the object executing it. The execution of the command is usually independent of the application context, therefore, the class encapsulating the command execution behavior is highly reusable. See Figure 6.27.

Mediator: Requires the communications among a set of client or colleague objects to go through the mediator object. This pattern leads to a highly cohesive mediator object and to lower coupling among the client objects. However, the communications are centralized leading to a more complex mediator object rather than complex and highly coupled interacting clients or colleagues. Consequently, mediator classes are not reusable, however colleague classes are normally reusable. See Figure 6.28.

Observer: Allows the decoupling between observer client objects and monitor objects. Monitor objects can be added dynamically when needed. Observer objects are notified whenever an event is observed by any of the associated monitor objects. The monitor class then implements an abstract monitor class. Client observer objects implement the observer interface. Many monitor objects can be added to an observer object. Similarly, many observer objects can be notified by one monitor object. One potential drawback of this pattern is that the monitor object may become a bottleneck should there be too many observers' state changes or registered observer objects. See Figure 6.29.

State: Requires each state of a stateful context object to be represented by a concrete object that is an instance of a subclass of the abstract context state class. The context object determines its current state by including an attribute referring to the concrete object representing its current state. The number of states of the context object can be modified easily. See Figure 6.30.

Strategy: Allows the definition of related algorithms in concrete strategy classes that are subclasses of an abstract strategy class. A client object delegates a functionality to the abstract class without being concerned about the existing subclasses or strategies. Additional strategies can be included in the design easily. The strategy classes can be reused in other application designs. See Figure 6.31.

Template method: Allows the designer to write an abstract class with some concrete methods and other abstract methods. The abstract methods are made concrete in subclasses of the

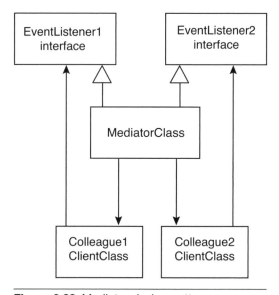

Figure 6.28 Mediator design pattern

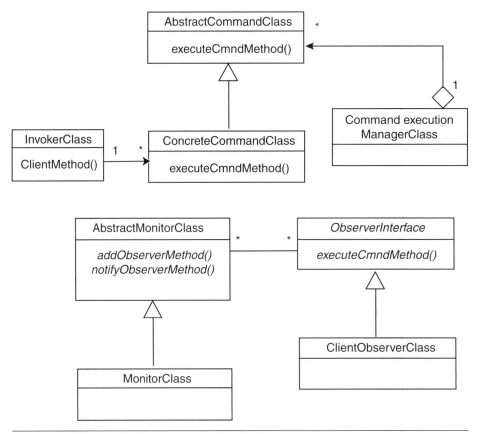

Figure 6.29 Observer design pattern

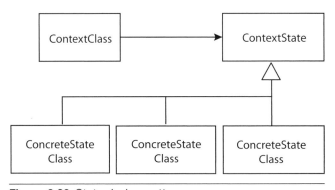

Figure 6.30 State design pattern

abstract class. A template method class provides a design structure that is refined later. See Figure 6.32.

Visitor: Requires the creation of a visitor class that encapsulates methods operating on objects in a complex class structure without disturbing the logic of the classes in the structure. Subclasses of the visitor class can also be defined to distinguish between visitor objects. See Figure 6.33.

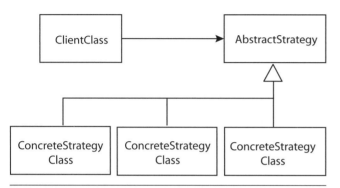

Figure 6.31 Strategy design pattern

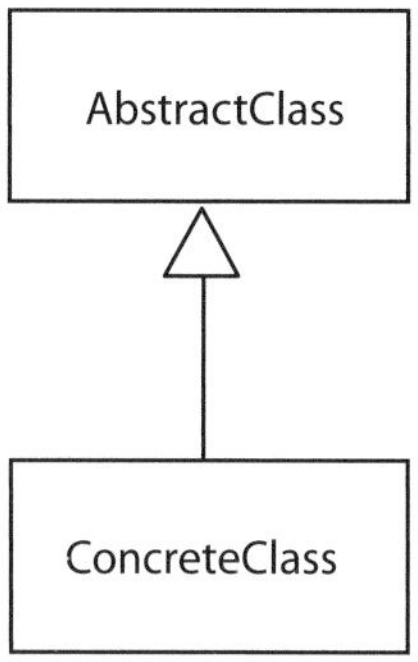

Figure 6.32 Template method design pattern

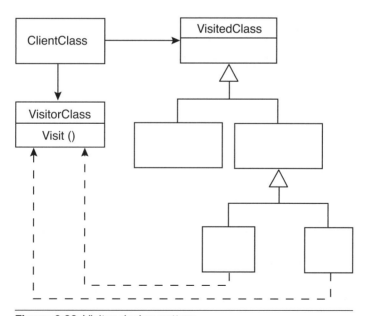

Figure 6.33 Visitor design pattern

6.5 DOCUMENTING AN OBJECT-ORIENTED DESIGN

A high-level OOD can be described using various types of UML diagrams. At the behavioral modeling level, sequence, timing, and communication diagrams can be used to describe the behavioral aspects of the design. The sequence and communication diagrams show the sequence of messages and interactions between the various objects involved in the design. However, at the structural modeling level, package, component, and deployment diagrams can be used to describe the static architecture of the high-level design model.

Package Diagram

A **package diagram** includes the packages used in the system, along with their elements and relationships. Package elements include class diagrams, use case diagrams, and possibly other UML diagrams. Classes related by aggregation and inheritance are normally included in the same package. Packages can be connected using the import or merge relationships. Also, packages can include other packages resulting in nested packages. A package is represented by a folder containing its elements and their relationships.

Component Diagram

A **component diagram** includes the software and hardware components that make up the system and the relationships. A software component is normally composed of many classes that are linked at run-time. A component is represented by a rectangle with the <<component>> stereotype. Components can also include ports through which bidirectional communication with other components can occur. The assembly connector symbol connects two components such that one component provides a service to the related component through a well-defined port or interface. Figure 6.34 shows an example of a component diagram. In the figure, the customer component provides customer information to the ATM component which in turn provides audit log information to the audit logger component.

Deployment Diagram

A **deployment diagram** describes the system and software architecture at run-time. It shows how the system elements or nodes are deployed in the physical locations of the system. A system element or node is either a hardware, software, or data element, and is shown as a three-dimensional box. Aggregation and communication association relationships and their related multiplicities and stereotypes can be used to link the nodes in a deployment diagram. Figure 6.35 shows a deployment diagram, including an application server, a database server, client machines, an intranet, and a firewall as nodes.

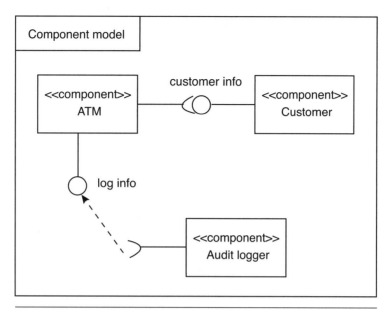

Figure 6.34 Component diagram example

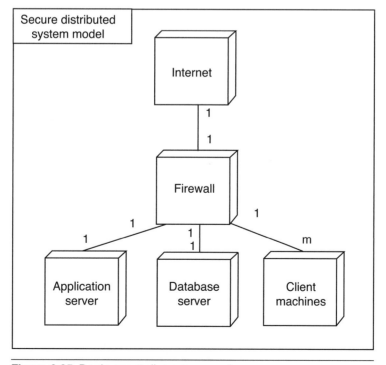

Figure 6.35 Deployment diagram example

6.6 DOCUMENTING OBJECT-ORIENTED DETAILED DESIGN

Once the high-level architectural design of the software is completed and reviewed, the detailed OOD process can begin. This process consists of the detailed description of each method included in every class of the architectural design. Techniques similar to those introduced in Chapters 4 and 5 can be used to describe and document the logic of each method. State machine, sequence, activity, and timing diagrams can be used to describe the internal behavior of an object. In addition, the entity relationship data model can be used to create the detailed database design. However, if **object-oriented databases** (OODB) are to be used to implement the application database, the entity objects identified in the OOA model (see Chapter 4) is mapped to the persistent object schemas in the OODB.

Once the detailed design is complete, a validation process based on review techniques can be used. Inspection checklists similar to those developed for the traditional design can be used to ensure that the design reflects both functional and NFRs. Moreover, object-oriented test plans can be developed. These test plans are executed later once the implementation is complete. The advantage of developing these plans at this point is to obtain unbiased testing based on the design rather than the implementation.

SUMMARY

After reviewing and approving the deliverables of the OOA phase, the object-oriented design provides a solution domain model that is used as the basis for software implementation and utilizes an object-oriented programming language. The deliverables of the object-oriented design are the high-level architectural design, the detailed design, and the database design. In addition to the object model identified in the analysis phase, the appropriate design patterns and architectural styles must be selected and reused to produce a high-level architectural object-oriented design by refining the object model.

KEY TERMS

abstract factory	component diagram	interface
adapter	composite	layered architecture
adapter pattern	delegation	mediator
architectural pattern	deployment diagram	mobile object architecture
behavioral patterns	design pattern	multi-tier architecture
bridge	distributed object architecture	object-oriented database
builder	façade	object-oriented design
chain of responsibility	factory method	orchestration
client/server architecture	fundamental patterns	package diagram
command	immutable	peer-to-peer architecture

pipe-and-filter architecture	singleton	template
problem domain	solution domain	three-tier architecture
prototype	state	transaction processing
proxy	strategy	visitor
service-oriented architecture	structural patterns	

REVIEW QUESTIONS

1. Identify three design patterns in which the delegation pattern is used.
2. What is the main difference between the façade pattern and the bridge pattern?
3. What is the main difference between the pipe-and-filter architectural style and the layered architectural style?
4. What are the main differences between architectural patterns and design patterns?
5. What are the benefits of design patterns?
6. List two design patterns that help to reduce the coupling among classes in an OOD.
7. List two architectural patterns that help to reduce the coupling among classes and that improve testability and maintainability.

EXERCISES

1. Consider the OOA model you obtained for the Web-based order processing system described in Exercise 6 in Chapter 4. Justify the selection of an appropriate architectural style that can best resolve the problem. Which design patterns can be reused in the OOD? Refine the analysis you obtained to produce a high-level OOD model.
2. Consider the OOA model you obtained for the milk delivery system described in Exercise 8 in Chapter 4. Justify the selection of an appropriate architectural style that can best resolve the problem. Which design patterns can be reused in the OOD? Refine the analysis you obtained to produce a high-level OOD model.
3. Develop an inspection checklist to validate a high-level and detailed OOD.
4. Provide examples in which the façade, proxy, strategy, and bridge design models can be used.
5. Provide an example in which the composite design pattern can be used.

BIBLIOGRAPHY

Books

Booch, G. *Object-Oriented Analysis and Design with Applications*, 3d ed., Reading, MA: Addison-Wesley Professional, 2007.

Booch, G., J. Rumbaugh, and I. Jacobson. *Unified Modeling Language User Guide*, 2d ed., Reading, MA: Addison-Wesley Professional, 2005.

Bruegge, B. and A. Dutoit. *Object-Oriented Software Engineering: Using UML, Patterns and Java*, 2d ed., Englewood Cliffs, NJ: Prentice Hall, 2003.

Coad, P., and E. Yourdon. *Object-Oriented Design*, Englewood Cliffs, NJ: Prentice Hall, 1991.

D'Souza, D. F., and A. C. Wills. *Objects, Components, and Frameworks with UML—The Catalysis Approach*, Reading, MA: Addison-Wesley, 1999.

Erl, T. *Service-Oriented Architecture (SOA): Concepts, Technology, and Design*, Englewood Cliffs, NJ: Prentice-Hall, 2005

Fowler, M. *Patterns of Enterprise Application Architecture*, Reading, MA: Addison-Wesley, 2003.

Gamma, E., et al. *Design Patterns: Elements of Reusable Object-Oriented Software*, Reading, MA: Addison-Wesley, 1995.

Grand, M. *Patterns in Java*, vol. 1., New York: John Wiley, 1998.

Jacobson, I., G. Booch, and J. Rumbaugh. *The Unified Software Development Process*, Reading, MA: Addison-Wesley, 1999.

Larman, C. *Applying UML and Patterns: An Introduction to Object-Oriented Analysis and Design,* 3d ed., Englewood Cliffs, NJ: Prentice-Hall, 2004.

Lethbridge, T. and R. Laganiere. *Object-oriented Software Engineering*, 2d ed., New York: McGraw Hill, 2005.

Meyer, B. *Object-Oriented Software Construction*, 2d ed., Englewood Cliffs, NJ: Prentice-Hall, 1997.

Nelson, J. *Programming Mobile Objects with Java*, New York: John Wiley, 1999.

Page-Jones, M. *Fundamentals of Object-Oriented Design in UML*, Reading, MA: Addison-Wesley, 2000.

Rumbaugh, J., et al. *Object-Oriented Modeling and Design,* Englewood Cliffs, NJ: Prentice-Hall, 1991.

Shalloway, A., and Trott, J. *Design Patterns Explained: A New Perspective on Object-Oriented Design*, 2d ed., (Software Patterns Series). Reading, MA: Addison-Wesley Professional, 2004.

Wirfs-Brock, R., Wilkerson, B., and Wiener, L. *Designing Object-Oriented Software*, Englewood Cliffs, NJ: Prentice-Hall, 1990.

Article

Pree, W., and Sikora, H. "Design patterns for object-oriented software development," *Proceedings of the 19th International Conference on Software Engineering*, 663–664, 1997.

Wieringa, R. "A survey of structured and object-oriented software specification methods and techniques," *ACM Computing Surveys*, 30(4): 459–527, 1998.

Software Implementation

7

After finalizing, reviewing, and approving the software design, one or more programming teams begin coding the software. Ideally, if the software design is clear and unambiguous, implementation is a straightforward process of mapping the design into code. However, there are many issues related to software implementation or coding that need to be addressed. Many software errors are caused by poor implementation and testing that fails to detect implementation errors; therefore, guidelines and standards for writing clear and secure software have been developed. In addition, prior to the use of dynamic testing techniques, a manual and static review of the code is conducted to remove known vulnerabilities and to enforce the adherence of the implementation to some coding guidelines and standards.

> ## *Learning Outcomes*
>
> In this chapter you will learn:
> - Mapping design into code
> - Coding style and documentation guidelines
> - Fault tolerance and exception handling in implementations
> - Software libraries and the use of Application Programming Interface
> - Guidelines for writing secure software
> - Code reviews

7.1 MAPPING DESIGN INTO CODE

After approving the software design deliverables consisting of both high-level and detailed design documents, the implementation phase begins. Software implementation or coding consists of the transformation of the design into an executable software implementation. Ideally, an application is implemented using a high-level programming language that is appropriate and suitable to the application domain. The choice of the programming language is typically made during the initial project planning phases. Some recruited team members would have been selected for their expertise in and knowledge of a specific programming language. The choice of the language is influenced by the type of software application under development. For example, to develop business application software, COBOL might be an appropriate and natural choice; however, COBOL is not suitable for real-time software applications. In large software development firms there is generally flexibility in hiring developers with specific programming skill sets; however, this flexibility might not exist and the manager will not have that expertise available. In that case, the project manager has to consider training existing developers in the use of a new programming language or justify the case for hiring the appropriate professionals. This requirement is normally included in the training and recruitment section of the software project management plan as discussed in Chapter 10.

Partial software implementations can be generated using integrated software development tools that are able to produce sizable parts of the software code from higher-level design representations. For example, there are many unified modeling language (UML)-based software

Table 7.1 C implementation of the FSM M in Figure 4.2

```
enum State { s0, s1, s2 };
enum Input { a, b, c };
enum Output { zero, one, errorMessage};
void sendMessage (Output msg);
void machine_M (Input i)
{       static State s = s0;
        switch ( s )
        {       case s0:
                        switch ( i )
                        {       case a:  s = s2;
                                        sendMessage(one);
                                default: // do nothing
                        }
                case s1:
                        switch ( i )
                        {       case a:  s = s2;
                                        sendMessage(zero);
                                        break;
                                case c:  s = s0;
                                        sendMessage(one);
                                        break;
                                default: // do nothing
                        }
                case s2:
                        switch ( i )
                        {       case a:  s = s1;
                                        sendMessage(one);
                                        break;
                                case b: // do nothing
                                        break;
                                default: // do nothing
                        }
        }
}
```

tools that are able to generate code from design artifacts modeled using UML. The extent of the code generation depends on the tool itself and the application being developed as well as its domain. It also depends on the completeness of the design itself. The advantage of automated code generation is that the generated code is well-documented and follows some internal coding standards homogeneously. However, the generated code might not be optimal and can require further work and testing. A typical illustration of automatic code generation can be seen when considering a finite state machine (FSM) as a design specification model. Due to the structured nature of an FSM, the generation of code implementing it is straightforward. As an example, see Table 7.1 that depicts a C implementation of the design level FSM shown in Figure 4.2 using nested switch statements.

It is clear that since the FSM M in Figure 4.2 is not completely specified, the implementation code is also incomplete. For example, at state s0, the code handles only input a. No actions are performed if at state s0 inputs b or c are encountered. To complete the machine, we can specify that for all possible inputs at a state other than the one shown in the figure, the output of the machine should indicate an error message for an invalid input and the machine remains at the same state. The default statement can be used to complete the implementation accordingly. Another possibility to complete the machine is to add a new state e that is directly reachable from all other states if an invalid input is present. An additional input reset applied at state e can be used to restart the machine at its initial state. Figure 7.2 shows the corresponding complete machine. Table 7.2 shows the implementation of the completely specified machine M shown in Figure 7.2.

7.2 CODING STYLE AND DOCUMENTATION GUIDELINES

As part of the software development plan, a **coding standard** specifying the style for writing code and documenting it should be adopted. A standard should be realistic, easy to learn, and practical. The main advantage of using a coding standard is that code written by various developers will look as if it is written by one person and, therefore, the readability of the code is enhanced. The standard should be adhered to by all developers without exception. Moreover, it should be adhered to during both the development and the maintenance of the software. Software code **inspection checklists** developed by the quality assurance group should include items related to the adherence to the organization's coding standard. Although adherence to coding and documentation standards can be time consuming and shortsightedly considered an overhead, in the long term, good code readability and documentation contribute positively to the quality of the produced software. In addition, the software understandability is enhanced and, consequently, the software maintenance cost is reduced as a result of good documentation practices.

Software coding standards can specify how various software elements are named, commented on, or formatted. Names constitute the basic components of a source code. Names can be keywords or reserved words used in the program. Defined names may be, among other

Table 7.2 C implementation of the FSM M in Figure 7.2

```
enum State { s0, s1, s2, e };
enum Input { a, b, c, reset };
enum Output { zero, one, errorMessage, restartedMessage };
void sendMessage (Output msg);
void machine_M (Input i)
{       static State s = s0;
        switch ( s )
        {       case s0:
                    switch ( i )
                    {       case a:  s = s2;
                                    sendMessage(one);
                            default:  s = e;
                                    sendMessage(errorMessage);

                    }
                case s1:
                    switch ( i )
                    {       case a:  s = s2;
                                    sendMessage(zero);
                                    break;
                            case c:  s = s0;
                                    sendMessage(one);
                                    break;
                            default:  s = e;
                                    sendMessage(errorMessage);

                    }
                case s2:
                    switch ( i )
                    {       case a:  s = s1;
                                    sendMessage(one);
                                    break;
                            case b: // do nothing
                                    break;
                            default:  s = e;
                                    sendMessage(errorMessage);

                    }
                case e:
                    switch ( i )
                    {       case reset:
                                    s = s0;
                                    sendMessage(restartedMessage);
                                    break;
                            default:  s = e;
                                    sendMessage(errorMessage);

                    }
        }
}
```

things, variable names, procedures, functions or methods, packages, classes, user-defined types, or table names in structured query language (SQL). For example, a naming standard might state that a name can be a concatenation of words in a sentence in which each word starts with a capital letter. An example of a name adhering to this rule would be AverageTemperatureDuring-

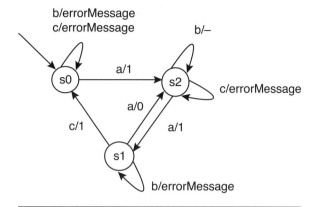

Figure 7.1 Completely specified FSM M

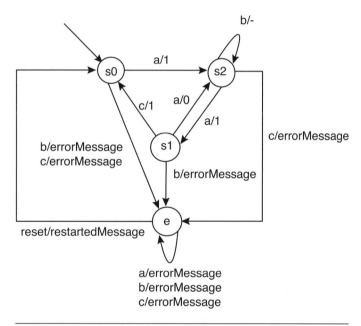

Figure 7.2 An alternative completely specified FSM M using an error state and a reset input

Daytime. Other standards might require an underscore (_) to separate the words. In this case, the same name would then be average_temperature_during_daytime. Obviously, any naming convention should be consistent with the syntax rules of the programming language used for software implementation. Comments standards can require that each variable name should be commented on within the same line to increase readability and code understandability.

Good practices for writing comments help reduce the future maintenance cost of the software, although their benefits might not be apparent when they are written. Comments must always be updated whenever the code is modified during maintenance to avoid inconsistencies. Coding standards for formatting the code include rules related to the indentation of the code, spacing, including separation lines and white spaces, and the use of fonts as well as other styling rules.

7.3 SOFTWARE LIBRARIES AND APIs

When developing large scale software, the concept of reusability of software components should be thoroughly explored. The reuse of trusted and already operational components adds to the trustworthiness of the software system being developing. Conceptually, reusability at the implementation level can be useful in two separate but complementary ways: writing code for reuse in future projects and writing code using existing reusable code. Writing code for reuse requires careful development of modules and components with clear **application programming interfaces** (APIs). This requires more investment at the beginning, but the payoffs are higher in the long term. Writing code with reuse requires the proper identification and use of existing components. This normally leads to saving in development cost and potentially more reliable software provided that **reusable components** are obtained from trusted sources.

Reusable components can exist in software libraries embedded in the integrated development environment or obtained from outsourced components or off-the-shelf software components. Regardless of the source, a good API for each module developed or reused is the key to successful reusability. Software companies consider reusable modules with properly designed APIs corporate assets. A good API is easy to learn, read, and use, additionally, it is secure and hard to misuse and is easy to extend and adapt. Moreover, any code using it is easy to maintain. Typically, an API is stable with almost no modification made to it once it is made public. It is obvious that an API can also be a corporate liability if it is not reliable, well tested, and stable. The key to a successful reusable module with an API is to ensure that the requirements are properly and completely elicited and managed so that both API and implementation reflect the requirements. An API should be functional, doing one simple function, and should be properly protected by maximizing the amount of hidden or private information, enforcing the least privilege principle. The module and its API must be well-documented with readable and consistent names to increase its usability and reusability. Most of the desirable quality properties and non-functional requirements (NFRs) must be reflected in both module and API design and coding. For documentation purposes, a typical API must be accompanied by a template as shown in Table 7.3.

In Table 7.4, the documentation of the method generateKeyPair of the class KeyPairGenerator inside the Java package java.security is shown.

Table 7.3 Template for documenting an API

API name	
Brief description	
Syntax or prototype (name and header)	
Typical use scenario	
Usage example	
Detailed description	
Arguments details	
Superclass(es)	
Error messages produced	
Exceptions thrown out	
Returned value	
Prerequisite or preconditions	
Special notes or warning on API use	

Table 7.4 Documentation of the method generateKeyPair

API name	generateKeyPair
Brief description	This method generates a key pair made of a private key and a public key using a given algorithm
Syntax or prototype (name and header)	public KeyPair generateKeyPair ( )
Typical use scenario	Used to create a key pair to be used in an application requiring asymmetric keys; one for encryption and the other for decryption

Usage example	// first create a KeyPairGenerator object using the
	// RSA algorithm
	kpg = KeyPairGenerator.getInstance ("RSA");
	// require 512 bytes long keys
	kpg.initialize (512, new SecureRandom( ));
	// generate a key pair object
	KeyPair kp = kpg.generateKeyPair( );

Detailed description	After initializing an object of class KeyPairGenerator with a key generation algorithm, a call to this method returns a new key pair every time it is called; if no explicit initialization was done prior to calling the method, a default algorithm and key sizes will be used
Arguments details	No arguments needed
Superclass(es)	KeyPairGeneratorSpi
Error messages produced	none
Exceptions thrown out	none
Returned value	Object of class KeyPair
Prerequisite or preconditions	KeyPairGenerator class must be constructed using a specific key generation algorithm
Special notes or warning on API use	

A clear API description allows the user or caller to use it properly and unambiguously. Many API abuse errors exist because of the ambiguity or lack of clarity of the API description. API abuse errors are discussed later in this chapter.

APIs are now becoming an essential part of a programming language system supporting the development of applications with reusable components. The popularity and usefulness of a language increases if it has a rich, usable, and robust collection of APIs and software libraries. For example, Java, C++ and C# have rich libraries, including a large variety of APIs covering useful and reusable functionalities needed in most software systems. Examples of such APIs bundled in different packages are security, communications and networking, file management, database connectivity, and graphical user interface (GUI) support functionalities.

7.4 FAULT TOLERANCE

Fault tolerant software is able to deal with some errors or abnormal conditions by first detecting them and then continuing to perform its intended functions normally. Fault tolerant software is also referred to as error-recoverable software or self-stabilizing software. Typically, the software deals with the error and continues working normally thereafter. Fault tolerance should be considered at the requirements specification and design phases of a software development model.

One approach to **fault tolerance** is embedding **checkpointing** procedures that continuously save the state of the software. In the case of a failure, a recovery procedure, known as a backward recovery, is applied to continue operating from the last checkpoint saved earlier. However, there is another approach to recovery, a forward recovery, in which the software deals with the error and steps forward to a future desirable state. In this case, care should be taken so that no critical functionality is skipped.

Another approach to fault tolerant software is called **N-version programming**. In this approach, given one software design, we provide N implementations of the design by N independent development teams. Assume that an algorithm that produces results for its invoker is implemented. Each implementation of the algorithm provides its result (vote) to an arbiter who compares the collected results, and the result obtaining a majority of votes is considered the correct one. This approach assumes that the algorithm design is correct and only a minority of implementations among the N implementations can be faulty. Therefore this approach fails if the design itself is erroneous or if the majority of implementations are erroneous. A solution to the design error can be addressed by having an M-version software design. In this case, we can have different M design solutions leading to MN software implementations. Each of the M designs is implemented by N programming teams independently. This solution is costly, however, and requires numerous computations occurring in real time. Delays in making timely decisions might not be tolerated in real systems such as space probing or nuclear reactor control systems.

Finally, the **recovery block** approach, introduced by Randell, requires the saving of the current valid state of the system before entering the recovery block. Inside the block, N software versions are listed in order of their desirability or confidence in their correctness. The result produced by the first version is evaluated by a *judge* procedure or predicate and if it is found not to match the expected result, the saved valid state is used to reset the current state and the next less desirable version is executed, and so on. Once one version in the sequence gives the desired result, the recovery block is exited. If none of the alternative versions provide a correct answer, a procedure is invoked to deal with the error. A typical recovery block looks like the following pseudocode:

ensure judge-procedure or judge-predicate
by invoke-first-version
else by invoke-second-version
else by invoke-third-version
else by ....
else invoke-error-handling

It is clear that developing fault tolerant software requires extra effort to produce the various versions, including their design, coding, and testing. However, software fault tolerance contributes positively to many desirable software properties such as reliability, availability, and, therefore, security, robustness, and trustworthiness.

7.5 EXCEPTION HANDLING

Simple run-time errors can be encountered during the execution of a program. For example, accessing an array element beyond the array boundaries or a divide by zero can lead to a program crash if left to the operating system to handle. In this case, the program has to be re-executed. For critical software systems and real-time applications, these simple run-time errors should not be ignored by the program and should be treated to avoid a program crash. **Exception handling** is a programming mechanism used to detect and deal with run-time software errors. Exceptions can be generic, such as a Run_time_exception, or specific, such as Array_out_of_bound_indexing. In an object-oriented programming language, an exception is an object generated when an exception occurs. Exception classes form a hierarchy of objects. An exception object of class Exception is the most generic type of object since the class Exception is the top superclass in the exceptions class hierarchy. The programmer should list all possible exception objects that can be generated by the code if other handling is necessary, otherwise generic handlers can be declared and used. When there are multiple catch blocks, these blocks are normally listed in order of increasing generality.

A typical implementation of an exception handler that uses the try-catch-finally blocks follows:

```
try
{ // code that may cause or generate an exception
}
catch (class X) // exception of class X
{ // code for handling an exception of class X
}
catch (class Y) // exception of class Y
{ // code for handling an exception object of class Y
}
finally
{ // code to execute after the exception handling code is executed
// and before returning to the caller if no exception has occurred
}
```

A catch block that does not specify the class of exception to catch will catch all raised exceptions in the corresponding try block.

The try block includes the code that will, under certain abnormal input conditions, lead to the creation of an exception object either thrown explicitly by the try code or by a method called within the try block. If an exception object is generated inside the try block and detected at run-time, the corresponding catch block is executed to deal with the exception. Depending on the type of exception, the catch block code might deal with the exception locally inside the module where the exception occurred, or it can decide to deal with the exception partially and throw it to the calling module. Additionally, it can throw it to the calling module without any other handling. If an exception is thrown by a handler inside the main module, the operating system takes over and the software shuts down.

The finally code will typically include cleanup code such as freeing memory and other resources or closing files. This code is always executed whether or not exceptions have occurred in the try block. Moreover, the finally block is executed after a return statement is executed inside the try block. Consequently, the finally block code allows the avoidance of resource leaks in the software implementation.

A module that may throw an exception in one or more of its try or catch blocks should indicate this fact as part of its signature. A proper use of the module requires the calling module to be aware of a possible exception thrown and to deal with such raised exception. In the Java code that follows, the method readUserProfile might throw an exception of class IOException and no handling of this exception exists in the method itself. Any method calling readUserProfile is now aware that an exception can be thrown and must be handled by that method or thrown outside. In this case, the compiler enforces the handling of the exception thrown out of the method. The challenge is to deal with an exception properly at a particular level to allow the recovery from the exception without propagating the error further, or by providing the user meaningful information about the error and how to fix it.

```
public void readUserProfile (String fileName) throws IOException
{
    if (fileName == null)
    {
        throw IOException();
    }
    ....
    InputStream input = new FileInputStream(fineName);
    ....
}
```

7.6 WRITING SECURE SOFTWARE

Security in software should be considered early in the software development process. As discussed in Chapter 3, security requirements are NFRs that must be specified at the requirements phase. However, there are **software security** vulnerabilities that could have been introduced during the implementation of the software. These vulnerabilities can be avoided if good software security coding practices are followed. However, they can also be eliminated in a code review using an up-to-date software security checklist. Taxonomies of varying complexity for software security errors have been developed.

Input/Output Validation and Representation Errors

The lack of input validation can lead to errors caused by external inputs supplied by a malicious user. **Buffer overflow** is one of the most common vulnerabilities created by the lack of input validation. A buffer overflow is caused by statements allowing the user to input data that is stored outside the allocated memory locations. Typically, a buffer overflow causes the corruption of possibly critical memory, such as the run-time stack and, therefore, leading to run-time errors. A simple C code example of an input validation coding error that can cause a buffer overflow is:

```
char command[maxSize];
gets (command);
```

The gets function can get more maxSize characters from the user into the fixed-size array named command, leading to the overriding of memory.

Other input validation vulnerabilities include **command injection**, denial of service, log forging, cross-site scripting, operating system injection, integer overflow, cookies, and hidden fields. Command injection is characterized by a malicious inputted user command, such as

SQL query or a system command that is not validated by the application software before being executed. Moreover, a non-validated user input can lead to a denial of service attack if, for example, the user input is inputted as the number of seconds a thread is asked to sleep. A large integer can make an application thread remain idle for a long time, hence denying service to the application user.

Security Violations

Failure to use the proper software functions to ensure the three security goals of confidentiality, integrity, and availability, is characterized as a software **security violation** error. Examples of security violations include improper or lack of access control, the use of weak random number generators, the violation of the least privilege principle, the misuse of private information, the improper management of user passwords, the improper creation and use of temporary files, and the file access race condition error.

The code must reflect the software detailed design which in turn must meet all software requirements, including security requirements. For example, each access to database records must be controlled. The user issuing an SQL query must be identified, authenticated, and authorized to view a particular record. The code must check whether the user issuing the SQL statement is allowed to view the results of the issued query. The use of a standard pseudorandom number generator is considered to be weak when faced with a cryptographic attack especially when the generated key remains active for some time in the database. It is also possible that the application elevates the privilege level of a user to perform some system operations. It is important that the privilege level be dropped after executing these operations, otherwise a low privilege user would be running as an admin or super user. The code should not be allowed to save any private-user information such as password or credit card numbers in plaintext. Saving such private information in a log file, transmitting it in plaintext, or obscuring it using weak encoding schemes can be illegal, according to legal and regulatory security requirements. Moreover, the hard coding of such private-user information should not be allowed in the code because a disassembler might be able to discover them in the object code. The use of improper procedures by an application to create and use temporary files would make the application and the system on which it runs vulnerable to malicious attacks.

API Abuse

An API is a contract between a caller and a callee. A caller is expected to use the callee according to the API abstracting it. Any deviation from the callee's API is considered an **API abuse**. An API abuse is normally introduced during the implementation of the caller module. The abuse can be known or unknown. These abuses typically should be detected during code review meetings. An example of a simple API abuse is a caller ignoring a returned value by the callee. The returned value of a module is part of the API contract. Ignoring a returned value by a caller module can lead to integrity problems if the returned value indicates that an error has occurred or a bad state has been reached. Such problems must be dealt with accordingly.

Coding Errors and Code Quality

Coding errors include those that can be detected by a static checker and can lead to erroneous outcomes. Typically, these errors are not detected by a compiler and, therefore, should be discovered in a thorough code review or using a static checker program. Examples of such errors include: invalid test conditions; dead code; returning an address in stack; memory leak; type mismatch; null dereferencing; redundant initialization of variables; declared, initialized, and unused variables; undefined local parameters; uninitialized variables; unreleased memory; and referencing freed memory.

Error Handling Errors

The poor handling of **errors and exceptions** that occur at run-time can lead to program shutdown and affect the availability of the application and, consequently, overall security. Typical error handling problems include ignoring a raised exception, throwing a generic exception, catching and dealing with exceptions in a generic way, catching a null pointer exception instead of fixing the reason for which this exception is raised, and returning inside a finally block causing the raised exception to be lost.

7.7 CODE REVIEW

Once the software is implemented, it should be reviewed in code review meetings. A typical **code review** is a non-automated process performed by a group of developers and other stakeholders. A code review aims at finding as many coding errors as possible prior to performing elaborate testing that involves the dynamic execution of the software under test. The code review process is normally based on a multitude of techniques, including code **walkthrough** and inspection checklists. The code walkthrough typically consists of scanning the code to verify that it follows coding standards and is free from known software vulnerabilities that can affect its robustness and security. Inspection checklists are used to verify that specific desirable coding requirements are observed.

When a code review meeting is arranged, the code to be reviewed is distributed ahead of time along with the design the code under review is supposed to implement. Participants in a typical code review meeting include the programmer(s) involved in the code under review, one or more of the creators of the design reflected in the code under review, a representative of the software quality assurance group, possibly a representative of the testing team, and a review moderator. The software quality assurance (SQA) group is responsible for ensuring adherence to the standards. In addition, the SQA group is responsible for developing and maintaining the various checklists used during the review meetings. Code review is considered a static testing technique since it does not involve the execution of the code under review. More information on code reviews is given in Chapter 8.

SUMMARY

After approving the detailed software design, the implementation phase of the software begins. When implementing software, the development team must adhere to internal coding standards related to naming, formatting, and commenting the code. In addition, the proper use of the APIs and the software libraries must be strictly observed. Moreover, writing secure and fault tolerant code should be seriously considered to produce trustworthy applications. Appropriate code reviews includes code walkthroughs and comprehensive inspection checklists to ensure that the reviewed code follows standards and is secure and robust.

KEY TERMS

API abuse
application programming
    interfaces
buffer overflow
checkpointing
code review
coding errors

coding standard
command injection
errors and exceptions
exception handling
fault tolerance
inspection checklists
N-version programming

recovery block
reusable components
security violation
software security
walkthrough

REVIEW QUESTIONS

1. List some guidelines for coding.
2. List items that can be included in a code inspection list.
3. What is the difference between code inspection and code walkthrough?
4. What is the difference between developing software for reuse and developing software with reuse?
5. List some known categories of software security vulnerabilities.
6. Why should a module user know whether the called module throws an exception?
7. What is the relationship between software fault tolerance and software trustworthiness?
8. What is an API and an API abuse?

EXERCISES

1. Write the code corresponding to the FSM in Figure 7.1.

2. Complete the FSM in Figure 7.3 using the two ways shown in the chapter. Write the corresponding code. Make the necessary assumptions when completing the machine. Compare and comment on the two ways.

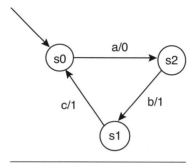

Figure 7.3 Exercise 2

3. Explain the file access race condition error and provide an example illustrating it.
4. Provide an example of each of the coding errors and code quality errors listed in the chapter.
5. Provide an example of each of the error handling mechanisms listed in the chapter.
6. List and discuss three types of API abuse of varying severities.
7. Compare the functionalities provided by the C# and Java APIs.
8. List five coding standards related to each of naming, commenting, and code formatting.
9. Consider one technique for software fault tolerance and compare it with its hardware counterpart.
10. Consider an API of a method in a programming language of your choice and assess whether the description is complete and unambiguous.
11. Write the template corresponding to the API of the method deleteRow of the interface ResultSet inside the Java package java.sql.
12. Search the Web for two code inspection checklists. Compare them and assess their completeness.

BIBLIOGRAPHY

Books

Barker, T. T. *Writing Software Documentation: A Task-Oriented Approach*, Boston, MA: Allyn & Bacon, 1998.

Beck, K. *Test-Driven Development: By Example*, Reading, MA: Addison-Wesley, 2002.

Bentley, J. *Programming Pearls*, 2d ed., Reading, MA: Addison-Wesley, 2000.

Fowler, M., et al. *Refactoring: Improving the Design of Existing Code*, Reading, MA: Addison-Wesley, 1999.

Grembi, J. *Secure Software Construction: A Security Programmer's Guide*, Florence, KY: Delmar Cengage Learning, 2008.

Howard, M., and D. C. Leblanc. *Writing Secure Code*, Redmond, WA: Microsoft Press, 2002.

Humphrey, W. S. *Introduction to the Personal Software Process*, Reading, MA: Addison-Wesley, 1997.

Hunt, A., and D. Thomas. *The Pragmatic Programmer*, Reading, MA: Addison-Wesley, 2000.

Kernighan, B. W., and R. Pike. *The Practice of Programming*, Reading, MA: Addison-Wesley, 1999.

Maguire, S. *Writing Solid Code: Microsoft's Techniques for Developing Bug-Free C Software*, Redmond, WA: Microsoft Press, 1993.

McConnell, S. *Code Complete: A Practical Handbook of Software Construction,* 2d ed., Redmond, WA: Microsoft Press, 2004.

Meyer, B. *Object-Oriented Software Construction*, 2d ed., Englewood Cliffs, NJ: Prentice Hall, 1997.

Mili, A. *An Introduction to Program Fault Tolerance*, Englewood Cliffs, NJ: Prentice Hall, 1990.

Sethi, R. *Programming Languages: Concepts & Constructs*, 2d ed., Reading, MA: Addison-Wesley, 1996.

Sommerville, I. *Software Engineering*, 7th ed., Reading, MA: Addison-Wesley, 2005.

Papers

Ounce Labs. "The path to a secure application: A source code security review checklist." 2007.

Randell, B. "System structure for software fault tolerance." IEEE Transactions on Software Engineering, 1(2): 220–232, 1985.

Stipenyuk, K., B. Chess, and G. McGraw. "Seven pernicious kingdoms: a taxonomy of software security errors", IEEE Security and Privacy, November-December 2005, 81–84.

Standards

IEEE Std 1028-1997 (R2002), IEEE Standard for Software Reviews, IEEE, 1997.

IEEE Std 1517-1999, IEEE Standard for Information Technology-Software Life Cycle Processes-Reuse Processes, IEEE, 1999.

IEEE/EIA 12207.0-1996//ISO/IEC12207:1995, Industry Implementation of Int. Std ISO/IEC 12207:95, Standard for Information Technology- Software Life Cycle Processes, IEEE, 1996.

Software Testing and Quality Assurance

Testing and quality assurance include activities that have significant impact on the quality of delivered software. In particular, testing safety-critical software and real-time software applications has to be carefully planned and must be performed effectively and efficiently. Since allocated resources are limited, the use of sound testing techniques during the planning and execution of these activities is crucial. In this chapter, various aspects involved in the testing process are introduced. Testing techniques, approaches, and strategies are explained. Finally an introduction to software quality assurance is provided.

Learning Outcomes

In this chapter you will learn:
- Basic terminology in software testing
- White box testing techniques
- Black box testing techniques
- System-level testing
- Integration testing approaches
- Approach to test object-oriented software
- Testing techniques to generate and select test cases to include in a test plan
- Software quality assurance and control activities implemented throughout the software development life cycle

8.1 TESTING AND TEST COVERAGE

Testing is a critical process within any software development and maintenance life cycle model. Testing is becoming increasingly important to the software development industry because of its implications to the quality of the produced software and the reputation of the producing company. Today, reputable software companies spend a great deal of resources on their testing activities. Testing activities include testing specifications, designs, and implementations.

Testing implementations is often referred to as software testing, or simply testing. In this chapter, we are concerned mainly in testing implementations.

In the early days of software development, testing was performed in ad hoc and informal manners. People involved in testing were not properly trained to perform their testing tasks. They were not motivated because they perceived the testing task as cleaning up other people's mistakes. The importance of testing was often downplayed and few resources were allocated. This has changed since it was realized that the quality of the produced software is greatly affected by the quality of the testing performed. Moreover, the reputation and marketability of the software is affected by the type and number of errors discovered after the software is released and deployed, therefore, it is beneficial to resolve all issues with the software before it is placed on the market. The outcome of performing a thorough testing is the generation of software error reports. A comprehensive error report can be useful in understanding, classifying, or prioritizing the error, and reproducing it in a test environment and then fixing it. Ideally, testing reveals all software failures caused by errors or faults. However, revealing all failures and, hence, removing their resulting errors or faults is optimistic.

Theories in software testing lead us to believe that unless an exhaustive testing technique is used, we cannot claim having obtained error-free software. Exhaustive testing is impractical because it could take years to complete, even for testing small programs. To illustrate the impracticality of exhaustive testing, consider testing the software when a first name text field of 20 characters maximum is filled by a user. Exhaustive testing requires that the software is tested for all possible correct and incorrect field input values. If it is assumed that there are 80 possible correct and incorrect characters, the number of possible combinations for a valid or invalid first name would exceed 80^{20}, using a computer that takes, say, 50 nanoseconds to process one combination. The testing, then, would take approximately 10^{11} years to complete for all possible combinations. It is indeed impractical!

With the absence of exhaustive testing, there are no formal guarantees that the software is error-free. In fact, in practice, even when all errors have been detected during testing, they might not be fixed due to the lack of time and will be fixed in future releases of the software. The difficulty in software testing is the inability to quantify the errors existing in software and, therefore, predict how many errors are left undiscovered. A random testing experiment was conducted in which errors of different levels of complexity were inserted in the software under test (SUT); all errors, except for one, were discovered progressively. There was no indication on how much more testing should be done before the remaining error would be discovered. The lesson learned is that finding errors is an asymptotic nonlinear function of time as shown in Figure 8.1.

Software economics tell us that it is unfeasible to attempt to continue testing forever. The other lesson learned is that even knowing the number of errors to start with, we are unable to find all of them. How, then, can it be feasible to expect to discover all errors when realistically we do not know the number of existing errors. Errors that are not discovered prior to the re-

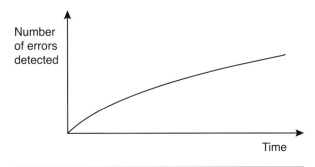

Figure 8.1 Testing time versus number of errors detected

lease date remain dormant until they are discovered and reported by users or by those testing for a second release of the software. One would hope that all safety-critical errors have been discovered and fixed or that these types of errors manifest themselves under restricted and rare circumstances. Published software project metrics show that discovering and fixing errors during the testing phase, and prior to the software delivery and deployment, would save costly maintenance efforts and resources.

It is the ethical responsibility of the software development company to ensure that (1) adequate and appropriate resources are allocated to the testing activities, (2) employees are properly trained to perform their testing tasks, (3) state-of-the-art testing tools are available for use by trained employees, and (4) an environment emphasizing the importance of software quality and dependability is being promoted internally. On the other hand, it is the ethical responsibility of the software tester to ensure that they remain up-to-date on their testing knowledge and that they are constantly looking for better testing tools and techniques. Furthermore, they must put their best efforts and mental capabilities toward discovering as many errors as possible. After all, human well-being and physical safety can be at stake.

8.2 DYNAMIC AND STATIC TESTING

Dynamic and static testing are two major testing approaches that can be clearly distinguished. **Dynamic testing** includes all testing activities that are performed by executing the SUT.

Static testing includes all testing activities that are performed without executing the SUT. Static testing can be done manually or automatically. Software code can be examined statically and manually during code review meetings. Moreover, code can be applied as input to a static analysis tool that generates error reports and pinpoints deficiencies in the code. Clearly, static testing does not reveal operational and configuration errors that manifests only when the software is executed in a specific run-time environment or platform. Static testing can also be achieved using quality assurance activities such as walkthrough and checklists performing

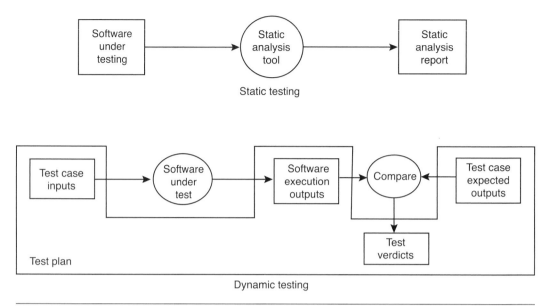

Figure 8.2 Static and dynamic testing

specific code quality audits, including **conformance** to coding standards for documentation, security, fault-tolerance, and error handling. A **test oracle** produces the test verdict after judging whether the SUT produced the correct output. Figure 8.2 shows the settings for both dynamic and static testing.

8.3 ANATOMY OF A TEST CASE

Planning for dynamic testing begins with the development of a **test plan** document appropriate to meet the goals and level of the desired testing. The main part of the test plan includes the **test suites** that need to be applied to the SUT. A test suite consists of a group of related **test cases** that are executed in a dynamic test setup. Given a set of test cases, each of the test case inputs is applied to the SUT while it is running, and outputs are observed and manually or automatically compared with the expected outputs as specified in the test cases. **Test verdicts** are then reached. Each test case can be described in details using a template similar to the one shown in Figure 8.3.

The test reference allows the backward traceability to the software requirements and software design documents. This reference is useful when maintenance and regression testing are needed. The test priority is useful when limited time and resources are allocated for the testing process. Assigning a priority to a test case is based primarily on the severity of the error the test case is attempting to uncover. It can also be linked to the threat or vulnerability we are trying

Test case number	
Test name	
Test reference	
Test priority	
Test precondition(s)	
Test preamble	
Test input	
Test expected output	
Test observed output	
Test verdict	
Remarks	

Figure 8.3 Template for detailed test case description

Table 8.1 A template for summarizing test plan execution results

Test case #	Test name	Test reference	Test priority	Test input	Test expected output	Test verdict
...						
...						

to avoid. High priority test cases generally reveal the more critical and frequent errors. These test cases are also called high-yield test cases. The test preconditions normally include all the operational and state conditions that must be satisfied and enforced for the test to be executable. These conditions could be meeting some memory or operating system requirements, or being at a particular state. The test preamble includes the test cases or inputs that must be applied prior to the proper execution of the current test case. For example, to execute a particular transaction, the successful logon test case must be executed as a test preamble. Both observed output and verdict can be filled only after applying or executing the test case on the SUT and analyzing the resulting output. A test verdict could be a pass, a fail, or inconclusive. An inconclusive test verdict might be reached if, for example, the test was interrupted due to an operational error or the test is unachievable due to incorrectly specified preconditions or preamble.

The test cases included in a test plan can be summarized for quick reference using a table template as shown in Table 8.1. This table can be manipulated and sorted to provide various metrics and indicators to the software development group and test managers. Also, if the test inputs and expected and observed outputs are simple, they can be included in the test plan summary template.

8.4 BLACK BOX, WHITE BOX, AND GREY BOX TESTING

A dynamic **black box testing** technique is applied to a running SUT without any prior knowledge of its source code. The concept of a black box applies to the entire software application or to one unit or function/method of the software. In either case, only the functionality and the interface specification of the black box are known. Black box testing is also referred to as functional testing. At the system level, the entire software is considered as a black box, and test cases are generated and selected based on the functional specifications or the use case model description of the software. However, at the unit level, a function or method is considered as a black box, and test cases are generated and selected starting from the functional specification and the description of its interfaces. System-level black box testing techniques include use case-based scenario testing. Both system-level and unit-level black box testing techniques include **boundary value analysis**, equivalence class testing, decision table- or tree-based testing, cause and effect graphing, and state-based testing. Also, use case-based scenario testing can be used for system-level testing. Ideally, black box-based system level test cases are written after finishing the software specifications. However, black box-based unit level test cases are written by the designers after finishing the unit design. The objective of the early development of these test cases is to avoid biased testing should these test cases be developed later in the development process.

A dynamic **white box testing** technique is applied to a running SUT when the code structure or data and control flows are known to the tester. White box testing is also referred to as **structural testing**. At the system level, the complete source code and software documentation are provided and test cases are generated and selected based on this knowledge. At the unit level, both the interface specification to the unit and the unit code are provided. Test cases are then generated based on the data and control flow structure of the code. Normally, white box unit testing is performed by the software developer who wrote the unit or a tester within the same development team. It also complements the static white box testing or quality assurance activities relying on the examination of the code without executing it. Various white box unit testing techniques are discussed in detail later in this chapter.

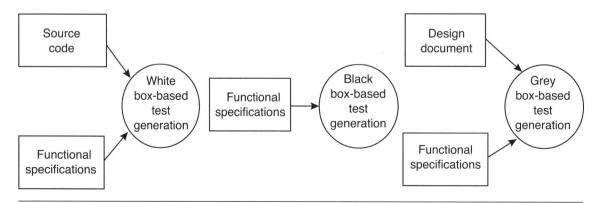

Figure 8.4 White, black, and grey box-based strategies and inputs

Grey box testing assumes that the software architecture and design documents are available to the test plan designer. Hence, providing hints on the inner working of the software and allowing the design of more interesting high-yield and fault-revealing test cases. Figure 8.4 shows the three test generation strategies and their respective inputs.

8.5 BLACK BOX-BASED UNIT TESTING TECHNIQUES

Given the functional specification of the unit under test (UUT) and its access interface specifications, black box-based testing techniques provide a systematic approach to the generation and selection of effective test cases. Techniques in this classification include **boundary value analysis**, **equivalence class testing**, **state-based testing**, and decision table- or tree-based testing.

Boundary Value Analysis

This black box-based **functional testing** technique suggests that effective testing should concentrate on applying test inputs obtained from the boundaries derived or elicited from the given functional specifications. The main idea is that serious errors hide at the boundaries. To detect these errors, should they exist, test case inputs must be selected. For example, simple boundary values for an input of integer data type would include $-INT\_MAX$, $-INT\_MAX + 1$, -1, 0, $+1$, $INT\_MAX - 1$ and INT_MAX. However, for complex and composite data types, boundary values become more difficult to generate and can require more ingenuity to obtain them. Moreover, if the interface specification includes more than one input, different test cases considering possible feasible combinations of boundary values for each input must be considered in the test plan.

Example 8.1

Suppose you are given an executable code, including a function called digitCount, whose functional interface specification states that digitCount takes an integer n as an input parameter and returns an integer representing the number of digits in n. Test cases whose test inputs are selected based on boundary value analysis are partially shown in Table 8.2. We are assuming that for a 32-bit integer, INT_MAX is $+2147483647$.

Table 8.2 Testing function digitCount based on boundary value analysis

Test case #	Test input	Expected output
1	−INT_MAX	10
2	−INT_MAX +1	10
3	−1	1
4	0	1
5	1	1
6	INT_MAX -1	10
7	INT_MAX	10

Example 8.2

Suppose you are given an executable code, including a function called search, whose functional interface specification states that search takes an array A of integers and an integer value *v* to search for inside array A. The function search returns an integer *r* representing the index at which *v* was found in array A; otherwise it returns −1 if *v* is not found in array A. In this example, we have three interface values: two are input values, one of which, array A, is a composite structure; and one output value, which is the returned integer value from the search function. Assuming that the size of the array A is held in a variable called size, the boundary values for the output variable *r* are −1, 0, 1, size −1 and size. However, obtaining boundary values for A requires more

ingenuity. One can think of the size of the array as an implicit variable worth considering testing its boundaries. So we can include test inputs in which the array size = 0 (empty array), size = 1, size = max − 1, and size = max, where max is the largest array size possible according to the specification. Moreover, if we know that the function search implements the binary search algorithm (in this case the given array is assumed to be sorted), we could think of testing around the boundaries of the middle of the array, the quarters of the array, and so on. Table 8.3 shows the test plan for testing a function search based on boundary value analysis. In this plan, we have assumed a maximum array size of 10. The plan includes combinations of possible boundary values for input and output interface variables.

Table 8.3 Testing function search based on boundary value analysis

Test case #	Test input		Expected output (returned value)
	Array A	Value v to search for	
1	{ }	5	−1
2	{1}	1	0
3	{1}	2	−1
4	{1,3,5,8,12,17,18,4,19}	7	−1
5	{1,3,5,8,12,17,18,4,19}	1	0
6	{1,3,5,8,12,17,18,4,19}	3	1
7	{1,3,5,8,12,17,18,4,19}	19	8
8	{1,3,5,8,12,17,18,4,19}	4	7
9	{1,3,5,8,12,17,18,4,19,45}	7	−1
10	{1,3,5,8,12,17,18,4,19,45}	1	0
11	{1,3,5,8,12,17,18,4,19,45}	3	1
12	{1,3,5,8,12,17,18,4,19,45}	19	8
13	{1,3,5,8,12,17,18,4,19,45}	45	9

Equivalence Class Testing

The **equivalence class testing** technique is based on the partitioning of the input domain into disjoint subsets. This technique is also referred to as equivalence partitioning testing. An equivalence class or partition of a given set of values includes values that are related. All values in an equivalence partition can be treated similarly. In the context of software testing, the basic idea is that a class or partition can be covered by considering only one representative value from the partition. At least one test case, including representative test inputs from each partition, would be selected. The choice of these subsets or partitions is problem-dependent and requires some ingenuity from the test designer. Formally, the equivalence partitioning of a given set of values is based on an equivalence relation that makes all elements of the partition related according to that relation. An equivalence relation is a symmetric, reflexive, and transitive relation.

Example 8.3

To test the digitCount function using equivalence class testing, we can partition the input integer values into disjointed subsets based on the number of digits in the integers of each subset. In this case, the equivalence relation based on which we partition the domain of all possible input values is $R =$ having the same number of digits, meaning that the values in each partition have the same number of digits. It is clear that for any a, b, and c belonging to the same partition, we have: $a\ R\ a$, $a\ R\ b$, implying $b\ R\ a$, and $a\ R\ b$, $b\ R\ c$, implying $a\ R\ c$. Hence R is an equivalence relation. If we assume that the largest integer has 10 digits, then we can have 10 disjoint subsets and from each we can draw one element. Hence, we consider that the 10 test cases shown in Table 8.4 are enough to test the digitCount function.

If we test function digitCount using the above test cases, one would think that if the function has passed all 10 test cases, we can conclude that the function is correct. However, we have seen earlier that using the boundary value analysis test selection technique would include a test case for $n = 0$. If the function digitCount is implemented as shown in Figure 8.5, the boundary value analysis test case for $n = 0$ (test case number 4) would detect a mismatch between the observed output of 0 and the expected output of 1. Consequently, an error would be revealed when that test case is executed. Hence, we can conclude that for the implementation given in Figure 8.5, the boundary value analysis-based test cases shown in Table

Table 8.4 Testing function digitCount based on equivalence class testing

Test case #	Test input	Expected output
1	5	1
2	16	2
3	124	3
4	2345	4
5	26756	5
6	123654	6
7	1456321	7
8	12345678	8
9	123456789	9
10	1357924680	10

8.2 are more effective in detecting errors in the implementation than the equivalence class-based test cases shown in Table 8.4.

For other problems, we might want to partition the integer domain into one of or a combination of the following: even and odd integers; positive and negative integers; power of 2 and non-power of 2 integers; prime and non-prime integers; fibonacci and non-fibonacci integers, and so on.

```
1   int digitCount(int n)
2   {
3       int count =0;
4       while (n != 0)
5       {   n = n / 10;
6           count++;
7       }
8       return count;
9   }
```

Figure 8.5 Code for implementing function digitCount

Decision Table- and Decision Tree-Based Testing

As explained in Chapter 4, a decision table specifies the stateless behavior of a process implemented in a function. For testing purposes, we can have one test case to correspond to a rule or column of the decision table.

Example 8.4

Given the decision table shown in Table 4.1, the test plan shown in Table 8.5 includes the test cases that would be selected based on the decision table coverage technique. The test plan includes eight test cases. Since the three conditions/predicates P1, P2, and P3 are mutually independent of each other, and their outcomes are binary (true or false), we have $2^3 = 8$ possible combinations of outcomes.

As an exercise, you should be able to select test cases based on a combination of decision table, boundary value analysis, and equivalence class techniques.

Similarly, if the specification is provided as a decision tree, one test case must exist to cover each path from the root of the tree to a leaf node of the tree. The decision tree that is equivalent to the decision table is shown in Figure 4.23.

Note that test cases 4, 6, and 8 can be omitted because in the corresponding combinations, the outcome of predicate P3 is not affecting the decision. They are included only to show that we have considered all possible combinations of the outcomes.

Table 8.5 Test cases based on decision Table 4.1

Test case #	Test input			Expected output	
	Age	Speeding history	Speed	Penalty	Points
1	20	Y	130	100	−2
2	20	Y	110	75	−1
3	19	N	130	50	0
4	19	N	110	50	0
5	23	Y	130	150	−3
6	23	Y	110	150	−3
7	35	N	130	125	−1
8	35	N	110	125	−1

State-Based Testing

The state-based testing technique starts from a given functional specification based on the input/output (IO) finite state behavior. This behavior is typically described by a finite state machine introduced in Chapter 4. Under this testing approach, test cases consist of input test sequences and the corresponding expected observable output sequences. Any mismatch between a test case expected output sequence and the observed output sequence is flagged as a test case failure. The test sequences must cover all possible states and traverse all specified transitions in the specification state machine. Executing test inputs to cover all states and transitions can detect problems in the SUT when considered as a black box. State-based testing is useful for testing communications protocols, graphical user interfaces, and web pages connectivity, among other types of systems whose behavior can be modeled by finite state machines.

The transition tour (TT) method generates a test sequence called a transition tour. For a given finite state machine (FSM), a TT is a sequence that takes the FSM from an initial state, traverses every transition at least once, and returns to the initial state. The TT-method allows the detection of all output errors. However, it does not guarantee that all state transfer errors are detected. This method has limited error detection capability compared to other methods because it does not consider state, checking to verify that the proper state was reached. However, an advantage of this method is that the test sequences obtained are usually shorter than test sequences generated using other methods. To further optimize a TT, we find the shortest path through the FSM which covers all transitions using a variation of the Chinese Postman algorithm.

Example 8.5

The FSM specification of an interaction system is shown in Figure 8.6. A test case, including a TT test sequence covering all transitions in the given FSM, is shown in Table 8.6.

A **distinguishing sequence** (DS) is used as a state identification sequence. An input sequence is a DS for an FSM if the output sequence produced by the FSM is different when the input sequence is applied to each state. The test sequences obtained by the DS-method are able to identify a particular FSM from all other FSMs. These sequences provide full-fault coverage because they are able to detect both state transfer and output errors. However, the disadvantage of this method is that a DS might not be found for a given FSM. Also, applying a fixed-length sequence might not lead to the shortest state identification sequence.

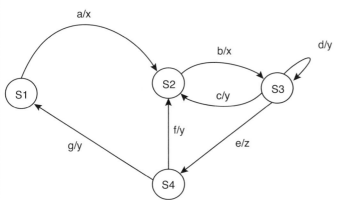

Figure 8.6 FSM specification of an interaction system

Table 8.6 Test case using the TT-method for the FSM in Figure 8.6

Test case #	1
Purpose	Covering all states and transitions using TT-method
Input	a b d e f b c b e g
Expected output	x x y z y x y x z y

Example 8.6

Figure 8.7 shows an FSM that has a DS $s = a\,a$. Table 8.7 shows the test case generated by the DS-method. Input $a\,a$ at states s1, s2 and s3 lead to the generation of $c\,d$, $d\,c$, and $c\,c$, respectively. We assume that input reset brings the machine to state s1.

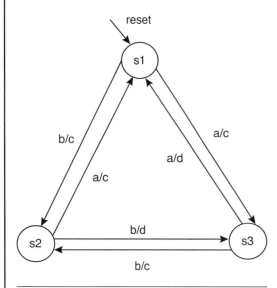

Figure 8.7 FSM with a distinguishing sequence $s = a\,a$.

Table 8.7 Test cases covering all states and transitions of the FSM in Figure 8.7 using the DS-method

Test case #	1
Purpose	Covering all states and transitions using DS-method
Input	reset a a reset b a a reset a a a
Expected output	− c d − c c c − c d c

apply the reset input to bring the machine to s_0, then apply the sequence taking the machine from s_0 to s_i. To ensure that s_i, has been reached, apply the DS for s_i. If, according to the observed outputs, s_i was reached properly, then apply all the possible inputs of transitions emanating from s_i and check that each of the transitions is correctly implemented, meaning that it reaches the right state according to the specifications.

Algorithms for optimizing the test sequence such as the Chinese Postman can be used. In addition, algorithms from digital systems theory can be used to find homing, distinguishing, and synchronizing sequences for a given FSM, should they exist. Also from protocol testing theory, optimized test sequences can be obtained using the variable-length unique input/output (UIO) sequences.

A more powerful but longer test sequence can be used to test each state and the proper implementation of each of the transitions originating at each state. The method used to generate such test sequence is called the W method. The W method assumes the existence of a DS and a reset sequence for the FSM. The reset input sequence takes the machine to an initial state s_0. To test that state s_i was implemented properly, first

A variation of state-based testing is syntax testing or language compiler testing. Given the specification of a language syntax or grammar rules, test programs can be generated that cover all the language rules specifications. As a result, the conformity of the compiler to the language specification for which it was developed can be tested.

Black Box-Based Robustness Testing

Black box-based robustness testing is based on testing the complete system or a unit of it, as a black box, when incorrect or illegal inputs are applied or unexpected operational errors or situations occur.

For boundary value analysis, select inputs that are just at the external boundaries of the domain of valid values. In Example 8.1, because it is not possible to input integer values INT_MAX + 1 or −INT_MAX − 1, the idea of testing beyond the boundaries is not applicable. However, in Example 8.2, if the effective size of the input array is v, two test cases should be included in the test plan for testing the function when the input values for variable v, denoting the size of the input array, are $v + 1$ or -1. The two test cases must specify the software reaction to these erroneous inputs according to the specified software requirements.

For equivalence class testing, select one input that does not belong to any of the identified equivalence classes or partitions. For example, if the input must be an odd number, no partition would include an even number. Therefore, assume that there exists one illegal partition that includes all illegal values and specify a test case that tests for this invalid input.

For decision table- or decision tree-based testing, select some invalid combinations of input values. These combinations could include inconsistent or ambiguous input conditions or values. This idea is not applicable if the condition outcomes are discrete and drawn from a finite set of possible values. Again, for these abnormal combinations, the test cases must specify the action to be taken according to the specification.

For state-based testing, if starting from completely specified state machines, the specification must indicate the behavior of the system when subjected to an unexpected input at each state. Because we would be covering all transitions and states of the machine, test cases that include unexpected inputs at each state should be included in the test plan. The SUT must behave according to its state-based specification. As we have seen in Chapter 4, the machine given in Example 8.5 is not completely specified. However, let us assume that at each state, for any input other than the ones shown, the system should remain at the same state (self-loop transition) and should output an error message. The state-based test case generation methods described would then be dealing with each of those invalid inputs at each state. It can be concluded, then, that testing a completely specified machine allows us to test the machine when both good inputs and unexpected inputs are received.

8.6 WHITE BOX-BASED UNIT TESTING TECHNIQUES

Given the source code of a function or module to test, white box-based testing techniques rely on generating test cases by constructing a control flow graph representing the control structure of the given source code. Two types of test generation techniques, the control flow-based and data flow-based techniques can then be applied.

Control Flow Graph

A **control flow graph** provides a graphical representation reflecting the control flow structure of a given source code. A flow graph is similar but simpler than a flow chart. A flow graph consists of directed edges and nodes. Nodes represent one statement or a block of sequential statements, or a decision statement. Directed edges represent the control flow between nodes. Nodes can be sequential, join, fork, decision, or mixed nodes. A join node represents a point in the program at which two or more sequential flows or paths meet to continue as a unique flow. A decision node represents a point at which two or more options of outgoing flows originate in the program. A mixed join/decision node represents a point at which two or more flows meet and at the same time a decision is made and two or more optional flows or paths originate. A fork node represents a point at which two or more parallel paths are executing concurrently. Figure 8.8 shows the types of nodes in a control flow graph. Also, in Figure 8.9, the main high-level programming language control structures and their corresponding flow graphs are shown.

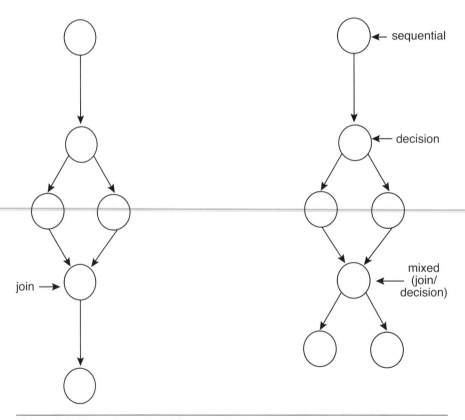

Figure 8.8 Nodes in a control flow graph

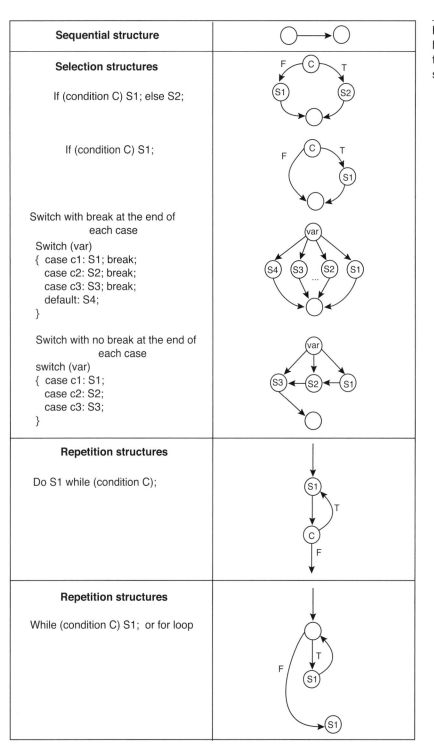

Figure 8.9 Programming languages control structures and their corresponding flow graphs

---

Example 8.7

The control flow graph corresponding to the code of function digitCount given in Figure 8.5 is shown in Figure 8.10.

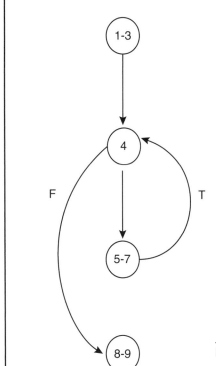

Figure 8.10 Control flow graph for function digitCount

Control Flow-Based Techniques

Given a control flow graph representing some source code, two basic criteria for selecting test cases exist, namely, statement and decision coverage. The **statement coverage** criterion is based on the selection of test cases that ensure that all program statements are traversed as a result of the application of the inputs of all test cases. This means that all nodes in the representative flow graph must be covered. The decision or branch coverage criterion is based on the selection of test cases covering all outcomes of every decision in the flow graph. A decision can be a simple one, using a single variable condition, or based on multiple conditions composed, using more than one variable. For example, if $(k < 3)$ is a simple single-decision condition and if $(k < 3$ and (&&) $m > j)$ is a composite multi-condition decision.

Example 8.8

To illustrate the idea of test coverage using control flow-based techniques, consider the function digitCount and its corresponding flow graph shown in Figure 8.10.

The only test case whose input is $n = 123$ and its expected output is 3, ensures that both statement and branch coverage criteria are satisfied. All nodes of the flow graph are visited and all edges are traversed at least once. The path traversed by executing this test case is 1-2-3-2-3-2-3-4. The condition is evaluated four times and the loop body (node 3) is executed three times. It is clear that the test case would pass because it produces the same expected output. Therefore, based on the control flow-based testing and the given test case input, we would assert that the code is correct. However, as shown earlier, for $n = 0$, the expected output does not match the observed output. Hence, a single test case based on statement and decision coverage failed to detect the error in the given code. In fact, the code does not deal with the special case when $n = 0$.

We can argue that extending the control flow-based test cases by considering the boundaries of the number of times each loop body is executed can provide more effective and elaborate testing. For example, in the first version of digit-Count, test cases can execute the loop body zero times, one, nine, or ten times. Executing the loop zero times requires the application of $n = 0$ as a test case input, whereas the loop condition fails immediately. In this case, the error is detected after executing this test case. Table 8.8 shows the extended test cases after executing them on the incorrect code of digitCount. The corrected code is shown in Figure 8.11. This code would pass all of the test cases.

In general, one of the main weaknesses of white box-based testing based on statement and branch coverage is that the generated test cases are based on the existing code structure. Hence, these techniques are not suitable for discovering missing functionalities, code, or behavior in the software being tested.

Table 8.8 Extended control flow-based test cases for digitCount after their execution

Test case #	Test input	Expected output	Observed output	Test verdict
1	0	1	0	Fail
2	9	1	1	Pass
3	123	3	3	Pass
4	123567667	9	9	Pass
5	1357924680	10	10	Pass

```
1    int digitCount(int n)
2    {
3        int count = 0;
4        if  (n == 0) return 1;
5        while (n != 0)
6        {    n = n / 10;
7             count++;
8        }
9        return count;
10   }
```

Figure 8.11 Corrected code for digitCount dealing with the case when n = 0

Example 8.9

To illustrate another weakness of decision coverage when the decision is a composite multicondition decision, consider the following code and its corresponding flow graph shown in Figure 8.12.

For the test case with inputs $x = 1$ and $y = 1$, and $z = 3$, statement coverage is guaranteed. After its execution, x and z becomes 2 and 4, respectively. However, if due to a logical error, && should have been an or (||) in the decision code, statement coverage would not have detected it. Using the decision coverage criteria, an additional test case is needed whose input forces the execution of the false outcome of the decision. Such use case would include $x = 1$ and $y = 3$ as inputs, and $z = 3$. In this case, x becomes 2 and z remains unchanged at 3.

Simple decision coverage is not enough because if the operator $<$ in $y < 2$ should have been $>$, because of the && operator, the decision outcome is evaluated false without considering the second part of the decision. This situation occurs when using a programming language in which short-circuit evaluation of Boolean expressions is unavoidable. In short-circuit evaluation, the outcome of the expression can be determined without the evaluation of all parts of the expression. For example, if two parts of an expression are linked by the && operator, if the first part evaluates false, the evaluation of the second part is skipped because its evaluation does not change the overall evaluation of the expression. Similarly, if parts are linked by an *or* operator, if the one part evaluates true, the evaluation of the parts to the right are skipped. **Short-circuiting** may lead to side effects when the unevaluated part includes some operation that must be executed regardless of whether the overall expression is true or false. For example, in the expression $(i < j)$ && $(k++ < 10)$, k is not incremented if $i < j$ is false and that causes related logic errors in the program.

To remove this problem with simple decision coverage when the decision is a composite one, consider **multiple condition coverage** in which all combinations of outcomes of every condition of the decision must be covered. If the decision is composed of three independent binary conditions, $2^3 = 8$ different paths must be covered in this case. Another solution is to rewrite the code to avoid the side effects of short-circuiting. If using ADA, Java, or the C programming language, the version of the Boolean operators that ignores short-circuiting and forces the evaluation of all parts of the expression can be used. For example, in ADA we use operator *and* instead of *and then*, and *or* instead of *or else*. In C and Java, we use & and | instead of && and ||, respectively. In summary, remember when using short-circuiting, although we would have produced faster executable software, additional testing must be performed to ensure the avoidance of side effects and potential logic errors.

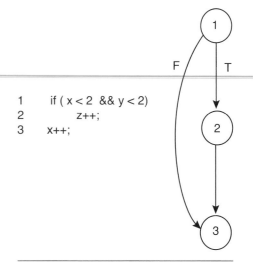

```
1     if ( x < 2  && y < 2)
2          z++;
3     x++;
```

Figure 8.12 Code and its corresponding flow graph

Example 8.10

The control flow graph is shown in Figure 8.13a, using multiple-condition coverage for the code in Figure 8.12. However, if the decision is ($x < 2$ || $y < 2$) instead, the control flow graph looks like Figure 8.13b. The number of test cases for covering the control flow graph in Figure 8.13a is 3, and for covering the flow graph in Figure 8.13b it is 4. These test cases are illustrated in Table 8.9.

In summary, when we have a composite decision, instead of representing it by one node in the control flow graph, depending on the type of connecting operators, the appropriate number of simple condition nodes are placed in the graph. This allows the generation of additional test cases that force the execution of all possible execution sequences in the graph.

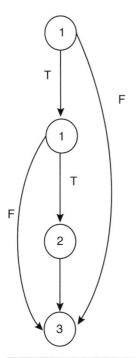
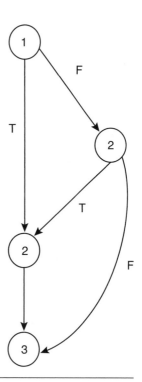

Figure 8.13 Control flow graphs

Table 8.9 Test cases using multiple-condition coverage criteria

Test case #	Input	Expected output
1	x = 1 y = 1	x = 2 z = 4
2	x = 1 y = 3	x = 2 z = 3
3	x = 3 y = 1	x = 2 z = 3

(a) Condition (x < 2 && y < 2)

Test case #	Input	Expected output
1	x = 1 y = 1	x = 2 z = 4
2	x = 1 y = 3	x = 2 z = 4
3	x = 3 y = 1	x = 2 z = 4
4	x = 3 y = 3	x = 2 z = 3

(b) Condition (x < 2 || y < 2).

Data Flow-Based Testing

Data flow-based testing techniques are based on the data flow graph. A data flow graph is obtained by first constructing the control flow graph then adding a label at each node of the graph for each variable specifying how that variable is manipulated or dealt with at this node. The data-related information added to the graph is needed to apply data flow-based testing techniques. The purpose of **data flow testing** is to detect **data flow anomalies**. Data flow testing is achieved by concentrating on the definition and handling or use of critical variables in the source code under test along the various execution paths. A variable must first be declared, then defined (i.e., assigned a value), before it can be used, defined again (redefined), or killed. A newly-declared variable x is denoted by x_{dcl}. A variable x that is rendered null or de-allocated from memory is denoted by x_{kill}. A variable x can be used in a computation or output statement, in this case we say x is c-used and is denoted by $x_{c\text{-}use}$. Variable x can also be used to evaluate a predicate, in this case we say x is p-used and is denoted by $x_{p\text{-}use}$. A definition free or def-free (also referred to as def-clear) execution path for a variable x is a path from an x_{def} to $x_{c\text{-}use}$ or $x_{p\text{-}use}$ that does not include another definition (or a redefinition) of x.

Example 8.11

A pseudocode and its corresponding data flow graph is shown in Figure 8.14.

An execution path that includes the definition and handling of variable x is: $x_{dcl}\, x_{def}\, x_{p\text{-}use}\, x_{c\text{-}use}\, x_{def}$ $x_{p\text{-}use}\, x_{c\text{-}use}\, x_{def}\, x_{p\text{-}use}\, x_{def}\, x_{kill}$. Data flow testing techniques analyze possible execution paths related to each of the critical variables to detect anomalies. For example, an execution path for x such as x_{def} x_{def} shows that there are two consecutive definitions of x without a use of x in between. This might be an indication of a data-related error that needs further examination. The error could be a missing statement that includes a c-use or a p-use of x. Alternatively, the error could be that one of the definitions of x is not needed. Other anomalous patterns that signal data-related errors could be: $x_{kill}\, x_{kill}$, $x_{kill}\, x_{c\text{-}use}$, $x_{kill}\, x_{p\text{-}use}$, $x_{def}\, x_{kill}$, $x_{dcl}\, x_{c\text{-}use}$ and x_{dcl} $x_{p\text{-}use}$. Also, x_{dcl} alone or $x_{dcl}\, x_{def}$ alone can be considered suspicious. This might signal either missing statements or unused variables.

```
1    int x;
2    x = 2;
3    while (x > 0)
4    { print (x);
5        x = x - 1;
6    }
7    print (x);
8    kill (x);
```

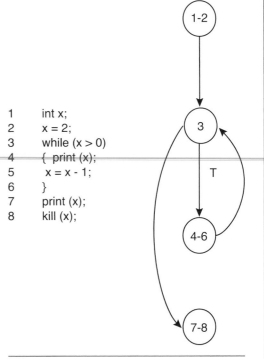

Figure 8.14 Pseudocode and data flow graph

When performing data flow testing, correctness of the source code is based on the satisfaction of data flow criteria. The du criterion requires the existence of a def-free path from every variable definition to each use of it. The existence of a du path that is not def-free is an indication of a data-related error in the code.

Data flow-based test case generation strategies are based on the selection of execution paths covering different aspects of data flow. Testing all paths in a given graph is ideal but exhaustive. The best and most practical strategy that comes closest to testing all paths is the all-du-path (adup) testing strategy. The **adup strategy** requires that every du path from every definition of every variable to every use of that definition be traversed after executing the test cases. The **all-uses** (au) **strategy** requires that at least one du path from every definition of every variable to every use of that definition be traversed after executing the test cases. The **all-p-uses** (apu) **strategy** requires that for every definition of every variable at least one def-free path from the definition to every p-use be traversed after executing the test cases. Similarly, the **all-c-uses** (acu) **strategy** requires that for every definition of every variable at least one def-free path from the definition to every c-use be traversed after executing the test cases. However, because in the apu strategy we might have variables that are never used in a predicate, we consider c-uses instead. This variation of apu strategy is called the all-p-uses/some-c-uses (apu/c) strategy. Similarly, because in the acu strategy we might have variables that are never used in a computation or output statement, we consider p-uses instead. This variation of the acu strategy is called the all-c-uses/some-p-uses (acu/p) strategy.

Example 8.12

To illustrate the test selection strategies, consider the following code fragment and its corresponding flow graph as shown in Figure 8.15.

The test cases generated using the adup strategy for variables i and j are shown in Table 8.10. In this example, let us assume that a and b are input variables, and k is an output variable. Variable i is defined then c-used at node 2, p-used at node 3, defined again at node 7, and c-used at node 9. Since there are 2 definitions and 3 uses of variable i, we could have a maximum of 6 du paths. The path going through nodes 1-2-3-9 is a def-free path and can be forced when $a = 5$. In this case, both the inner and outer loops are not executed.

However, some of these paths are not def-free. For example, the path going through nodes 1-2-3-4-7-3-9 is not a def-free path and can be forced when $a = 1$ and $b = 2$. By going through these 2 execution paths, we would have covered every definition and every use of variable i. Similarly, variable j is defined and c-used at node 2, defined at node 4, defined at node 6 and c-used at node 9. The 2 paths going through nodes 1-2-3-4-5-7-8-3-9 and 1-2-3-4-5-6-5-7-8-3-9 would cover every definition and every use of variable j. The first path can be executed if $a = 1$ and $b = 1$, and the second if $a = 1$ and $b = 2$. Because the second path would be executed when testing for variable i, it is omitted to avoid redundancy.

(*continues*)

Example 8.12 *(continued)*

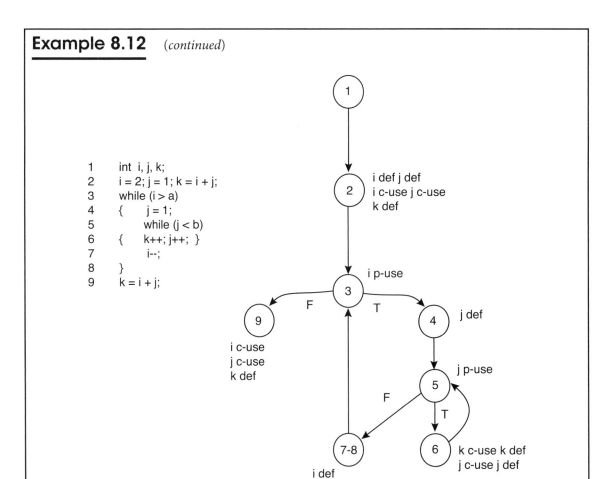

```
1    int  i, j, k;
2    i = 2; j = 1; k = i + j;
3    while (i > a)
4    {     j = 1;
5          while (j < b)
6    {     k++; j++;  }
7          i--;
8    }
9    k = i + j;
```

Figure 8.15 Code of Example 8.12 and its corresponding data flow graph

Table 8.10 Test cases generated using adup strategy for variables *i* and *j* from the code in Example 8.12

Test case #	Input	Expected output
1	a = 5 b = 2	k = 3
2	a = 1 b = 2	k = 3
3	a = 1 b = 1	k = 2

Path Expression

A **path expression** is an algebraic expression that is used to represent one or more possible execution paths in control or data flow graphs. In essence, a path expression representing a program captures all possible sequences of execution that the program can go through.

The operators that can be used to formulate path expressions are: '*', '+', '.', { }, and ( ). Suppose x and y are two path expressions, $\{x\}^*$ denotes a 0 or more repetition of x, $\{x\}+$ denotes a 1 or more repetition of x, $(x + y)$ denotes a choice between x and y, and $x.y$ denotes a new path expression resulting from the appending of y to x. To obtain a path expression from a given flow graph, label each edge of the flow graph, then, based on the control structure, appropriate path expressions are obtained.

8.7 INTEGRATION TESTING

Real-world software systems are developed in teams, therefore, each individual team member or programmer implements the assigned modules. These modules can be functions, methods, or complete classes. After each developer completes the unit test plans related to their own deliverable code and fixes all errors found, integration testing starts. The objective of **integration testing** is to ensure that all modules of the system under development interface properly, and consequently the system functionalities are provided as specified. Parameters mismatch between caller and called modules, inappropriate returned values, side effects due to the abuse of global and shared data, and data protection and visibility violations are typical errors that can be detected during integration testing.

Integration test planning is crucial to shorten the testing time. Because we are dealing with possibly integrating a large number of modules, a good integration test plan must consider, in addition to error detection, error diagnostics and localization. This is useful to shorten the time for fixing errors and proceeding with integration without further delays.

The simple big-bang integration testing based on compiling and linking all modules at once and running an executable (if we have a clean compilation) is inappropriate. We might have to deal with a large number of integration errors at once making the process unmanageable and time consuming. There are three possible approaches to plan and execute integration testing, namely, the top-down, bottom-up, and hybrid.

Top-Down

In the **top-down integration** approach, top-level modules in the caller-called hierarchy or high-level design are integrated first. Modules are integrated one-by-one, top-down, and from left-to-right until all modules of the hierarchy are integrated. Any integration error between a new module and the already-integrated modules is easily detected, diagnosed, and fixed. This approach requires the writing of many stub modules to be used while integrating modules. A stub module is a simple module faking the functionality of a module called by a module being integrated.

Example 8.13

Consider the following pseudocode and its corresponding flow graph shown in Figure 8.16. The transitions in the flow graph are labeled by s, a, b, c, d, e, f and g.

The path expression obtained from the graph is: s . (g + { a.b . (c + d) . e . f }*). Possible execution paths can be generated by unfolding the expression. From the above path expression, some of the possible execution paths are: s g, s a b c e f g, s a b d e f g, s a b c e f a b c e f g, and so on.

```
0    read x
1    while (x < 5)
2    {      m++;
3           if (y < 5)
4                   p++;
5           else  p--;
6                   p++;
7    }
8    x++;
```

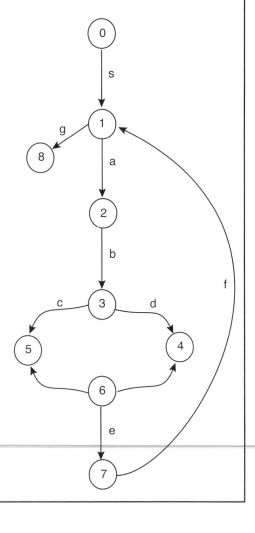

Figure 8.16 Pseudocode and its corresponding flow graph with labeled edges

Feasible execution paths can then be considered to generate test cases whose inputs should force the execution of the path under consideration. Path feasibility depends on the conditions at each decision node.

Path expressions can be useful in analyzing the control or data flow graph. For example, to obtain probabilities of a possible path, label the edges with assigned probabilities and use appropriate probability arithmetic. If interested in data flow analysis, label the nodes with use and definition information related to variables. Then data flow anomalies can be detected by parsing the labeled path expressions.

Example 8.14

In the simple hierarchy shown in Figure 8.17, to integrate modules M1 and M2, a stub replacing M3 is needed. Once M1 and M2 are integrated, the M3-stub is replaced with the real M3. At this time, when integrating M3 with M1-M2, two stubs must be written and used, namely, M4-stub and M5-stub.

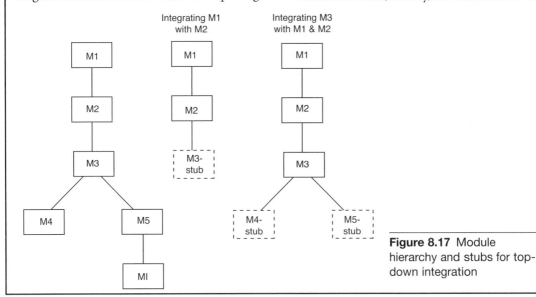

Figure 8.17 Module hierarchy and stubs for top-down integration

The complexity of a stub for module M depends on how complex the functionality of M is. The stub module header or signature for M is the same as that of the signature for M. It should simply pretend to do the work of M by returning expected values to its caller. For example, if M is to return 0 or 1, then the stub for M can be randomly generating 0 or 1 and returning it to the caller of M. However, it can get more complicated if M is returning complex data or data that is dependent on the data passed to the stub.

Knowing that top-level modules are typically user-interface modules and that low-level modules are IO and utility modules, top-down integration has several drawbacks. If given a limited time for testing, it is necessary to consider that more time is spent on integrating top-level modules and less time is spent on utility and IO modules. Utility and IO modules have higher fan-in and can be reused in future systems. Therefore, less testing of these modules leads to a lower reliability of the current system as well as future ones. Also, the late integration of input modules delays the use of real data in the modules integrated earlier. This problem can be solved by making an exception to the strict top-down module integration requiring the integration of input modules as soon as possible. In this case, for the hierarchy given, module M1 must be integrated earlier. The sequence of integrated modules would then be M1-M2-M3-M5-MI-M4. However top-down integration allows a more thorough testing of user-interface modules, hence, increased usability and a better user interface is obtained. Also, the morale of testers will be higher because the look and feel of the system is revealed earlier during the integration testing.

Bottom-Up

In **bottom-up integration** testing, lower-level modules are integrated first. Integrators tend to spend more time on testing the integration of lower-level modules, therefore, obtaining better quality utility and IO modules, making these modules highly-reusable and more reliable. However, the look and feel of the system is delayed until top-level modules are integrated. Also less time might be spent on top-level modules leading to more user-interface errors and consequently to less usable software. Bottom-up integration requires the integrators to write driver modules. A driver module is a module used to call the top-level module in the hierarchy being integrated so far.

It is hard to state which is simpler to write, a stub or a driver. It really depends on the functionality of the modules we are replacing with a stub or a driver. What is clear is that the writing of correct stubs and drivers is an overhead. However, the reward is producing a better and faster integration of software modules with easily detected and corrected errors.

Example 8.15

To integrate M5 and M4, we need a module M4-driver to make the call to M4. M4-driver passes meaningful data to M4 and receives returned data from M4. M4-driver does not need to have the same signature as M4. Also, M4-driver is much simpler than M3 because, unlike M3, it does not have to call modules other than M4. However, to be able to pass meaningful data to M4, it is ideal to either pass already-read data or to read data from a real data source or a test file. For example, if M4 is a sorting routine, M4-driver would loop over reading the test case inputs and pass them to M4. The driver also has to collect and analyze any returned values or modified parameters. Figure 8.18 shows the use of drivers when integrating bottom-up.

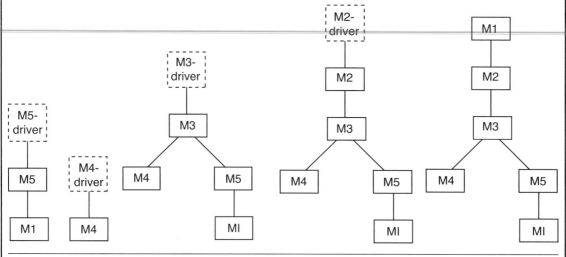

Figure 8.18 Bottom-up integration of the modules in the hierarchy of Figure 8.17

Hybrid

In the **hybrid** top-down/bottom-up approach, also called the **sandwich approach**, two teams of integrators work concurrently. One team performs top-down integration, whereas the other performs bottom-up integration. Ideally, user interface, IO, and utility modules would have received equal attention and time during integration testing. However, this approach requires additional coordination between the two testing teams.

8.8 SYSTEM-LEVEL TESTING

System-level testing refers to testing the software system as a black box. Normally, system-level testing aims at executing the acceptance test plan developed earlier at the end of the functional requirements phase. In addition, the various test plans targeting each of the non-functional requirements (NFRs) are also executed. The acceptance test plan (ATP) is normally user-centered and checks the conformance of the SUT to the functional requirements. The acceptance test plan includes test cases generated using the various black box-based testing techniques mentioned earlier. Other testing activities targeting the conformance to NFRs are described below.

Acceptance

Acceptance testing consists of the execution of the ATP developed at the end of the requirements phase of the software development project. The ATP includes test cases that are derived from the functional specifications and are mainly user-centered. Both the ATP and the functional requirements are formalized and approved by the client and the developer. Acceptance test cases are derived from considering the system as a black box. Hence, black box-based techniques can be applied to generate effective and representative test cases. If the system is user interface-driven, interactive, or real-time, state-based testing is used more frequently by modeling the user interface utilizing an extended FSM. If the system's interface is command line-driven or textual, then equivalence class testing and boundary value analysis techniques can be used to generate test cases. Finally, if we are dealing with a stateless, batch-based system, decision table- or tree-based specification of the system functionalities can be used as the basis for generating acceptance test cases.

Conformance to Non-Functional Requirements

System-level testing involves testing the conformance of the system, as a black box, to the NFRs. In the following, each type of system-level testing addresses a specific type of NFR. Other types of NFRs such as political, legal, and regulatory requirements must also be tested possibly using other non-automated techniques.

Load/Stress

The objective of load or **stress testing** is the evaluation of the SUT at or beyond the limits specified in the related NFRs. The expected behavior of the SUT should reflect the non-functional user requirements developed earlier in collaboration with other stakeholders and the client and users. For example, if the requirements state that the system must accommodate up to 100 users logging in simultaneously, then the corresponding test case requires the tester to have up to 100 users attempting to logon at the same time. Moreover, while testing the system under a heavy load, we should also test that the system can still handle normal and abnormal user interactions. For example, when testing for 100 users simultaneously logging in, some of the attempts should supply incorrect identification and passwords so that they would be rejected due to identification and authentication errors. The system should be robust and behave as expected when subjected to good or bad inputs regardless of the size of the input load. Also, other quality requirements such as performance must still be met regardless of load size and correctness of inputs. When subjected to more than 100 logon attempts, the system must behave according to the requirements. Load and stress testing can be performed effectively and efficiently using only automated testing tools.

Interoperability

The objective of **interoperability testing** is to evaluate the proper integration and operation of the SUT in its execution environment that can include operating systems, hardware platforms, or devices, as well as other software or hardware systems. Interoperability testing can be included as part of the system integration test plan.

Usability

Usability testing involves evaluative procedures that are performed to ensure that the SUT meets the specified usability requirements. These procedures can include questionnaires to potential users for the evaluation of the user-friendliness of the SUT. Usability testing can be performed without executing the SUT, (i.e., statically) but also can be done dynamically by inserting probes and indicators in the SUT to collect metrics on users' and system behavior and interactions. The latter can be achieved only if the source code is provided (i.e., white box-based).

Performance

Performance testing involves the application of test cases to ensure that specified performance requirements are met by the SUT. As mentioned in Chapter 3, performance requirements can include memory and response-time requirements. A response-time requirement statement might be: *Under no circumstances would the response time of the system to any user request exceed 10 milliseconds.* This requirement should be verified when a single user is interacting with the system or when the maximum possible number of users are interacting simultaneously. This scenario shows the interrelationship between performance and stress-related requirements and their related test cases. The technical feasibility of having consistent, nonconflicting, minimally restrictive, and realistic requirements was discussed earlier.

Security

Security testing ensures that the specified security requirements are met. Security testing is becoming increasingly critical in software and system testing. Security test cases can be developed based on the nature of the security threats and their associated risks. They can be based on the misuse or abuse cases that are identified while the use case model is being developed in the software requirements phase. Test cases are selected to cover all the specified security requirements discussed in Chapter 3.

Robustness/Fault Tolerance

Robustness testing ensures that the specified fault-tolerance and robustness requirements are met. As stated earlier in the boundary value analysis-based testing discussion, test cases should be designed to test the software system under both normal at the boundary conditions and abnormal just outside the boundary conditions. These abnormal conditions could be, in addition to bad inputs, abnormal operational and external conditions. For example, how does the software behave if a power failure occurs? a storage device failure occurs? a message arriving unexpectedly late from an external device? Is the software able to recover from the failure and continue its normal operation? The concept of robustness and fault-tolerance are linked with the concept of availability, survivability, and resiliency related to security requirements. This suggests that robustness and fault-tolerance testing could be integrated with the security testing discussed earlier.

Installation or Deployment

Installation or deployment testing aims at evaluating the validity of the software deployment and installation procedures provided to the client or user by the software developer. This testing must ensure that all specified steps of the procedures and their variations or options are exercised. Their outcomes must match the expected outcomes as specified in the installation test plan. The usability and user-friendliness of the installation procedures must also be examined.

8.9 OTHER TEST SELECTION STRATEGIES

Random and **probabilistic test** selection strategies can be used in combination with white box and black box techniques. However, these strategies used alone can lead to biased test inputs selection and an ineffective use of testing time.

Random

The **random testing** approach is based on the random selection of test inputs that are applied to the SUT. Random testing can be part of a brute force approach to testing. Its effectiveness relies on the randomness of the test input generation which can guarantee a uniform coverage of the input test domain, but may not. Random testing can be used in conjunction with other techniques. For example, after identifying the equivalence classes or partitions, we can use random testing to select test inputs from each of the identified equivalence classes. Random testing can be used in the context of black box-based testing. It can also be used for white box-based unit testing to randomly select execution paths when a decision is taken at a decision node of the control flow graph. If not used properly, and in conjunction with other strategies, random testing is equivalent to ad hoc and informal testing.

Probabilistic

The **probabilistic testing** approach is based on assigning a probability for every choice taken at a particular decision point. The sum of the assigned probabilities at a given point is 1. Decision points exist at a choice node in a control flow graph or at a non-final state that possesses outgoing transitions. An execution path has a probability that is equal to the product of the probabilities along its edges. After assigning probabilities to all edges, a tester can then compute the probability of occurrence of each of the test cases obtained earlier. Test cases can then be prioritized and classified under high-, medium-, and low-priority categories. High-priority test cases can be executed first followed by medium-priority test cases and then low-priority test cases. Strictly selecting test cases based on probabilities demands care. Experience shows that the most serious and critical software errors are frequently the ones that are least probable and difficult to reproduce. A combination of priority and criticality of the test case can be useful in addressing this concern. Remember the objective of testing is to effectively use testing time to discover the critical or most frequent errors—as many as possible and as early as possible. Frequent errors are annoying and affect the usability and reputation of the software, therefore affecting its economic bottom line.

One of the difficulties of the probabilistic approach is assigning appropriate probabilities. This requires inputs from an experienced tester and possibly an application domain expert. For example, at a given user-interface state, three possible outgoing edges exist: transition asking for help from the system; providing erroneous input and getting an error message; or providing the correct input and getting the requested service. Based on experience with similar systems, an expert tester could decide to assign 0.3 to the first possibility, 0.2 to the second, and 0.5 to the third. This assignment affects the probability of certain test cases and hence the priority classification of the test cases as described earlier.

Mutation

Mutation testing is based on the execution of test case inputs on several mutant programs. A mutant program is a small modification of a supposedly correct program under test and written by an experienced programmer. The basic assumption is that the program under test contains errors. These errors would be caused by simple variations of the program. If all mutants give outputs that are different from the output generated by the program, we can conclude that the program under test is probably correct. However, if one or more mutant programs and the program under test generate the same output, then a further investigation is necessary. It is either due to the inadequacy of the test inputs or that the program under test is incorrect. By adding more test inputs, we hope to distinguish the program from additional mutants. We say that more mutants are killed. The effectiveness of the test data is measured by computing the mutation score, which is the number of killed mutants over the total number of executed mutants. This strategy relies on the generation of a large number of mutant programs, which can be an exhaustive task.

8.10 POTPOURRI OF TESTING ISSUES

In this section some important software testing issues that can be considered by interested readers for further research are discussed.

Architectures

When testing distributed software applications such as communications protocols and web services, different test setups and architectures can be considered for test purposes. In the protocol testing literature, local, remote, and distributed **test architectures** are used. Each architecture has it own merits, limitations, and difficulties. For distributed test architectures, test synchronization becomes problematic and more complicated because there is a need to have distributed synchronization as to when the distributed test inputs are applied. Also, each architecture has its own points of control and observations (PCOs). The placement of a test oracle to produce proper verdicts for each test case is crucial in a **distributed testing** architecture.

Correctness

According to some reported statistics on errors and their frequency, 2 percent of reported testing errors are due to erroneous test cases. For example, if the test case expected output is incorrect, and then if the software is correct and delivers a correct output, the test verdict is incorrect because a mismatch exists between observed output and expected output. After analyzing this *wrong* error, the tester might discover that the error is in the test case itself. This type of error is classified under **test case design error**. Other test case errors include incorrect test case preambles or preconditions and incomplete test case descriptions among others. These test errors often lead to inconclusive test verdicts.

Developers and the quality assurance group can avoid these test design errors by a careful peer review of the test cases. Test plans can also be reviewed using appropriate walkthrough and checklists.

Description Language

The automatic application of test case inputs and the automated analysis of test outputs and verdicts can be facilitated by using a formal description of the test cases and their inputs. Special purpose languages serve that goal. In addition to being executable, basic checking of the test cases can be performed to ensure test case correctness and perhaps completeness. In the area of communications protocols and distributes systems, an ISO standard **test description language** is used. The Tree and Tabular Combined Notation (TTCN) is a test description language that allows the structured specification of test suites. Various automated test tools have been built to execute TTCN-specified test cases and to analyze the test results.

Software Testability

Software testability refers to the ease with which a given software can be tested. Software testability adopts some of the concepts of hardware testability, namely, controllability and observability.

A software is **controllable** if special testing functions can be used to control the execution of the software during testing. For example, a reset function available to a tester is useful to return the software to a specific state—normally the start state. This reset function is useful in state-oriented systems such as communications protocols with a known initial state. Additionally, a set function is useful to set the system to specific critical states. In the context of state-oriented systems, the existence of a homing sequence is useful. Independent of the current state, this sequence would lead to a specific state.

A software is **observable** if a tester can observe the execution of key and critical activities. The software includes probes at which logs are generated. These logs are available to testers and are useful in diagnosing errors during testing or in production. These probes can be enabled or disabled by a tester or before delivering the software. The number, granularity, and location of these probes in the code are important decisions that the tester needs to make because probes influence the diagnostics power and the number of saved logs analyzed.

Regression Testing

Regression testing is performed every time maintenance activities are performed on a given software. The extent of work involved in regression testing depends on the type of maintenance activity, and on the coupling between the modified modules or methods and the rest of the software. Low-module coupling makes regression testing simpler because side effects are reduced. The complexity and number of test cases re-executed depends on the scope of effect and control of the modified modules. Any time a new software release or upgrade is installed in a production system, the appropriate regression test plan has to be developed and executed. The main challenge in regression testing is that the tests have to ensure that all unwanted side effects of the modifications made are detected and resolved.

8.11 OBJECT-ORIENTING TESTING

The strategies for testing non-object-oriented software apply for testing object-oriented software also. Object-oriented software encapsulates related modules or methods in separate classes. The first step involves the testing of classes individually. Then, classes can be integrated and all relationships between classes are verified. Once all integration errors have been resolved, system-level testing is performed.

Testing Classes

Classes encapsulate methods and attributes or data. Methods and attributes have separate visibility specifications. For example, in Java, classes and methods can be private, public, packaged, or protected. To test a class, each of the methods (or units) inside the class have to be tested. White box-based and black box-based testing techniques can be used to produce cases to test these methods. When testing a method in a class under test that calls another method in the same class or outside the class, a stub method must be created. Method drivers also have to be created to start testing individual methods. Furthermore, conformance to method visibility specification can be verified during method testing. It is recommended that entity classes tests are performed first because they tend to be simpler to test and highly usable by other interface and control classes.

Integrating Classes

Once each individual class has been tested completely, integrating classes together begins. When integrating two classes, stub methods (inside stub classes) and driver methods are needed. The class interaction diagram shows the interclass communication associations and facilitates the selection of classes for integration. If this diagram resembles a hierarchy, then a top-down or bottom-up integration strategy is used, which is similar to the module hierarchy discussed earlier in this chapter.

System-Level Use Case Testing

Once classes of the software have been integrated, the software is tested at the system level as a black box and acceptance test plans are executed. In addition, the various test plans for checking conformance of the software to NFRs are executed. An acceptance test plan for object-oriented software is based mainly on the use cases and their related scenarios. NFRs such as security requirements can be checked by executing scenarios from the misuse or abuse cases.

8.12 SOFTWARE QUALITY ASSURANCE

Software quality assurance (SQA) and software testing are related with respect to their goals. They both aim at producing better quality software. While software testing addresses mainly the

SUT as a product, SQA addresses the processes with which, and the environment in which, the product is being developed and maintained. For example, testing activities involve the design and execution of test cases and the management of the testing process. However, testing-related SQA activities ensure that proper training for testers, concisely documented testing procedures and test plans exist, and that proper management of the testing activities is taking place.

Plan and Activities

Software Quality Assurance (SQA) consists of life cycle activities that are performed by a dedicated SQA group along all phases of the software development processes. Normally, a software quality assurance plan is devised for each software development project.

A recommended standard template for an SQA plan is provided by **IEEE 730**-1998. According to the standard, the plan should include sections to:

- Deal with SQA management issues, including SQA resources and risk management
- Identify product and process quality assurance tasks and activities
- Provide an SQA schedule, identify the standards, practices, conventions, and metrics
- Identify the list of documentation to be audited and reviewed
- Identify the roles and responsibilities with respect to testing-related activities
- Identify the problem reporting and resolution procedures and their related metrics
- Identify the tools, techniques, and methodologies used
- Provide procedures for code, media, and supplier control
- Identify procedures for records collection, maintenance, and retention
- Identify the training needs for the SQA personnel

The main responsibilities of the SQA group during the software development phases include:

- Audit and review of all product deliverables
- Execution of test plans according to the SQA plan; reporting software problems
- Dealing with new or modified standards and practices during the project
- Ensuring the proper handling of media and code and their libraries
- Ensuring quality control over supplied, subcontracted, and outsourced products
- Collection of process and product quality-related metrics
- Execution of the SQA plan, updating its schedule, and ensuring its progress
- Assessing and auditing the main SQA responsibilities listed

Audit and Review

With respect to the audit and review responsibilities, the SQA group basically checks all process deliverables against specific quality requirements. Deliverables must conform to internal company standards, professional standards, and possibly regulatory (country) and international standards. Company standards can include document layouts, coding standards, screen or GUI design standards, specific software development procedures, and any other quality requirement that the company deems appropriate for its business. Professional standards can include, for example, the IEEE project management standard and other specific software development and information processing standards. Other standards include national standards such as ANSI, international standards such as ISO or IFIP, or software-related military standards.

Each deliverable of the software development process is checked for adherence to the adopted standards. Checking for conformity to the standards is at the core of the SQA activities. Checking can be performed automatically or manually. Automatic checking is performed with automated static checker tools. These tools are useful to check for adherence to internal coding standards and for avoiding serious software security errors.

Non-automated SQA activities are mainly performed during a deliverable review meeting such as the design document review meeting. These activities involve walkthrough and inspection of the deliverable under review. Any software deliverable, including code, document, prototype, or even review report is normally submitted to the SQA group for review. A meeting is scheduled by the SQA group. This meeting is normally attended by a representative from the group responsible for authoring the deliverable under review, the group who is going to be the user of the deliverable, and two other developers: one acting as a meeting moderator and another acting as a recorder. As a result of this meeting, a complete review report should include the items to address in the deliverable and the person assigned to work on each item. In addition, a decision regarding the status of the deliverable is made. The decision can be to accept the deliverable as is, accept with minor changes with or without a new review, accept with major changes and a new review, postpone the decision, adjourn the review and schedule a continuation review, or deliverable should be reworked and resubmitted and a new review scheduled.

Each SQA review meeting should have a concise agenda, including the parts of the deliverable to review and the expectations from the review. The moderator ensures the review is progressing effectively and professionally. An SQA group within the software development organization acts like the military police within the army, keeping order during its operation. In some organizations, SQA can be outsourced to save internal resources and produce higher-quality deliverables because reviews are critical and should be as unbiased as possible. The resources allocated to an SQA group depend on the size, number, and complexity of the deliverables, in addition to the emphasis on quality as part of the organization culture.

Inspection Checklist and Walkthrough

The **inspection** of a deliverable involves the reviewing of the deliverable against a **checklist** that is pre-designed as part of the software development processes. A checklist can also be considered an internal standard to use during SQA reviews. Typically, there is a checklist for each deliverable identified in the adopted development process. Typical checklists include coding standards, design document, GUI or usability, test plans, and requirements document. Moreover, specific checklists can be adopted to review software security, performance, and fault-tolerance checklists.

These checklists provide an emphasis on the specific requirements that are critical to the software under development. These checklists must be reviewed periodically or at any time there are changes to the standards upon which they are built.

A deliverable **walkthrough** consists of checking the deliverable incrementally and linearly, unlike the non-linear checking performed during checklist-based reviews. For example, if the deliverable is a design document, the document is distributed ahead of the meeting time. During the meeting, the document is examined page by page and checked against the various design quality standards. The problem with walkthrough when it involves a large document is the loss of concentration after a while. This can be addressed by scheduling several review meetings for the same deliverable. However, discontinued meetings can lead to missing the detection of inconsistencies within the same large document.

In addition to adherence to standards, reviews should be able to detect incompleteness, inconsistencies, and contradictions in the deliverable under review and across deliverables. For

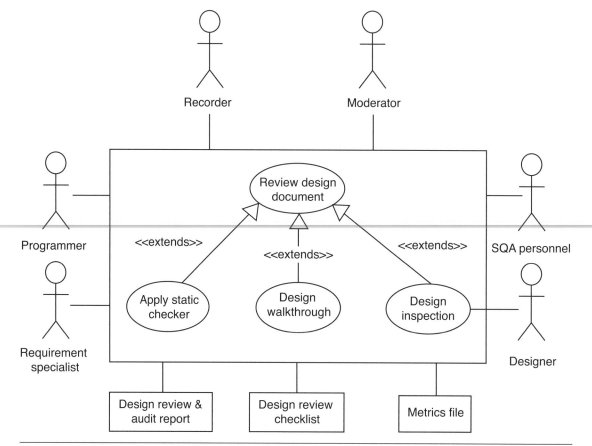

Figure 8.19 Actors and use cases involved in an SQA design review meeting

example, the design review by the SQA should catch inconsistencies between the design document under review and the already-reviewed requirements document. One may argue that these inconsistencies must have been detected by the design team during internal design team meetings and reviews. However, if these errors remain undiscovered then, the SQA review is the last chance for discovery. Otherwise, these design errors would manifest themselves later in the code and hopefully be discovered during software testing. Errors caused by design inconsistencies are costlier to fix, especially if they are due to requirements errors.

Metrics

Metrics collected by the SQA group is useful for future software process improvement, hence future product quality improvement. SQA metrics can be product-related or process-related metrics. Product-related metrics can be based on the IEEE Standard for a Software Quality Metrics Methodology that provides a methodology for collecting product-related metrics. Process-related metrics can be based on the IEEE Standard for Software Productivity Metrics. This standard describes the conventions for collecting and measuring the various development processes. Also, metrics collected about the activities of the SQA group and their outcomes can be used later for assessing the performance and effectiveness of the SQA process. For example, the number of design inconsistencies discovered in an SQA design review versus the number of inconsistencies discovered later in production and found to originate from design inconsistencies would be a good indicator of the effectiveness of the SQA design review meeting and could be the target for future internal SQA process improvement.

Figure 8.19 shows a unified modeling language (UML) diagram illustrating the actors and use cases involved in an SQA design review meeting.

SUMMARY

In this chapter, we have addressed various issues related to the testing of software and software quality assurance. Software testing and quality assurance activities are performed all along the software development life cycle. Planning for testing starts as early as the requirements specifications phase when the acceptance test plan is developed and approved. Also, planning for quality assurance activities starts during project planning. The execution of software test plans can start once the first module is written and tested using their respective unit test plans. However, the execution of the quality assurance plan starts immediately after its approval.

The main element of a test plan is the test case. A test case consists of test inputs and expected outputs. The test case inputs are normally obtained systematically using sound **test generation** and selection strategies and techniques. Three main types of testing can be used. White box testing is based on the given source code tested, black box testing is based on the executable of the software tested and its functional specifications, and grey box testing is based on the executable of the software, its specifications, and design documentation. Four black box-based test generation and selection techniques have been discussed, namely, boundary value analysis, equivalence class testing, decision table- or tree testing, and state-based testing. White box-based test generation and selection techniques based on the concept of control and data flow graphs have been presented. Control flow-based testing techniques based on statement, decision, and multiple condition coverage have been discussed. Also, data flow-based testing techniques that built upon the control flow graph have also been studied.

Various types of system-level testing have been discussed. They address the conformance of the system under test as a black box to its documented functional and NFRs. Acceptance testing deals with the system as a black box and checks conformance to its functional requirements. However, load testing, performance testing, security testing, and usability testing, among other testing activities, deal with the system as a black box and check the system's conformance to its NFRs.

In the white box-based testing, mutation testing can be used to ensure test adequacy and effectiveness. Also, when using white box or black box test generation and selection techniques, random or probabilistic testing strategies can be used.

The planning for SQA and its importance, elements of the SQA plan, and the activities performed as part of the plan were discussed. Finally the audit and review processes that are key activities of the quality assurance functions were presented. Inspection and walkthrough activities used during a review process of a deliverable were also discussed.

KEY TERMS

acceptance testing	distinguishing sequence	mutation testing
adup strategy	distributed testing	observable
all-c-uses strategy	dynamic testing	path expression
all-p-uses strategy	equivalence class testing	performance testing
all-uses strategy	functional testing	probabilistic testing
black box testing	grey box testing	random testing
bottom-up integration	hybrid	regression testing
boundary value analysis	IEEE 730	robustness testing
checklist	inspection	sandwich approach
conformance	installation	security testing
control flow graph	installation or deployment	short-circuiting
controllable	testing	software quality assurance
data flow anomalies	integration testing	software testability
data flow testing	interoperability testing	state-based testing
decision table-based testing	metrics	statement coverage
decision tree-based testing	multiple condition coverage	static testing

stress testing	test description language	top-down integration
structural testing	test generation	usability testing
system-level testing	test oracle	walkthrough
test architectures	test plan	white box testing
test cases	test suites	
test case design error	test verdicts	

REVIEW QUESTIONS

1. What are the main differences between black box, white box, and grey box testing?
2. What is the main weakness of white box testing techniques? black box testing techniques?
3. What are the advantages and disadvantages of top-down integration testing?
4. What are the advantages and disadvantages of bottom-up integration testing?
5. Discuss the difficulties in obtaining stubs and drivers in integration testing.
6. What is the difference between control flow graph and data flow graph?
7. How can path expressions be used to perform data flow testing?
8. Describe the general strategy to test object-oriented software.
9. What are the main differences between checklist- and walkthrough-based reviews?
10. How can static analysis tools help in performing some of the quality assurance tasks?
11. List some metrics that can be collected by SQA and how they can be useful for process improvement.
12. What are the main activities of the SQA group?

EXERCISES

1. Draw the control flow graph of the corrected code for digitCount given in Figure 8.5. List the test cases that can ensure statement and branch coverage. Show the path traversed for each test case.
2. You are given an executable of the greatest common divisor (gcd) function. This function accepts two integers and returns their gcd. Produce test cases based on a combination of black box-based testing techniques.
3. Consider an implementation of the gcd function that you can find in a textbook or on the Web. Show its corresponding flow graph. Provide test cases based on control flow-based testing techniques.
4. You are given an executable of the bubbleSort function. This function is a void function and accepts an array of integers. The function terminates after sorting the integers in the array in ascending order. Provide test cases based on boundary value analysis. Provide test cases based on equivalence class testing.

5. Consider the function bubbleSort. This function takes an array of integers A and sorts it:

```
void bubbleSort(int A[])
{        int nswaps = 1;
         int temp;
         while (nswaps != 0)
         {        nswaps = 0;
                  for (int i = 0; i < A.length-1; i++)
                       if (A[i] > A[i+1])
                       {              nswaps++;
                                      temp = A[i]; A[i] = A[i+1]; A[i+1] = temp;

                       }
         }
}
```

Produce a control flow graph. Provide control flow-based test cases. For each test case, show the path traversed when executing the test case.

6. Consider the following mysterious C code:

```
public static void main (String args[])
{        int row = 10, column;
         while (row >= 1) {
                  column = 1;
                  while (column <= 10) {
                           System.out.println(row % 2 == 1 ? "<" : ">" );
                           ++column;
                  }
                  —row;
                  System.out.println( );
         }
}
```

Produce a control flow graph. Write its equivalent path expression. Write the path expression corresponding to the data flow of variable row and variable column.

7. Given the following function for trimming a string:

```
function trim(instring: string) : string;
const blank = ' ';
var i,j : integer, found : boolean, result : string;
begin
        i := length (instring);
        found := false;
        while (not found) and (i >= 1) do
        begin
                if instring[i] <> blank then
                        found := true
                else
                        i := i - 1
        end;
        for j := 1 to i do result[j] := instring[j];
        return result;
end;
```

Briefly describe the main purpose of this function. Produce a black box-based test plan using both boundary value analysis and equivalence class testing given the function interface and its functional description. Produce a control flow graph. Produce a white box-based test plan to catch the maximum number of errors. Produce a path expression from the obtained flow graph. Produce 2 path expressions describing the data flow for variables i and found. Is there any data flow anomaly? show it? Suppose instead of i := i - 1 we have written i := i + 1, which test cases developed earlier would detect the error and how? Suppose instead of i >= 1 we have written i <= 1, which test cases developed earlier would detect the error and how? Suppose instead of instring[i] <> blank, we have written instring[i] = blank, which test case would detect the error and how? Suppose instead of and in (not found) and (i >= 1), we have written or, which test case would detect the error and how?

8. Given the following informal specification: The program prompts the user for a positive integer in the range 1 to 20 and then for a string of characters of that length. The program then prompts for a character and returns the position in the string at which the character was first found or a message indicating that the character was not present in the string. The user has the option to search for more characters. Produce black box-based test cases using both boundary value analysis and equivalence classes techniques.

9. The method findArray takes two parameters, smallArray and largeArray, both are arrays of characters. The method returns −1 if smallArray is not found contiguously in largeArray,

otherwise it returns the position in largeArray at which smallArray starts. For example, findArray({'b', 'd'}, {'a', 'b', 'c', 'd', 'e'}) returns −1. However, findArray({'b', 'c'}, {'m', 'a', 'b', 'c', 'd', 'e'}) returns 2. Write a test plan to test an implementation of this method using boundary value analysis and equivalence class testing.

10. A student implemented the method findArray as follows:

```
int findArray(char [] smallA, char [] largeA)
{
        int savedk,m;
        for (int k = 0; k < largeA.length-smallA.length; k++)
        {
        savedk = k;
        for (m = 0; m < smallA.length; m++)
        if (smallA[m] != largeA[savedk++]) break;
        if (m == smallA.length) return k;
        }
        return -1;
}
```

Draw the flow graph of the method code. Add test cases to A if needed to do branch and statement coverage. Does the above code pass all test cases?. The code includes a logical error that you might or might not have found in your testing, what is it? Which test case can discover it? and if not in your plan, write it. Can you optimize the code?

11. Given the module hierarchy shown in Figure 8.20, provide one possible sequence of modules when integrating top-down. Give one possible sequence of modules when integrating

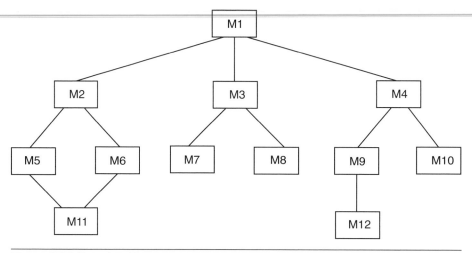

Figure 8.20 Exercise 11

bottom-up. How many stubs and drivers are needed to test module x3 on its own? How many stubs and drivers are needed to test module a on its own? How many stubs and drivers are needed to test module x1 on its own?

12. The method primeNumber takes an integer k > 0 and returns true if k is a prime number. For example, System.out.println(primeNumber(13)); will print true and System.out. println(primeNumber (9)); will print false. A prime number is an integer k ≥ 2 that is divisible only by 1 and itself. The first few prime numbers are: 2, 3, 5, 7, 11, 13, ... Based on the 2 black box testing techniques boundary value analysis and equivalence class, write a test plan to test the method primeNumber.

13. A student implemented the method primeNumber as follows:

```
boolean primeNumber(int k)
{        if ( k % 2 == 1) return false;
         for (int I = 2; I < Math.sqrt(k); I++)
         {        if (k % I == 0)
                           return false;
         }
         return true;
}
```

Show the flow graph corresponding to the above code. Then, based on path testing, write a test plan that tests the method primeNumber using multiple-condition and statement-coverage techniques. Execute the test plans by completing the last two columns of the two test plan tables you have written in A and B. If your test cases were complete, the above code should not pass all the test cases, i.e., the code does not work in all situations. Why? How do you fix the code to pass all test cases?

14. Write the path expression for the control flowgraph in Figure 8.15. Produce a test plan to cover selected feasible paths in the flowgraph.

BIBLIOGRAPHY

Books

Beizer, B. *Software Testing Techniques*, 2d ed., Boston, MA: International Thomson Computer Press, 1990.

Binder, R. V. *Testing Object-Oriented Systems Models, Patterns, and Tools*, Reading, MA: Addison–Wesley, 2000.

Craig, R., and S. Jaskiel. *Systematic Testing*, London, UK: Artech House Publishers, 2002.

DeMillo, R., et al. *Software Testing and Evaluation*, Reading, MA: Addison-Wesley, 1987.

Graham, D., et al. *Foundations of Software Testing: ISTQB Certification*, London, UK: International Thomson Business Press, 2008.

Haug, M., et al. *Software Quality Approaches: Testing, Verification and Validation*, Berlin: Springer, 2001.

Hutcheson, M. *Software Testing Fundamentals: Methods and Metrics*, New York: John Wiley and Sons, 2003.

Jorgensen, P. C. *Software Testing: A Craftsman's Approach*, Boca Raton, FL: CRC Press, 1995.

Kaner, C., J. Bach, and B. Pettichord. *Lessons Learned in Software Testing*, New York: John Wiley and Sons, 2002.

Mathur, A., *Foundations of Software Testing*, Reading, MA: Addison-Wesley Professional, 2008.

Myers, G. J., et al. *The Art of Software Testing*, 2d ed., New York: John Wiley and Sons, July 2004.

Patton, R. *Software Testing*, 2d ed., Toronto: SAMS Publishing, 2005.

Perry, W. E. *Effective Methods for Software Testing*, 2d ed., New York: John Wiley & Sons, 2002.

Pezze, M., and M. Young. *Software Testing and Analysis: Process, Principles and Techniques*, New York: John Wiley and Sons, 2007.

Schulmeyer, G. C., and J. I. McManus. *Handbook of Software Quality Assurance*, 3d ed., Englewood Cliffs, NJ: Prentice Hall, 1999.

Spillner, A., et al. *Software Testing Foundations: A Study Guide for the Certified Tester Exam*, 2d ed., Rocky Nook, MA: Rocky Nook, 2007.

Wysopal, C., et al. *The Art of Software Security Testing*, Reading, MA: Addison-Wesley Professional, 2006.

Papers

Ackerman, F. A. "Software inspections and the cost effective production of reliable software." *Software Engineering, Vol. 2: The Supporting Processes*, Richard H. Thayer and Mark Christensen, eds. Wiley-IEEE Computer Society Press, 2002.

Boujarwah, A. S., K. Saleh, and J. Al-Dallal. "Testing syntax and semantic coverage of Java language compilers." *Journal of Information and Software Technology*, 41(1): 15–28, January 1999.

Boujarwah, A., and K. Saleh. "Compiler test case generation methods: a survey and assessment." *Journal of Information and Software Technology*, 39(9): 617–625, September 1997.

Boujarwah, A., and K. Saleh. "Compiler test suites: Evaluation and use in an automated test environment." *Journal of Information and Software Technology*, 36(10): 607–614, September 1994.

Chow, T. S. "Testing software design modeled by finite-state machines." *IEEE Transactions on Software Engineering*, vol. 4, 178–187, 1978.

Clarke, L., et al. "A formal evaluation of data flow path selection criteria." *IEEE Transactions on Software Engineering*, 15(11): 1318–1332, November 1989.

Dssouli, R., K. Saleh, El M. Aboulhamid, A. En-Nouaary, and C. Bourhfir. "Test development for communication protocols: Toward automation." *Computer Networks and ISDN Systems*, Special issue on Advanced Topics on SDL and MSC, 31(17): 1835-1872 June 1999, pp. 1835–1872.

Dssouli, R., K. Karoui, K. Saleh, and O. Cherkaoui. "Communications software design for testability: specifications transformations and testability measures." *Journal of Information and Software Technology*, 41(11/12):729–743, August 1999.

Frankl, P., and E. Weyuker. "A formal analysis of the fault detecting ability of testing methods," *IEEE Transactions on Software Engineering*, 19(3): 202, March 1993.

Probert, R. L., and O. Monkewich. TTCN: "The international notation for specifying tests of communications systems." *Computer Networks and ISDN Systems* 23(5): 417–438 (1991).

Rapps, S., and E. J. Weyuker. "Selecting software test data using data flow information." *IEEE Transactions on Software Engineering*, 11(4): 367–375, April, 1985.

Rothermel, G., and M. J. Harrold. "Analyzing regression test selection techniques," *IEEE Transactions on Software Engineering*, 22(8): 529, August 1996.

Saleh, K. "Testability-directed service definitions and their synthesis." Proc. of the *Eleventh IEEE International Phoenix Conference on Computers and Communications (IPCCC-92)*, 674–678, March 1992.

Saleh, K., and R. Probert. "Issues in testing E-commerce systems." *Electronic Commerce Technology Trends: Challenges and Opportunities*. K. Dong, eds. IBM Press, 273–282, February 2000.

Saleh, K., A. Boujarwah, and J. Al-Dallal. "Anomaly detection in concurrent Java programs using dynamic data flow analysis." *Journal of Information and Software Technology*, 43(15): 973–981, 2001.

Saleh, K., R. Probert, W. Li, and W. Fong. "An approach to high-yield requirements specifications for e-commerce and its application." *International Journal on Digital Libraries*, 3(4): 302–308, May 2002.

Ural, H., K. Saleh, and A. Williams. "Test generation based on control and data dependencies within system specifications in SDL." *Computer Communications*, vol. 23, 609–627, 2000.

West, C. H. Protocol validation by random state exploration. In *International Symposium on Protocol Specification, Testing and Verification*. 1986.

Weyuker, E. J. "Assessing test data adequacy through program inference." *ACM Trans. on Programming Languages and Systems*, 5(4): 641–655, October 1983.

Whittaker, J. A. "What is software testing? And why is it so hard?" *IEEE Software*, 70–79, January/February 2000.

Standards

IEEE Std 730, *IEEE Standard for Software Quality Assurance Plans*, IEEE, 2002.

IEEE Std 1008, *IEEE Standard for Software Unit Testing*, IEEE, 1987.

IEEE Std 1028, *IEEE Standard for Software Reviews*, IEEE, 1997.

IEEE Std 1044, *IEEE Standard for the Classification of Software Anomalies*, IEEE, 1993.

IEEE Std 1059, *IEEE Guide for Software Verification and Validation Plans*, IEEE, 1993.

IEEE Std 1061, *IEEE Standard for a Software Quality Metrics Methodology*, IEEE, 1998.

ITU-T Recommendation Z.140, Testing and Test Control Notation version 3 (TTCN-3): Core language.

Software Maintenance

Once the software is delivered and deployed, its intended users will begin to report the newly-discovered software errors. Also, users will demand modifications and additions to reflect new requirements or operating environments in addition to desired features that were known but were left out of the original specifications. Software maintenance encompasses all activities related to software enhancements performed after the software is deployed. The IEEE standard defines software maintenance as the modification of a software product after delivery to correct faults, improve performance or other attributes, or adapt the product to a modified environment. The standard also defines a process through which a maintenance activity moves. Another ongoing activity supporting software maintenance is software configuration management (SCM). The IEEE standard for SCM defines the activities involved in the configuration of the software and the management of the configuration items. The SCM plan is part of the project plan and its processes are part of the generic life cycle model processes.

Learning Outcomes

In this chapter you will learn:
- Software maintenance activities
- Software maintenance processes
- Software maintenance management processes
- Reengineering and reverse engineering
- Software configuration management and change management

9.1 IMPORTANCE OF SOFTWARE MAINTENANCE

It is estimated that the cost of software maintenance is about 70 percent of the overall cost of developing and maintaining software. Billions of dollars are spent around the world on software maintenance activities every year. The extensive cost and effort needed for maintaining software necessitates the development and use of formal maintenance and **maintenance management** processes and automated tools designed to reduce the maintenance cost.

In the previous chapters, the issue of maintainability in the preceding software development phases has been addressed. Maintainability is defined as the ease with which software maintenance can be performed. Software development for maintainability should be considered a long-term approach to reduce maintenance cost. Enhancing the software requirements engineering processes eliminates high-cost maintenance errors. Design for future reuse and with reusable components also reduces maintenance cost. Moreover, developing properly-documented, modular, robust, and secure code reduces future maintenance cost. There are many reasons for the high cost of software maintenance. They are either due to management or they have a technical basis.

Management frequently misunderstands software maintenance, which leads to poor management decisions. For example, frequently inexperienced software engineers are assigned to complex maintenance activities. In fact, large companies tend to hire recent graduates and assign them to the maintenance tasks. Corrective maintenance tasks are also viewed as being the *dirty work*, and maintenance engineers feel that their work is not appreciated and is of low visibility to upper management. Upper management should make an effort, therefore, to change the attitudes toward maintenance efforts.

The technical reasons for the high cost of software maintenance include a lack of understanding of the software due to its complexity, lack of documentation, the unexpected side effects of the software changes, the lack of formal techniques for **regression testing**, and the absence of the original developers. The concept of design for change and maintainability is becoming important as the cost of maintenance is rising. Unfortunately, as software goes through numerous modifications, there is a tendency to neglect updating the various documents to reflect these modifications. This leads to inconsistencies between specification and design documents and code. These inconsistencies result in more expensive maintenance of the software. Also, the developers involved in the original release of the software might not be present during the maintenance of the software. Another common problem with maintenance is that when one error is fixed other errors can be introduced as a side effect. Similarly, when a new feature is introduced, the interactions among and with the other features can be affected leading to new errors. Finally, there is a lack of formal software testing theory dealing with determining the necessary and sufficient amount of testing needed to ensure that the new software is meeting the software requirements specifications. Failure to test the new code and how the code is possibly affected by the software changes leads to the introduction of subsequent new errors that have to be resolved. Moreover, retesting the entire software is costly if the effect of the software maintenance activities can be localized and bounded. Proper regression testing should replace random or ad hoc testing of the software.

Maintenance of software cannot be avoided if the software company that has developed it wants to remain in the market. Even continuously evolving the software to deal with new requirements and environments is becoming critical for a software development company to survive and remain competitive in the market. Moreover, current research suggests that software maintenance should be dealt with as a service performed on the software after being deployed. The maintenance of software can then be outsourced to specialized service companies, allowing the development company to concentrate on the production of high-quality software products.

9.2 TAXONOMY OF SOFTWARE MAINTENANCE ACTIVITIES

There are four types of maintenance activities: adaptive, corrective, perfective, and preventive. Typically, adaptive, perfective, and preventive activities are scheduled maintenance activities. However, corrective maintenance activities can be either scheduled or unscheduled. Unscheduled corrective maintenance activities are referred to as emergency maintenance. The effort needed to perform a maintenance activity depends on its type, scope, effect, severity, and priority.

Adaptive

Adaptive maintenance activities involve adapting the software to another operating environment or to a new software or hardware paradigm or technology. Configuring the software to deal with a new user interface technology or to be ported to another operating system are considered adaptive maintenance activities as well. Typically, these activities are wide in scope and effort and are triggered by upper management decisions influenced by market- or technology-driven choices. Ideally, these activities require new or modified interface specifications followed by design and code changes as well as a complete system testing. Adaptive maintenance activities could be scheduled activities according to a long-term software evolution and market penetration plan for the software development organization.

Corrective

Corrective maintenance activities involve the diagnosing of reported software errors and making the necessary changes to fix them. Typically, software errors are reported by the users after encountering them during software use. Other errors might have been found by software testers prior to the delivery and deployment of the software in the market and these reported errors are scheduled by the maintenance team manager for resolution. However, sometimes high-impact and critical errors affecting the software operation or high-profile users are encountered and reported by the client. Due to their importance, the maintenance team manager might initiate an unscheduled corrective maintenance activity to deal with these errors. Normally, **unscheduled maintenance** activities are costly because they have to be given higher priority that disrupts the execution of other scheduled activities and causes unexpected delays. Software errors leading to corrective maintenance activities can be caused by specification, design, coding, or testing errors in addition to the errors introduced during previous maintenance activities. The latter error types are due to the so-called *imperfect debugging*.

Based on reported statistics, fixing a specification error discovered after the system has been deployed costs many times more than fixing it had it been discovered during the design phase. Fixing a specification error requires changes to the specification, design, and code. Specification errors can be caused by missing requirements, capturing the requirements incorrectly, or specified requirements that are not thorough. Design errors can be caused by making poor design choices, including the choice of algorithms, data structures, or high-level architectural style. In addition, simpler design errors include logic errors in the data or control flow in the selected algorithms or data structures. Coding errors are due to incorrect mapping of the design into an implementation. Normally, coding errors are simpler to fix than design or specification errors. Testing errors are due to the misinterpretation of the test results or the bad design of a test case that led to the error introduced during the code testing phase and was undiscovered.

Perfective

Perfective maintenance activities involve software changes leading to improving the functional and non-functional aspects of the software. For example, modifying the user interface to optimize the user interactions and increase the system usability is considered a performance maintenance activity. Modifications dealing with enhancing the response time, reducing the memory requirements, or adding advanced search capabilities and other advanced features are also the result of perfective maintenance activities. These are scheduled maintenance activities initiated by external users or clients. They can also be initiated by product managers as a result of market studies and surveys that clearly indicate a need for product revision and evolution. Depending on its scope, a perfective maintenance activity can require specification, design, and code modifications.

Preventive

Preventive maintenance activities involve software changes intended to improve the future maintainability of the software and reduce the possibilities of finding more errors. These maintenance activities are normally triggered internally by the maintenance team manager or upper management. The impact is to reduce the maintenance cost in the long term. Examples of preventive maintenance activities include software restructuring, changing the algorithm and data structures used, and enhancing the software documentation. Typically, most preventive maintenance activities impact the non-functional aspects of the software. Similar to adaptive and perfective maintenance, preventive maintenance activities should be considered part of the software evolution plan aimed at the long-term software economics. Finally, **reverse engineering** and **design recovery** are two activities that can eventually lead to preventive maintenance activities.

Statistics indicate that about 75 percent of maintenance activities are adaptive and preventive, 20 percent are corrective, and the remaining 5 percent are preventive. It is clear that preventive maintenance is given a low priority because they are not triggered by the software users or clients. They are scheduled by the managers only when no other maintenance activities are to be scheduled and to avoid idle time for the team members.

9.3 SOFTWARE MAINTENANCE PROCESS

The software maintenance standard introduced in IEEE Standard 1219-1993 describes the process for managing and performing software maintenance activities. The software maintenance process described has seven phases (Figure 9.1):

Phase 1: Problem and modification identification, classification, and prioritization. In this phase, a software change request (SCR) is first assigned a number, classified as requiring scheduled or unscheduled corrective, adaptive, perfective, or preventive maintenance. The request is then validated for completeness and correctness. If it is found to be a valid request, it is assigned a priority and an initial estimation of the resources required to execute it is completed.

Phase 2: Analysis. In this phase, both the economic and technical feasibilities of the requested change are analyzed. The impact of the changes is determined and possible alternative solutions are identified and possibly prototyped. The software code, databases, and relevant documentation are analyzed to identify and locate the parts that need to be modified. A strategy for testing, including unit, regression, and acceptance testing should be in place to perform the needed testing of the change. A tentative plan is then prepared for performing the design, coding, testing, and delivery of the change in the software. Risk analysis is performed by considering the change needed, the estimated effort needed, and the results of the feasibility of the change. The outcome of risk analysis is the decision whether to move to the design phase. Clearly, the complexity of the analysis phase depends on the type of maintenance activity and its scope. Risk analysis is suitable for complex maintenance requests such as adaptive and extensive corrective maintenance involving the addition of complex features to the existing software.

Phase 3: Design. In this phase, the change is designed, which means that all changes needed to the code and documentation are outlined in an action plan. The software modules that are

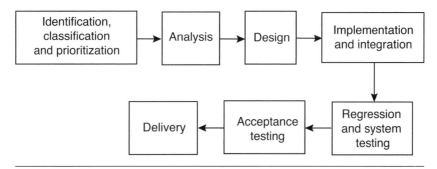

Figure 9.1 Seven phases of the software maintenance process

affected by the required change are identified. The design documentation of the affected modules is modified. Unit test cases and regression test cases are developed. The implementation and testing plans are updated if necessary. The modified specification and design documents are reviewed using walkthrough and inspection checklists. In addition, the modified test plans, including unit and regressions test plans, are reviewed.

Phase 4: Implementation and integration. In this phase, changes to code are performed according to the design action plan. The unit test plans are executed and the code is modified if needed. The modified code is reviewed in code review meetings using code walkthroughs and code inspection checklists. The code is also verified to reflect the design changes. The code is integrated again and the modified code is placed along with all modified documents in the software library.

Phase 5: Regression and system testing. In this phase, the regression test plan is executed to ensure that the modified software did not affect other related software features. System level testing is performed to ensure that the modified or newly-introduced features have been successfully incorporated into the new modified version of the software. System testing includes functional testing and interface testing. Once the system testing is completed and all reported errors have been fixed, the software is ready for acceptance testing.

Phase 6: Acceptance testing. This phase is performed to ensure that the code and documentation are acceptable to the client. Acceptance tests are executed on the full system including the modified software and the systems and subsystems with which it interfaces. Acceptance testing can be performed at the developer or client premises or both.

Phase 7: Delivery. This phase follows the approval of the software by the developer and client representatives.

9.4 SOFTWARE MAINTENANCE MANAGEMENT

Due to the complexity of software maintenance activities and the cost and effort needed to perform them, proper management of these activities is essential. As for any management process, maintenance management includes planning, organizing, staffing, leading, and controlling functions.

Planning of maintenance activities is needed to ensure that resources are being used efficiently and that timely actions are performed as prescribed in the schedule included in the plan. Project management and, in particular, software project management is presented in detail in Chapter 10. The IEEE Standard 1219 for software maintenance recommends a template for a software **maintenance plan**. The plan includes sections on organization and management, the maintenance process, maintenance reporting requirements, administrative requirements, and documentation requirements. The organization and management section describes the organizational structure of the maintenance team, scheduling priorities, resources and responsibilities, and the tools and techniques used to perform the maintenance tasks. The section on the maintenance process describes the actions that are performed during each of the seven phases of the software maintenance process. The section on reporting requirements describes how a software error or maintenance request is reported and how all related documents are communicated to the various maintenance personnel. The section on administrative requirements describes the standards and guidelines used for reporting, tracking and controlling, and ensuring the quality of the software maintenance activities. The final section on documentation requirements provides templates used to document all outcomes of the software maintenance process.

The proper execution of the maintenance activities requires an organizational structure that clearly identifies the responsibilities, roles, and authorities of each of the maintenance personnel. Three types of organizational structures, functional, project, and hybrid, can be adopted to perform maintenance activities. These structures and their advantages and disadvantages are described in Chapter 10. The functional organization divides the maintenance activities into functionally-related activities such as help desk, software modification, **configuration management**, integration and regression testing, and maintenance quality assurance. Software change includes modifying or extending requirements, specifications, design, and code. Similar to the development activities, maintenance activities can be either ongoing, such as configuration management and quality assurance, or executed during a specific phase such as the software modification activities. Each functionally-related group of activities is performed by a team of maintenance personnel. Figure 9.2 shows the functional organizational structure of a maintenance group in a software development company.

In addition to a proper and appropriate organizational structure, the maintenance groups must be staffed with personnel having the appropriate background. The execution of the various functionally-related activities requires various skill sets. For example, the help desk personnel require a different background and experiences than the quality assurance personnel.

The proper management of a maintenance team requires a motivating leadership style to ensure that team members feel that their maintenance work is appreciated. As we mentioned

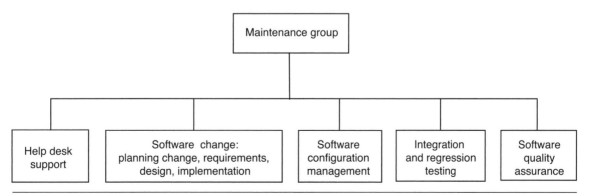

Figure 9.2 Functional organization of a maintenance group

in Chapter 8, maintenance personnel feel that they are doing secondary work fixing other colleagues' errors. A **maintenance team** leader must ensure that this myth is eliminated by motivating and appropriately rewarding team members.

A maintenance team manager must continuously monitor the execution of the maintenance project plan and schedule. Corrective actions must be taken when needed to ensure the timely execution of the plan and to assure adherence to the budget and quality requirements.

To emphasize the importance of maintenance and to deal with maintenance in a more specialized way, software maintenance is now viewed as a service. Software companies specializing in maintenance are emerging. Their services are being sought by software development companies and other client companies. Typically, a software maintenance company interfaces with various maintenance stakeholders to provide its services. These stakeholders include customers and users, software developers, suppliers and software vendors, outsourced help desk providers, and deployment and operations groups. To ensure timely and trustworthy delivery of **maintenance services**, it is important to provide clear definitions of the mechanisms for interfacing between a maintenance group and the other maintenance stakeholders. In addition, other interfaces exist among the various stakeholders. For example, an important interface exists between customers and users and the help desk providers.

9.5 SOFTWARE CONFIGURATION MANAGEMENT

A large number of objects are produced during the development and maintenance of a complex software system. To ensure that these objects are properly controlled and maintained during the software development and maintenance processes, a proper software configuration management (SCM) is needed. SCM is defined as a tool for tracking and controlling the development and evolution of a complex software system. SCM deals also with the control of multi-version software and software **change management** as part of the software evolution process.

SCM allows for reporting of software development and maintenance efforts more easily and the secure access to various software configuration items that are generated. Moreover, SCM provides a framework for the management of software changes, including planning, tracking, and controlling change activities. Additionally, SCM allows for ease of coordination among the software developers and maintenance personnel. Consequently, SCM enhances the overall productivity of the software organization by reducing the time to market (TTM) for software releases and fixes, leading to a decrease in the software production cost and better customer and user experiences.

SCM is normally supported by appropriate tools that are often integrated in the software development and maintenance environment used. A typical SCM tool provides functionalities dealing with software revision and version management, software build and release management, software change management, and software auditing. A secure access to these functionalities is required to meet the security and auditability requirements needed for these types of software tools.

Table 9.1 Template of a traceability matrix

Requirement	Specification	High-level design	Detailed design	Code	Unit test cases	System test cases	User manual	Maintenance request
...								

SCM is supported by automated tools that facilitate the various activities in SCM. Real SCM tools started to emerge in the 1990s. The main challenge of SCM tools is the seamless integration within the software development process and tools. A typical SCM tool includes a rich model for the various types of configuration items, consistent version control for the various item types, **configuration control**, scalable workspace management for distributed systems, scalable concurrent engineering, and process control and management.

A software **traceability matrix** is a useful tool for analyzing the cost and impact of an SCR. Ideally, this matrix is initially constructed at the requirements level and is continuously updated during the lifetime of the software. A software requirements traceability matrix allows the forward traceability for every requirement, including business rules, use cases, and non-functional requirements (NFRs). For each requirement element, the related detailed specifications, high-level and detailed design sections, code, unit and system level test cases, user manual sections, and maintenance requests are included in the matrix. As explained later in the chapter, all related elements are also called software configuration items. Additionally, the matrix allows for backward traceability. Every configuration item can be traced back to a software requirement. Table 9.1 shows a typical template of a software traceability matrix.

Planning for SCM can be considered an integral part of a project management plan. A standard for configuration management planning is defined by the IEEE. IEEE Standard 828 describes the minimum-required contents of an SCM plan. The standard recommends the inclusion of six sections in the SCM plan. SCM is a key process area in Level 2 of the capability maturity model (CMM). Table 9.2 shows the template of an SCM plan as recommended by the IEEE Standard 828.

In the following section, we concentrate on the SCM activities. These activities are included in Section 2 of the recommended standard for SCM plan template described in the previous section.

9.6 CONFIGURATION MANAGEMENT ACTIVITIES

A typical standard implementation of an SCM system in the software development and maintenance organization includes activities related to configuration item identification, configuration changes control, configuration items status accounting, software audits and reviews, interface control, and subcontractor and vendor control. Figure 9.3 shows the configuration management activities and the sub-activities of both **configuration identification** and configuration control.

Table 9.2 Content of an SCM plan

1. Introduction to the plan
   a. Overview of the software project for which SCM plan is developed
   b. Identification of the software configuration objects (SCI)
   c. Identification of other related software to be covered by the SCM, e.g., testing tools used
   d. Relationship of the SCM to the system configuration management
   e. Limitations for the application of the SCM plan related to the life cycle phases covered and other time and resource constraints
   f. Assumptions that affect the success of the SCM plan execution, including the availability of tools and the proper training of the involved personnel and stakeholders
2. Activities of the SCM plan
   a. Configuration identification
   b. Configuration control
   c. Status accounting
   d. Audits and reviews
   e. Interface control
   f. Subcontractor/vendor control
3. Management of the SCM plan
   a. Project organization, including all groups involved in performing SCM activities, the roles these groups play within the project, and relationships between these groups with respect to the execution of the SCM
   b. Responsibilities of people or group for each SCM activity are clearly identified
   c. Applicable policies, procedures, and guidelines that affect the SCM plan
4. Schedule
   a. Sequencing of SCM activities and interdependencies
   b. Relating SCM activities to software project plan activities and milestones
   c. Identifying milestones for SCM; baselines, launching the implementation of change control process, and starting the audit process
5. Resources
   a. Personnel needed to perform the SCM activities
   b. Techniques, software tools, and equipment needed
   c. Training requirements
6. Maintenance of the plan
   a. Monitoring the execution of the plan
   b. Procedures for requesting and approving changes to the plan
   c. Communication and implementation of changes to the plan

Item Identification

A software **configuration item** (CI) is any software-related item that is produced during the development and maintenance activities or used to support such activities. A CI can be a documented source code, design, specifications and requirements; data models, data design, and databases; executable code; software documentation, including user and installation manuals; plans for test project management and quality assurance; support elements, including compilers, operating systems, integrated development environments, computer-aided software engineering tools; and test environments.

The first activity in configuration management consists of identifying, naming, describing, and acquiring the configuration items. In addition, procedures for modifying, tracking, searching, and accessing the configuration items must be developed. Configuration items and their

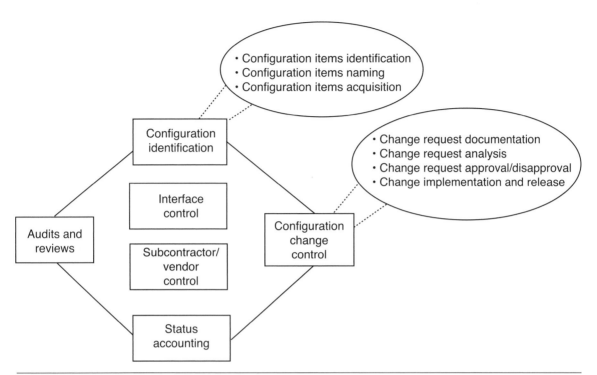

Figure 9.3 SCM activities

relations to the various project phases, activities, and their deliverables should be specified. This allows a proper control of the items that can be and need managed at each of the software development and maintenance activities. The identification of CIs can be performed by an elicitation process based on checklists, interviews, or brainstorming sessions. Once identified, CIs must be named and assigned a unique identifier. Naming conventions for the various types of configuration items must be adopted. Storage medium, their physical locations, and their access control mechanisms should be specified for each CI. Procedures and plans for ensuring resiliency and high availability of critical CIs must be developed. Retention and disposal policies must also be specified for the CIs. Plans for the acquisition of some CIs such as development and maintenance support tools must also be outlined.

Control and Change Management

Configuration control deals with procedures to manage changes to the various CIs identified for the software project. A change management procedure should specify how a change request can be initiated, reviewed, approved, tracked, and implemented. An SCR form should be developed and used any time a software change is needed. A software change refers to any of the four types of maintenance activities. The way a change request is handled can depend on the extent and impact of the change. Accordingly, the change management plan can provide variations for the handling of a change.

To initiate the process of software maintenance, an SCR form is filled out by the change originator. A change originator is the person or organization initiating the change. A typical SCR includes the identity of the initiator, date of initiation, the version or release implicated, the configuration item(s) affected, the change type, the reason for the change, the priority assigned for the request, and a description of the change. A change request number and a change status field are also assigned for tracking purposes. The change type indicates whether the change is a requirement, specification, design, or code change. The reason for the change indicates the main driver for the change, including new or modified business rules, legal or regulatory requirements, modified running environment, performance improvement, or fixing a software error.

Once submitted, a change request should be evaluated. The change management plan should specify the evaluation process and the criteria for evaluation and the review process needed for the evaluation. The criteria for evaluation can include technical aspects such as the impact of the change on other configuration items and its technical feasibility, and management aspects such as the impact on the available resources and its economical feasibility. Two outcomes of the evaluation are time estimates to make the necessary changes at all levels and to all affected configuration items, and an impact analysis related to the effect of the change on the schedule, resources, usability and, other non-functional aspects of the software such as security, maintainability, and performance.

After reviewing the evaluation of the requested change, a decision on whether to approve or disapprove the change request is made. A configuration control board (CCB) is normally responsible for making such decisions. Depending on the extent and impact of the requested change, approval of CCBs at varying levels of authority might be needed. A CCB can include one or more maintenance personnel, depending on the complexity and criticality of the configuration items for which the CCB is responsible. The configuration management plan should include the process for dealing with request changes for the configuration items and the CCBs involved and the level of authorities.

Once approved, the activities described in the configuration management plan for implementing the software changes are performed. For tracking purposes, each new version of the software should include a version identifier, the related change request numbers, the affected configuration items, the change verification date, and the release and deployment dates. The activities performed during the release and deployment of the new version is also described in the release plan included in the configuration management plan.

Status Accounting

The configuration management plan should include activities related to the periodic reporting on the status of the CI with respect to changes performed in separate releases. The plan also provides a template for the generated status reports and specifies the levels of security needed for storing, communicating, and processing the reports. For each CI, the report should include a reference to the changes and change requests and their status. These activities are normally performed within an automated configuration management tool.

Audits and Reviews

A **configuration audit** assesses the level of conformance of a configuration item to the specified functional and NFRs. An audit can be performed periodically during the development and maintenance of a software product. However, the most critical audit is the one performed prior to establishing a new software release baseline. The IEEE Standard 610 identifies two types of audits: the functional configuration audit (FCA) and the physical configuration audit (PCA). An FCA is conducted to assess whether a configuration item has been developed properly according to the stated functional and NFRs, including performance and security requirements. A configuration audit is typically conducted to provide an input to a review process. A PCA assesses the conformance of a configuration item to the technical documentation that defines it in the configuration management plan. In addition, PCA checks whether all needed configuration items with the correct versions are included in the software baseline to be released and deployed.

Once all configuration items have been audited and reviewed, a new software version is ready for release and deployment. The release control and deployment plan of the configuration plan is then executed.

Interface Control

When dealing with complex and embedded software that requires interfacing with outsourced or off-the-shelf hardware and software components, the configuration plan should ensure that proper coordination exists between the internally developed configuration items and the external items. The plan should first identify all such external configuration items. Each interface item should be described and the procedures for approving it and integrating it within the new software release should be specified. Each external CI should be handled similarly to the internally developed CIs with respect to status accounting, auditing, and reviewing. A CCB with clear responsibilities and authorities can also be assigned to deal with external interfaces.

Subcontractor and Vendor Control

Complex software can require off-the-shelf software components or software components to be outsourced to external software companies. The SCM plan should clarify the activities needed to control the proper acceptance, integration, and deployment of the outsourced or purchased software within the overall software system. The SCM plan should first identify the external CIs that are part of the project CIs and should specify the procedures to monitor the compliance of the external CI to the internal project requirements. In addition, the plan should specify the procedures for change control, configuration audits, and reviews related to these external CIs. For purchased software components, the procedure for dealing with proprietary software should be specified.

9.7 SOFTWARE MAINTENANCE TECHNIQUES

Many techniques have been developed to assist in the maintenance of software systems. There are techniques that deal with the major software deliverables and aim at enhancing the understandability and maintainability of the software. Examples of these techniques are reverse engineering, design recovery, **restructuring**, and **reengineering**. Other techniques help in the proper testing and integration of software modules that have been modified. Examples of these techniques are regression testing and debugging techniques. Tools supporting these software maintenance techniques have been developed and are being used to automate the maintenance process. The maintenance of software is performed continuously until it is deemed unfeasible due to the complexity of the software and the negative side effects that are attributed to any, even minor, software maintenance. At this point management makes a decision regarding retiring the software.

Reverse Engineering and Design Recovery

The term reverse engineering has its origins in hardware systems. It refers to the extraction or deciphering of a digital hardware component. Viewing the software like it was a black box, reverse engineering leads to the discovery of its functional specification and the deconstruction of the software.

The inverse of reverse engineering is forward engineering. The systematic process for producing software that we have studied in this book is a forward software engineering process. Forward engineering is based on the use of techniques, tools, and standards for producing software products starting with the requirements specifications. In contrast, in reverse engineering, we start from a finished software product and we move backward step by step until we obtain the requirements specifications that are met by the subject software.

Reverse engineering can be beneficial for many reasons. Many existing **legacy software** systems lack effective and up-to-date documentation. The software is hard to maintain because the specification and design documents are either nonexistent or were not updated. These problems can be avoided if a configuration management system is in place. Reverse engineering is a technique that aims at making the software product more maintainable. As a result of a reverse engineering process, the software has a documented design and documented requirements specifications. Because these documents reflect the current state of the software, they can be considered collectively as a workable and maintainable baseline that can be saved in a configuration management system. In general, the aim of reverse engineering is to examine existing software rather than modifying or improving it. However, the results of the reverse engineering process can be used to make software maintenance decisions related to preventive, perfective, or adaptive maintenance.

Other reverse engineering techniques can be used to obtain the specification and design of executable software as a black box without having access to the code itself. This process can help in program understanding and producing user manuals or input/output specifications. These techniques rely on the synthesis of higher-level abstractions such as design specification by observing and collecting execution traces. However, in this case, there is no guarantee that we have observed all possible traces and, therefore, the synthesized higher-level abstraction might be incomplete.

One form of reverse engineering is **re-documentation**. After obtaining a higher-level abstraction, the existing documentation might have to be revised or re-written to reflect the reverse engineered abstraction. Moreover, the re-documentation can be obtained directly from the lower-level abstraction using some automated tools; for example, obtaining finite state machines (FSMs) from source code. Another form of reverse engineering is design recovery that starts from either executable or source code and documentation to obtain all information related to the design of the software and its main functionalities. Design recovery is needed when the design documents are non-existent, out of date, or poorly developed. Recovered design artifacts allow a new designer joining the development team to understand the current software design. Understanding the design allows the team to make informative design and maintenance decisions such as restructuring or reengineering.

Restructuring and Reengineering

As a result of the reverse engineering process, the maintenance team can make decisions related to the extent of software changes needed. Unlike reverse engineering, restructuring leads to changes to the current software configuration items. Restructuring can occur at lower levels of abstractions, including code and design. Restructuring the source code refers to changes to the control structures used to improve the code efficiency and readability. Restructuring the software design refers to changes to the high-level design and the modules interrelationships intended to improve the coupling and cohesion of the software design in addition to enhancing its reusability. Restructuring code and design are often used in preventive and perfective maintenance changes.

After examining the reverse engineered software, a decision to pursue and plan for a more extensive maintenance process can be made. The software reengineering (renovation or rejuvenation) process results in obtaining new software abstractions at all levels. Starting from new requirements specifications, a forward software engineering process is started leading to new lower levels of abstractions, including new design and new code. The new reengineered requirements include requirements that already exist in the current system in addition to requirements that are needed but are not met in the existing system.

Although the effort needed differs, restructuring and reengineering are two maintenance techniques that can be used to enhance the functional and non-functional characteristics of an existing software product. Therefore, they are mainly triggered by perfective, preventive, and adaptive maintenance requests.

After software goes through extensive maintenance activities of the four types, it might be possible that new change requests are not accommodated without serious side effects on the existing aging software. Specifically, adaptive maintenance requests, in which the software has to accommodate new operating environments, might not be feasibly accommodated. In this case, management can decide to retire the software. In practice, the software company would be working on the development of a new system in parallel to servicing and maintaining the software being retired.

Regression Testing

After making a change to the source code as a result of a maintenance activity, the modified software should be tested. The complete testing of the software is expensive and time consuming. Regression testing techniques decreases the amount of software modules tested. Only potentially affected software components are tested prior to being integrated and delivered in a new software. Many techniques have been developed for determining the most appropriate test cases that can detect if any new errors have been introduced. Proper regression testing requires careful configuration management and coordination when dealing with a large maintenance team who is involved with multiple change requests. One specification-based black box regression testing technique requires the execution of test cases that are related to functionalities that, in case of failures, would put the offered services at high risk. Other techniques examine the source code using data flow analysis to determine all possible effects of a modified code on other unchanged modules in the software. Graves, et al. provides an empirical study of such techniques.

SUMMARY

After being developed and deployed in the market, a software system has to be maintained. Maintenance activities are triggered by change requests that originate from the various software stakeholders. There are four types of maintenance activities: corrective, preventive, perfective, and adaptive. Each type has its own complexity and scope. The IEEE Standard 1219 describes a process for managing and performing software maintenance activities consisting of seven phases, including problem identification and prioritization, analysis, design, implementation and integration, regression testing, acceptance testing, and delivery. Maintenance activities are managed most effectively using an SCM system. An SCM plan whose template is recommended in IEEE Standard 828 specifies how the software configuration items are handled during software maintenance. Configuration control describes the procedure to control and manage changes starting from the initiation of the change request to its review, approval, and implementation. Maintenance activities can require the application of reverse engineering and design recovery techniques prior to the use of restructuring and reengineering techniques.

KEY TERMS

adaptive maintenance	design recovery	re-documentation
change management	legacy software	reengineering
configuration audit	maintenance management	regression testing
configuration control	maintenance plan	restructuring
configuration identification	maintenance services	reverse engineering
configuration item	maintenance team	traceability matrix
configuration management	perfective maintenance	unscheduled maintenance
corrective maintenance	preventive maintenance	

REVIEW QUESTIONS

1. List the main activities in SCM.
2. List the types of software maintenance.
3. Provide an example of each type of software maintenance.
4. Describe the phases of the software maintenance process.
5. List the functions of a software maintenance group manager.
6. List the main parts of an SCM plan.
7. What is a configuration management audit?
8. What are the software maintenance techniques?
9. What is the main difference between design recovery, restructuring, and reengineering?

EXERCISES

1. Obtain an SCM checklist from the Web and assess its completeness with respect to the standard activities related to SCM.
2. Obtain a software maintenance checklist from the Web and assess its completeness with respect to the maintenance activities covering the seven phases of the software maintenance process.
3. Obtain an SCM plan from the Web and assess its completeness with respect to the IEEE standard for configuration management planning.
4. Obtain an SCM audit from the Web and assess its completeness.

5. Consider a case of a software system that was reengineered. Discuss the rationale for deciding to reengineer.

BIBLIOGRAPHY

Books

April, A., and A. Abran. *Software Maintenance Management: Evaluation and Continuous Improvement*, New York: John Wiley and Sons, 2008.

Arthur, L. *Software Evolution: The Software Maintenance Challenge,* New York: John Wiley and Sons, 1988.

Bennett, K. *Software Maintenance: A Tutorial, in Software Engineering*, Dorfman and Thayer, eds., New York: IEEE Computer Society Press, 2000.

Grubb, P., and A. Takang. *Software Maintenance: Concepts and Practice*, Singapore: World Scientific, 2003.

Pigoski, T. *Practical Software Maintenance*, New York: John Wiley and Sons, 1997.

Wills, L., and P. Newcomb, eds., *Reverse Engineering*, New York: Kluwer, 1996.

Papers

April, A., et al. "Software maintenance maturity model: a model and its architecture." 8th European Conference on Software Maintenance and Reengineering, 243–248, Tampere, Finland, March 24–26, 2004.

Banker, R., et al. "Software errors and maintenance management." Information Technology and Management, vol. 3, 25–41, 2002.

Bennett, K., and V. Rajlich. "Software maintenance and evolution: A roadmap." International Conference on Software Engineering, Proceedings of the Conference on the Future of Software Engineering, 73–87, Limerick, Ireland, 2000.

Chen, Y., and R. Probert. "A risk-based regression test selection strategy." 161–162, International Symposium on Software Requirements Engineering (ISSRE), 2003.

Chikofsky, E., and J. Cross. "Reverse engineering and design recovery a taxonomy." 13–17, IEEE Software, January 1990.

Estublier, J. "Software configuration management: A roadmap." International Conference on Software Engineering, Proceedings of the Conference on the Future of Software Engineering, 279–289, Limerick, Ireland, 2000.

Graves, T., et al. "An empirical study of regression test selection techniques." 188–197, 20th International Conference on Software Engineering, Kyoto, Japan, 1998.

Merant. "The benefits of software configuration management." White paper, Merant, 2001.

Niessink, F., and H. Van Vliet. "Software maintenance from a service perspective." *Journal of Software Maintenance: Research and Practice*, 12(2): 103–120, March/April 2000.

Royce, W. "Managing the development of large software systems." 1–9, *Proc. IEEE WESCON*, August 1970.

Saleh, K., and A. Boujarwah. "Communications software reverse engineering: A semi-automatic approach." *Journal of Information and Software Technology,* vol. 38 379–390, March 1996.

Westfall, L. "Software configuration management audits." The Westfall Team, www.westfall-team.com, 8 July 2006.

Saleh, K., R. Probert, and K. Al-Saqabi. "Recovery of CFSM-based protocol and service design from protocol execution traces." *Journal of Information and Software Technology*, 41(11/12): 839–852, August 1999.

Software Reverse Engineering, Special issue, *Journal of Systems and Software*, vol. 77, 2005.

Zhang, L., et al. "Identifying use cases in source code." *Journal of Systems and Software*, 79(11): 1588–1598 November 2006.

Standards

IEEE Std 828-1998, IEEE Standard for Software Configuration Management Plans.

IEEE Std 1028, IEEE Standard for Software Reviews, IEEE, 1997.

IEEE Std 1042-1993, IEEE Guide to Software Configuration Management.

IEEE Std 1074, IEEE Standard for Developing Software Life Cycle Processes, IEEE 1997.

IEEE Std 1219, IEEE Standard for Software Maintenance, IEEE, 1998.

Software Project Management

Software project management encompasses a set of activities that are performed during the phases of a typical software development project. The software project manager must continuously ensure that the software product is developed according to the client's business requirements, within the allocated time, and within budget. Many software projects fail because of poor management. The manager could have overlooked one or more of the crucial elements of project management. These elements include **risk engineering** and management, human resource management, effort and cost estimation, project monitoring, tracking and control, time and financial management, and the proper use of project management tools. The manager must develop a management plan to follow closely during the execution of the project. This plan must be monitored and necessary modifications made by the manager to ensure the timely delivery of a quality software product.

Learning Outcomes

In this chapter you will learn:
- Basic terminology in software project management
- Project management activities
- Software metrics for project management
- Cost estimation techniques
- Risk engineering activities
- Project scheduling and tracking techniques
- IEEE standard for the software project management plan document

10.1 PROJECT, PEOPLE, PROCESSES, AND PRODUCTS

Software project management is focused on the proper management of people and processes to enable the smooth execution of the project plan and the delivery of a high-quality product. The four main elements of software project management include (1) the **project** itself, (2) the **people** working on the project, (3) the **processes** used to produce the project **deliverables**, and (4) the final **product** delivered to the client. Software projects fail because of a deficiency in dealing with one or more elements. For example, an unrealistic project plan, the recruitment of people who lack the necessary knowledge and skills, inappropriate processes and tools, and a misunderstanding of the product requirements are some typical reasons for project failures. The Standish Group, a software market research organization, reported that in 2002, one-third of software projects were completed on budget with all features and that about one-eighth were complete failures.

A **project plan** is an important deliverable that must be developed carefully. In this chapter, a standard template for a software project management plan is described. Once written, the plan must be executed by the project manager. People involved in the execution of the plan should be well-versed. Progress of the plan activities must be closely monitored by the manager to ensure timely execution. Any delays in the execution of the plan and any foreseen or unforeseen risks that arise during the project progress must be detected. Proper project progress monitoring tools must be used to ensure the early detection of problems. Corrective actions must be taken by the manager to ensure the timely delivery of the product. A review of the project plan and its timeline can be needed as a result of a corrective action.

Obviously, people are the most important resources for the execution of a project. Engaging the proper people to perform the prescribed tasks according to the project plan is important. Training people on the proper use of tools and techniques is essential. Once engaged in the project, management must ensure that people are treated well and coached to ensure retention and continuity. Lines of communication and reporting must be well-defined to ensure a frictionless environment. Transparent and continuous monitoring of people involved in the project is critical for the early detection of problem symptoms.

Processes and phases that shape the project plan must be understood and defined because they determine deliverables and the efforts involved in their execution. An appropriate software life cycle model must be adapted for the project and the development team needs to be knowledgeable regarding that model. Industry-proven tools supporting the proper execution of the processes must be used and people trained in the most effective use of those tools. Also, industry standards must be understood and followed according to the software requirements. Metrics must be properly collected during the execution of the project phases. They can be used for enhancing future project plans and for estimating the cost of future development efforts.

The proper interactions among people and processes, using a feasible project plan, lead to the production of a high-quality product delivered on time and within budget. Projects can fail and delivery dates can be delayed because of the improper use of tools and techniques prescribed in the project plan and adapted as part of the life cycle model.

10.2 PROJECT MANAGEMENT ACTIVITIES

Once the software requirements are determined and elicited, the scope of the software project is defined and the project is initiated. The project planning process starts by selecting the appropriate development process and its phases, activities, and deliverables, and the software project plan is developed accordingly. The project plan includes a schedule of activities and **milestones**, and their respective resource allocations. A risk management plan is also an inclusive part of the project plan. It includes all anticipated risks the software project can face and specifies how to handle the risk should it happen during the execution of the project. The project plan should also indicate the quality assurance and management requirements related to the project as well as the precise description of the product being delivered. Additionally, the plan should describe how the project plan is executed and managed.

Once the project plan is approved by upper management, it is launched and the planned activities begin. The activities are monitored using the reporting and tracking methods specified in the management **control plan**. Controls are activated to detect any deviation from the plan and its schedule.

While the project is being executed, all measurement collection and quality management activities occur as stipulated in the plan. As the project is progressing, **quality control** must ensure that all deliverables meet the needed quality requirements. In addition, all basic project management activities are performed, including human resource management and review of the project schedule, among many other activities.

Once the activities of the project are concluded according to the plan, an official approval is obtained from the client after verifying the acceptance criteria stipulated in the product acceptance plan. The product is then shipped to the client. At this point, the project development phase ends. All project and product measurements are concluded, analyzed, and archived. Lessons drawn from the project are also documented.

Table 10.1 shows the software project management activities at project startup, during the execution, and at closeout.

Table 10.1 Project management activities

	Project management activities	
During project startup	• Estimation • Staffing • Resource acquisition • Training	• Developing the work plan: activities, schedule, resource, and budget allocation
During project execution	• Quality assurance control • Reporting and tracking • Metrics collection • Risk monitoring and mitigation • Reviews and audits • Configuration management • Process improvement	• Budget control • Schedule control • Requirements control • Verification and validation • Documentation • Problem resolution • Subcontractor management
During project closeout	• Product acceptance • Staff reassignment • User training • Product installation	• Archiving • Post-mortem evaluation and assessment • Integration and conversion

In the remainder of the chapter, **software metrics** and cost estimation techniques, software risk management, project scheduling and tracking, and a standard template for a software project management plan are discussed.

10.3 ESTIMATION TECHNIQUES AND SOFTWARE METRICS

One of the most critical activities of a software project manager during the project startup phase is to estimate the effort needed to complete the project tasks. Estimations affect many resource aspects. Financial and human resource decisions rely on **estimations** of the needed effort to produce the software. These estimations must be accurate and realistic. The common problems with estimation are either related to the overestimation or the underestimation of the effort needed. In general, the tendency in the software industry is to underestimate the effort and that leads to the realization during the project execution that the project milestones cannot be met. In that case, the manager has to review the project schedule and take the necessary control measures to keep the project on track as stipulated in the software risk management plan. In addition, the consequences of underestimation lead to low employee morale, decline in reputation, and a stressful work environment. On the other hand, overestimation can lead to losing the bid or making poor decisions related to outsourcing parts of the project versus developing it internally.

To estimate the effort, managers can use informal approaches, relying on one or more expert opinions or their own experiences or those of their peers or, perhaps, the opinions of hired consultants. Another approach is to use a decomposition process to break down the project into functional components and ask potential developers of these components to provide their own estimates based on prior experiences with similar components. The estimated effort is then the total of these factors.

Estimations can be performed at the macro-level or the micro-level. Macro-level estimation techniques consider the software product as a whole. On the other hand, micro-level estimation techniques attempt to decompose the product into the smallest possible components and then estimate for those components. Although micro-level estimations require more time to produce, they tend to produce more accurate estimates and smaller variations between the estimated values and the real values.

Estimation techniques can be classified under two broad categories. The first category includes black box-based or **requirements-based estimation** techniques. Estimations are obtained once the software **project scope** is clearly defined in terms of the required functionalities (see Chapter 3). The widely used estimation techniques, such as function points and use case points, are in this category. The second category includes techniques that are based on the projected size of the final software product in terms of number of **lines of code** (LOC). COCOMO is a widely-used technique in this category.

Estimation techniques could also be specification-based or implementation-based. In both techniques, the size of the project is the main factor. However, the determination of size differs. In **specification-based techniques**, the size depends on the interface specifications; and in implementation-based techniques, the size depends on the expected size of the code needed to implement the software.

In general, most **empirical estimation** models that are based on the size of the project use the following mathematical equation to compute an estimate of the effort (E) needed in person-months:

$$E = (a + (b \times \text{Size}^c)) \times F$$

where a, b and c are model coefficients that are empirically obtained, Size is the estimated size of the project in kilo (thousand) lines of code (KLOC) and F is a product of other factors that can influence the project estimates. In the Bailey-Basili model for example, the equation is:

$$E = (5.5 + (0.73 \times \text{Size}^{1.16}) \times F$$

The same general equation is also used to estimate the effort for projects where the Size is estimated in terms of function points needed. In the model introduced by Kemerer, for example, the equation is:

$$E = (-37 + 0.96 \times \text{Size}) \times F$$

Clearly, the product of factors F will play a role in differentiating among projects, depending on their complexities.

Function Points

Function point (FP) metrics, introduced by Allan Albrecht in 1979, are specification-based metrics that are used to estimate the effort needed to develop a software system. Because they rely on the requirements specifications, function points reflect the user's view of the system being developed and, therefore, they are as stable as the requirements themselves. Function points are implementation independent. Computing the number of function points, also called function point count, for the project is independent of the design choices taken, the tools used, or the programming language utilized to implement the system.

According to FP metrics, the complexity of software and the effort needed to develop it are a function of the number and type of five kinds of functional components that can be obtained and assessed at the requirements specifications phase. These five functional components include:

1. Internal files corresponding to the database files that are created and maintained within the application
2. External files corresponding to the files that are owned and maintained by other applications but used by the application
3. External inputs corresponding to the inputs that affect the control flow and internal logic of the application leading to the creation and maintenance of data

4. External outputs corresponding to the data leaving the application to different output devices, files, or external systems
5. External inquiries corresponding to simple user queries resulting in responses to them

The first two types of components are referred to as data-based components and the other three as transaction-based components. These functional components should also be classified under one of the three complexity levels: simple, average, and complex. Simple internal and external files include few records with simple structures. Complex internal and external files have a large number of records with complex structures. External inputs is information from the outside to the inside, originating from user interfaces or from other applications. Simple external inputs include control information and simple business information affecting one internal file. Complex external inputs contain business information originating from the outside to the inside and triggering the update of two or more internal files. Complex external outputs refer to many data subsets across many files. The complexity of an external inquiry is obtained by taking the greater of the complexities of the input and output parts of the inquiry. Various weighting factors are then used for each of the five types of functional components and for each of the three complexity levels. Table 10.2 shows the weighting factors for the three complexities of the five functional components.

The number of unadjusted function points (UFP) is obtained by summing up all factors assigned to an identified component according to its complexity.

Table 10.2 Weighting factors for function point metrics

	Simple	Average	Complex
External input	3	4	6
External output	4	5	7
User inquiry	3	4	6
External file	7	10	15
Internal file	5	7	10

Example 10.1

Table 10.3 shows an example of the use of function point estimation. Suppose the software being developed has 1 external input, 3 external outputs, and 1 user inquiry, all of simple complexities; the number of unadjusted function points would be $3*1 + 4*3 + 3*1 = 18$. In addition, it has 2 external inputs and 1 user inquiry of average complexity, and 1 external input, 1 external output, 1 internal file, and 3 external files of high complexity. Similar computations should be performed for the remaining average and complex components. The total number of unadjusted function points is: $(3*1 + 4*3 + 3*1) + (4*2 + 4*1) + (6*1 + 7*1 + 15*3 + 10*1) = 98$ UFPs.

(continues)

Example 10.1 (*continued*)

Table 10.3 Example of function point metrics

	Simple			Average			Complex		
	Weight factor	How many?	Product	Weight factor	How many?	Product	Weight factor	How many?	Product
External input	3	1	3	4	2	8	6	1	6
External output	4	3	12	5	0	0	7	1	7
User inquiry	3	1	3	4	1	4	6	0	0
External file	7	0	0	10	0	0	15	3	45
Internal file	5	0	0	7	0	0	10	1	10
Total	18			12			68		
Number of FPs	18 + 12 + 68 = 98 function points								

To take the context and the type of software project into account, Albrecht has introduced a list of 14 technical factors that influence the effort needed to complete the project. The product of these factors is then used to adjust the number of function points. Each of these factors must be rated on a scale 0 to 5. A rating of 0 means that the factor is irrelevant or has no influence, and a rating of 5 means that the factor is essential and has a strong influence. The 14 technical factors are shown in Table 10.4.

A rating from 0 to 5 is assigned to each factor. Their sum is computed to obtain a value for S. The overall complexity factor CF is then computed using the equation: $CF = 0.65 + 0.01 \times S$. CF is within the range 0.65 to 1.35. The number of adjusted function points (AFP), then, is $UFP \times CF$.

Table 10.4 Technical factors affecting the complexity of software projects

1. Reliable backup and recovery needed	8. Real-time update needed
2. Data communications needed	9. Complexity of the interfaces
3. Distributed functions required	10. Complexity of the processing
4. Performance required	11. Reusability
5. Heavily used configuration	12. Ease of installation
6. Real-time data entry needed	13. Multiple sites
7. Ease of use	14. Easy to change

To map the number of adjusted function points (f) to the needed effort in person-months, in 1995, Jones proposed a first-order estimation as a function of f and an exponent j to compute the effort in person-months using the equation: $m = f^{3*j}/27$ person-months. j depends on the type of the software application involved and the capabilities and expertise of the development team and varies from 0.39 to 0.48. In Example 10.1, if we consider $j = 0.43$, and use UCF = 1, the number of person-months is 13.71. A programming language dependent on mapping from function points to LOC was published by Quality Software Management. For example, the average number of LOC per function point in the C and Java programming languages are 162 and 63, respectively. The fact that less code needs to be written in Java is due to the extensive use of the application programming interface and libraries in Java programs. We can use these averages to estimate the size of the software that needs to be developed in terms of the number of LOC. In Example 10.1, the estimated number of lines is approximately 15 KLOC of C code or 6 KLOC of Java code.

An extension to the function point metrics called **feature point** metrics was introduced to deal with the algorithmic complexity of the software system under development. The number of algorithms in the software is determined. Each algorithm is assigned a weight of 3. The number of feature points is then computed as the sum of the function points and the total weights of all identified algorithms.

Another approach the manager can take to reduce the risk of underestimation is to produce estimates using various techniques and performed by experts. Differences between the estimated efforts can then be reconciled using statistical analysis techniques. For example, if the three estimates, E_{Low}, E_{High}, and E_{Mid} are obtained, such that $E_{Low} < E_{Mid} < E_{High}$, the value for E that can be used is computed using the equation:

$$E = (E_{Low} + 4 \times E_{Mid} + E_{High}) / 6$$

Use Case Points

The **use case point** (UCP) is a software effort estimation technique that was introduced by Gustav Kamer in 1993. It is an extension of the function point method based on the use cases existing in the use case model of a software system.

In UCP metrics, actors and use cases are classified under three categories: simple, average, and complex. For example, an external system interacting with the system using defined application programming interfaces is typically a simple actor. External systems interacting with the system using some standard protocols and data stores are typical actors of average complexity. A user interacting with the software using graphical-user interface components, such as forms and dialog boxes, is considered a complex actor.

The complexity assessment of a use case is based on the number of transactions or steps that are included in the use case description. These steps are included in the normal and alternative flow of events in the use case description. A use case is classified as simple if the number of transactions does not exceed 3. Similarly, an average complexity use case includes 4 to 7 transactions and a complex use case includes more than 7 transactions. Factors are assigned to the various complexities of both actors and use cases. The factors for both actors and use cases are shown in Table 10.5.

The unadjusted actor weight (UAW) is the sum of complexity values assigned to each actor. Similarly, the unadjusted use case weight (UUCW) is the sum of complexity values assigned to each use case. The total unadjusted use case point (UUCP) is the sum of UAW and UUCW. The number of adjusted use case points (AUCP) is computed by multiplying the UUCP with the product of two adjustment factors: the **technical complexity** factor (TCF) and the environmental factor (EF).

The TCF is obtained using the equation: $TCF = 0.6 + (0.01 \times TF)$, where TF is the sum of all the weighted values computed for each of the 13 technical factors listed in Table 10.6. Technical complexity factors are mainly related to the product and its complexity in terms of functional and non-functional requirements (NFRs). Each factor has its own weight, and a value ranging from 0 to 5 is assigned to a factor, depending on the technical complexity of the corresponding factor. For example, the technical factor related to the level of security requirements

Table 10.5 Actor and use case complexity values

Actor type	Value
Simple	1
Average	2
Complex	3

Use case type	Value
Simple: ≤ 3 transactions	5
Average: between 4 and 7 transactions	10
Complex: > 7 transactions	15

Table 10.6 Technical complexity and environmental factors for UCP metrics

Technical factor	Weight
Distributed system	2
Performance requirements	1
End user efficiency	1
Internal processing	1
Reusability of code	1
Installation ease	0.5
Usability requirements	0.5
Portability requirements	2
Changeability requirements	1
Concurrency	1
Security requirements	1
Direct access to 3rd party	1
User training facility	1

Environmental factor	Weight
Familiarity with project	1.5
Application experience	0.5
Object-oriented experience	1
Lead analyst capabilities	0.5
Motivation	1
Stability of requirements	2
Part-time staff	−1
Programming language difficulty	−1

is given a weight of 1. If the security requirements are complex, a high value of 5 is assigned to that factor yielding a weighted value of 5. It is left to the reader to compute, as an exercise, the smallest and the largest possible values of TCF.

Similarly, the EF is obtained using the equation:

$$EF = 1.4 - (0.03 \times ENVF)$$

where ENVF is the sum of all the weighted values computed for each of the 8 **environmental factors** listed in Table 10.6. Environmental factors are related to the people, process, and project aspects of the software. Each factor has its own weight, and a value ranging from 0 to 5 is assigned to a factor, depending on its relevance. For example, the stability of requirements is given the highest weight of 2 and if the requirements are felt to be volatile or not well-defined, a high value of 5 is assigned to it, making the weighted value 10. It is left to the reader to compute, as an exercise, the smallest and the largest possible values of EF.

The equation to obtain the number of adjusted use case points (AUCP) is:

$$AUCP = (UAW + UUCW) \times TCF \times EF$$

To obtain the estimated effort in person-hours needed to develop the software according to the UCP metrics, Kamer stated that 20 person-hours are needed for each use case point. However, other refinements and empirical studies of the UCP technique suggested a range between 15 and 30 person-hours per UCP. Assuming we use p person-hours per UCP and a work day of h hours, the number of work days would then be: $((p \times AUCP)/h)$ days.

COCOMO

The COnstructive COst MOdel (COCOMO) was first introduced by Barry Boehm in 1981 to provide an estimate of the effort in person-months needed to develop a software product. COCOMO is based on the estimation of the size of the software in terms of the number of lines of code. There are three versions of COCOMO with varying levels of detail. The basic COCOMO provides an estimate of the effort as a function of an estimate of the program size. In the intermediate COCOMO, the estimate is a function of both the program size and an effort adjustment factor (EAF) related to a set of contextual cost drivers. The detailed COCOMO allows for adjustment factors for the phases of the software development life cycle model.

The formulae used in the basic COCOMO model are:

$$E = a \times Size^b$$
$$D = c \times E^d$$
$$P = E/D$$

where E is the effort in person-months, D is the development time in chronological months, Size is the estimated number of KLOC, and P is the estimated number of persons needed.

Example 10.2

Assume that a software requirement based on the use case model includes only the use case Place Order described in Table 3.5. This use case is complex because the number of steps exceeds 7. There are also 3 actors. The buyer is a complex actor, and the warehouse and accounting are both simple actors. Hence the UAW is 5 and the UUCW is 15, making the UUCP = 20. The values assigned to the 13 technical complexity factors and 8 environmental factors are shown in Table 10.7. Then the TF = 38.5, and the TCF is $0.6 + (0.01 \times 38.5) = 0.985$. Also, the ENVF is 21.5 and the EF is $1.4 - (0.03 \times 21.5) = 0.755$. AUCP is $20 \times TCF \times EF = 14.87$. Assuming the estimated productivity is 25 person-hours per UCP and 7-hour work day, the effort in work days would be:

$$((25 \times 14.87)/7) = 53.11 \text{ days}$$

Table 10.7 Values of technical complexity and environmental factors

Technical factor	Weight	Value	Weighted value
Distributed system	2	3	6
Performance requirements	1	4	4
End user efficiency	1	4	4
Internal processing	1	1	1
Reusability of code	1	2	2
Installation ease	0.5	4	2
Usability requirements	0.5	5	2.5
Portability requirements	2	4	8
Changeability requirements	1	4	4
Concurrency	1	1	1
Security requirements	1	4	4
Direct access to 3rd party	1	0	0
User training facility	1	0	0
Total			38.5

Environmental factor	Weight	Value	Weighted value
Familiarity with project	1.5	4	6
Application experience	0.5	4	2
Object-oriented experience	1	3	3
Lead analyst capabilities	0.5	3	1.5
Motivation	1	4	4
Stability of requirements	2	4	8
Part-time staff	−1	0	0
Programming language difficulty	−1	3	−3
Total			21.5

Table 10.8 Coefficients a, b, c and d used in the basic COCOMO model

Product type	a	b	c	d
Organic	2.4	1.05	2.5	0.38
Semi-detached	3.0	1.12	2.5	0.35
Embedded	3.6	1.2	2.5	0.32

The coefficients a, b, c, and d are listed in Table 10.8. Depending on the type of the software product, various coefficient values are used. Three types of software products are considered in COCOMO: organic, semi-detached, and embedded. Organic products are relatively small and simple. Semi-detached products are average in size and simplicity. Embedded products are complex in the sense that they must meet the constraints of their embedding environment and interfaces, including software and hardware.

Example 10.3

For a given project involving the development of a semi-detached software, it was estimated that the size of the software in KLOC is 100. The estimated effort in person-months needed to develop the software product is computed as follows:

$$E = 3 \times 100^{1.12} = 521 \text{ person-months}$$
$$D = 2.5 \times 521^{0.35} = 8.93 \text{ months}$$
$$P \text{ is } E/D = 58.36 \text{ persons}$$

The formula used in the intermediate COCOMO model is:

$$E = a \times Size^b \times EAF$$

where coefficients a and b are given in Table 10.9, Size is the estimated number of KLOC for the project and EAF is the effort adjustment factor computed using the cost drivers rating table.

In the intermediate COCOMO model, the estimated effort is adjusted by considering 15 factors that can influence the development effort. These factors are related to the attributes of the product, the hardware used, the personnel working on the project, and the development environment and methodologies used. Each factor is rated on a scale ranging from very low to extra high. An effort multiplier is assigned for every attribute. Table 10.10 shows the 15 attributes and the effort multiplier for each rating.

The effort adjustment factor (EAF) is the product of all effort multipliers assigned to a particular project. The EAF makes the LOC-based estimation dependent also on the particular context in which the project is being developed.

Table 10.9 Table of coefficients used in the intermediate COCOMO model

Product type	a	b
Organic	3.2	1.05
Semi-detached	3.0	1.12
Embedded	2.8	1.2

Table 10.10 Table cost drivers ratings used in the intermediate COCOMO model

Cost drivers	Very low	Low	Nominal	High	Very high	Extra high
Product attributes						
Required software reliability	0.75	0.88	1.00	1.15	1.40	
Size of application database		0.94	1.00	1.08	1.16	
Complexity of the product	0.70	0.85	1.00	1.15	1.30	1.65
Hardware attributes						
Run-time performance constraints			1.00	1.11	1.30	1.66
Memory constraints			1.00	1.06	1.21	1.56
Volatility of the virtual machine		0.87	1.00	1.15	1.30	
Required turnabout time		0.87	1.00	1.07	1.15	
Personnel attributes						
Analyst capability	1.46	1.19	1.00	0.86	0.71	
Application experience	1.29	1.13	1.00	0.91	0.82	
Software engineer capability	1.42	1.17	1.00	0.86	0.7	
Virtual machine experience	1.21	1.10	1.00	0.90		
Programming language experience	1.14	1.07	1.00	0.95		
Project attributes						
Use of software tools	1.24	1.10	1.00	0.91	0.82	
Application of software engineering	1.24	1.10	1.00	0.91	0.83	
Required development schedule	1.23	1.08	1.00	1.04	1.10	

We have studied techniques to estimate the effort needed to develop a software product. The outcome of this estimation exercise should be used prudently by the project manager. Normally, a variation of $\pm 30\%$ of the obtained estimate should be expected. An overestimation is normally a safe recourse to avoid the risks of being late and over budget. An underestimation would affect the morale of the development team once project delays become imminent. Also, late projects affect the reputation of the development company and can lead to legal and financial consequences.

Example 10.4

For the same semi-detached software project, Example 10.3 considers the ratings and corre- sponding multipliers for each of the 15 factors as shown in Table 10.11. The EAF for this project is 1.63. The effort E in persons-months is $3 \times 100^{1.12} \times 1.63 = 849.78$ persons-months.

Table 10.11 Example of attribute ratings using the intermediate COCOMO model

Cost drivers	Rating	Effort multiplier
Product attributes		
Required software reliability	High	1.15
Size of application database	Very high	1.16
Complexity of the product	High	1.30
Hardware attributes		
Run-time performance constraints	Nominal	1.00
Memory constraints	Nominal	1.00
Volatility of the virtual machine	Low	0.87
Required turnabout time	Nominal	1.00
Personnel attributes		
Analyst capability	High	0.86
Application experience	Low	1.13
Software engineer capability	Nominal	1.00
Virtual machine experience	High	0.9
Programming language experience	High	0.95
Project attributes		
Use of software tools	Low	1.10
Application of software engineering	Low	1.10
Required development schedule	Low	1.08

10.4 RISK MANAGEMENT

One of the main reasons for the failures of software projects is the inability to deal adequately with both anticipated and unanticipated problems occurring during the execution of the project. Ideally, a project manager must be ready ahead of time to deal with problems that can occur while the software is being developed. A software project risk is a problem occurring during the development of the software and the consequence of that problem. Software **risk management** encompasses activities that deal with the continuous identification, classification, assessment, prioritization, avoidance, detection, and mitigation of software risks. In addition, for the activities to succeed, the project manager must be able to plan them thoroughly, communicate them clearly, and do so in a timely manner. Figure 10.1 shows all activities within the risk management cycle.

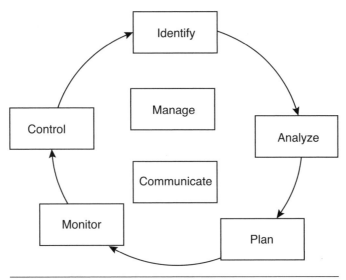

Figure 10.1 Risk management activities

The ultimate goal of software risk management is to make timely and informed decisions and take appropriate risk control actions when anticipated and unanticipated risks occur. The planned decisions and actions must be chosen after considering the risk impacts and costs—both in the short- and long-term—and all the available solutions and their costs.

Management Planning

Risk management planning involves startup risk management activities for the software project, including meetings for defining the risk efforts, risk management budget and schedule, assigning risk responsibilities within the development group and beyond, defining the interactions with other stakeholders, and deciding on the templates, risk taxonomies, and other standards and procedures to follow.

Identification

The first step in a risk management process involves the identification of risks. **Risk identification** requires the expertise of application domain experts in addition to general project management experience. The early identification of a risk reduces the costs that can be incurred should the risk materialize. Also, the late identification of a risk can limit the available risk mitigation solutions and make them costlier, less efficient, and less effective. A formal process for risk identification involving the various stakeholders are needed for complex, high stakes projects. This process involves: reviewing project documents to identify potential problems; conducting information gathering techniques, including brainstorming and interviewing; and performing checklist evaluation.

Risks can be either system-related or project-related. System-related risks are technical and non-technical risks related to system elements, including software, hardware, information, and people. Software risks include the following:

- The product and its capabilities at various stages of the development process. Examples of risks in this category are the unfeasibility of a requirement, the bad performance of a selected design solution, and the insecurity of an access control mechanism.
- The software development processes, the work environment, and the adopted **process model**. Examples of risks in this category are the unfamiliarity of the development team with the adopted process model, the unsuitability of the adopted process model, and the potential communication problem and lack of team coherence.
- The development system and the technologies used. Examples of risks in this category are the unfamiliarity of the development team with the development system and the lack of knowledge of the team in regard to the tools and techniques used.

Project risks are technical and non-technical risks related to project management style, project plan, effort estimation, risk planning, and project dependencies and constraints. Examples of technical project risks are the underestimation of effort for scheduled project activities, the inadequacy or lack of project progress monitoring methods, the unavailability of third-party software when needed, and the project constraints are unfeasible and overly-restrictive. Examples of non-technical people-related project risks include the lack of synergy among team members and the lack of communication among the various project stakeholders.

To cover all potential risks, the manager must be experienced, rely on the expertise of others in the organization, consider various published project risks taxonomies, and participate in brainstorming sessions with other project stakeholders to elicit potential software risks. Identified risks must also be well-documented and maintained. Each risk is assigned to an owner. The risk owner is a developer who is responsible for following up on the planning, tracking, and control of the risk.

Analysis

After identifying the risks, they must be assessed and verified for appropriateness and applicability. The likelihood of their occurrence and their impacts on the project schedule, cost, and quality must be evaluated either qualitatively or quantitatively. For example, in a qualitative assessment, the likelihood ranges from very low, low, medium, high to very high. The **risk impact** ranges from negligible, minor, tolerable, significant, to major. In a quantitative assessment, **risk likelihood** and risk impacts are continuous. In a quantitative assessment, the **risk exposure** is then computed as follows:

$$\text{Risk exposure} = \text{Risk likelihood} \times \text{Risk impact}$$

For example, if the likelihood of a risk is 0.25 (or 25 percent), and its impact is the loss of $1000, then the risk exposure is $250. Based on the risk exposure, identified risks can then be assigned priorities. A risk priority can be very low, low, medium, high, or very high. Obviously, high exposure risks should be dealt with thoroughly since they will likely be assigned a high priority. The main challenge in analyzing the risks is to find the correct likelihood of occurrence of each risk and its exact impact. Many techniques can be used to assess the risks and analyze them, including interviews and meeting with internal experts or consultants in the application domain.

The risks and their exposures can then be categorized and prioritized accordingly. A project risks table summarizing all project risks, their likelihoods, impacts and exposures, can be used to view and sort the risks in order to prioritize them. A typical template for a risks table is shown in Table 10.12.

Planning

A risk response plan must be designed for every risk identified. A risk response plan aims at enhancing the opportunities to counter the risk and to reduce the threats it poses to the project. The types of risk actions are developed and prioritized. Risk actions include:

- **Risk avoidance** actions to prevent the risk from occurring. Examples of risk avoidance actions are steps to improve the communications among team members and to increase by 20 percent the efforts estimated for critical activities in the project schedule to deal with the risk of project delivery delays.
- **Risk mitigation** actions to reduce the risk impact should it occur. Timely and planned actions to reduce the likelihood and impact of a risk are typically taken when the risk is unavoidable but its impact could be costly. An example of a mitigation action is the development of a disaster recovery plan to deal with the risk of a natural or man-made disaster leading to the interruption of the project development.
- **Risk acceptance**, meaning no action is to be taken should the risk occur. Typically, very low-impact and low-exposure risks are accepted and their costs are assumed without further actions.
- **Risk transfer** actions shift the responsibility of dealing with the risk and taking the appropriate action to a third party should the risk occur. The third party could be an insurance company or a financial institution. Risk transference is normally considered when dealing with non-technical risks such as contracts, financing risks, and natural disasters.

Table 10.12 Template for a project risks table

Risk ID	Risk name	Risk probability (RP)	Risk consequence (RC)	Risk exposure = RP * RC

The aim of a risk action is to reduce the risk exposure. The risk reduction leverage (RRL) can be computed for every risk action as follows:

$$RRL = (\text{Exposure before reduction} - \text{Exposure after reduction})/\text{Risk action cost}$$

For example, if a risk action costs $2000 and reduces the risk exposure from $100,000 to $20,000, the RRL would be 40. Clearly, for the same risk action cost, the higher the RRL the better is the return on investment leading to a lesser exposure. The RRL can be used to assess the effectiveness of the possible risk control actions and to decide on the most effective action with the highest return on investment.

Tracking

Risk tracking is an ongoing activity mainly based on the monitoring of the risks by continuously checking the conditions for their occurrences. Moreover, the proper implementations of risk actions are also monitored. Risk **tracking techniques** include periodic risk status reports and the monitoring of key risk indicators. The early detection of the imminence of a risk occurrence is desirable because it enhances the preparedness of the team to initiate, implement, and control the risk actions planned earlier. Once a risk is realized, the planned risk actions are activated to deal with that risk.

Control

Risk control is part of the overall project control dealing with the proper implementation of the control actions and risk plan. If corrections to the actions or to their implementations are needed, updates to the risk management plan are made. Risk control can involve risk reassessment, audits, and status meeting. These risk control activities are normally needed when some identified risks are not being dealt with according to plan or if the manager notices the occurrence of an unusual number of unanticipated risks.

Communication

Risks that are identified, assessed, and planned for must be communicated to the concerned stakeholders. Failing to communicate risks and risk plans gives a false sense of protection against the occurrence of these risks. To properly follow up and control risks, they must be communicated to various units within the organization and to the appropriate levels of management. In addition, risks need to be communicated to the client's organization. For example, the client must be aware of the risks related to changes to the requirements and the consequences of such changes on the project schedule.

A risk is typically raised or identified by any project stakeholder. The project manager will review the risk and check its validity. If it is found to be a relevant risk, the risk is saved in the risk registry. The project review team would then review the risk and prescribe the appropriate actions. The project team or the assigned risk owner is then responsible for implementing the risk actions.

Table 10.13 Template for a risk description

Project name:		Project manager:	
Risk ID:			
Risk description:			
Risk originator:		Risk origination date:	
Risk stakeholders:			
Risk likelihood:	Risk impact:		Risk priority:
Description of risk impact:			
Risk owner:			
Key risk indicators:			
Recommended avoidance actions:			
Recommended mitigation actions:			
Recommended control actions:			
Last risk review date:			

A typical template for documenting a risk is shown in Table 10.13.

10.5 SCHEDULING AND TRACKING PROJECTS

One of the main project management startup activities of a project manager is to develop a project schedule. The **schedule** has to be feasible in terms of the allocated time and resources. It also has to be easy to track. Tracking the progress of a project can reduce risks related to the late delivery of the product. To manage and track a large project, the project manager needs to divide the project work into related tasks. Tasks need to be structured around the phases of the life cycle model adopted by the development company. A task has an identity, a purpose, a duration, a start time, a list of predecessor tasks, if any, and the resources needed to complete it. Predecessor tasks are those tasks needed prior to the start of the task at hand. Resources include human, software, hardware, and possibly financial resources. A milestone is a particular point in time at which the task is completed. Breaking the project into small and manageable tasks allows the early detection of lateness in a project. In this case, early control actions can be taken to deal with the problem. The work involved in a task and the duration of a task should be reasonably short; otherwise an overhead dealing with the management of a large number of project tasks is needed. On the other hand, large tasks would increase the risks related to delays in project delivery. A typical template for describing a project task is shown in Table 10.14.

Table 10.14 Template for task description

Task ID:	Task name:
Task description:	
Scheduled start date:	Scheduled end date:
Task duration:	
Assigned human resources:	
Other needed system resources:	
Predecessors:	
Task completion percentage:	
Potential risks:	
Last task update:	
Nature of task updates:	
Recommended mitigation actions:	
Last task review date:	

Various techniques can be used to track the progress of a project. Monitoring the adherence to completion dates or milestones set for the project tasks can be achieved by conducting progress review meetings or by periodically **reporting** the progress achieved so far. Once early signs of lateness are detected, the manager can intervene to varying degrees, depending on the severity of the problem and the causes of lateness.

The project length is the duration in days of the longest path in the task network—the length of the project **critical path**. Given the available resources, including human and other system resources, and the dependencies between the tasks, the manager must exploit the concurrent execution of tasks to its fullest. The concurrent execution of tasks leads to better resource utilization and to shorter project length.

The **tasks** of a project can be summarized in both a tabular or graphical form. A typical template for the tabular representation of a project schedule includes one row per task. The columns of the table correspond to the attributes of the task, including the task identification, task name, duration, start date, finish date, and the predecessor task(s), if any. A task whose duration is 0 day is called a milestone task. It is used to represent the termination of a phase or a group of tasks in the project schedule.

A **task network** is a graphical representation of a project schedule table. It is composed of nodes and directed arcs joining them. A node in the network represents a task and includes the task name and its duration. A directed arc between two nodes represents the dependency of the sink node or task on the completion of the start node or task. The task represented by the sink node cannot start until all the predecessor tasks have successfully terminated. Predecessor tasks are those represented by the source nodes of all incoming arcs to the sink node. The number of incoming edges to a task represents the number of its predecessor tasks. Initial tasks are represented by nodes with no incoming edges. Final tasks are represented by nodes with no outgoing edges.

Example 10.5

Table 10.15 shows a project schedule table composed of 9 tasks, including a milestone task. Task A is the initial task and task H is the final task in the project. Figure 10.2 shows the task network equivalent to the project in Table 10.15.

A critical path on the task network is the longest duration path from start to finish. A task network can have more than one critical path, all

Table 10.15 Project schedule in a tabular form

Task ID	Task name	Duration	Start	Finish	Predecessor
1	A	1 day	Mon 01/10/07	Mon 01/10/07	
2	B	1 day	Tue 02/10/07	Tue 02/10/07	1
3	C	2 days	Tue 02/10/07	Wed 03/10/07	1
4	D	4 days	Thu 04/10/07	Tue 09/10/07	2,3
5	E	5 days	Thu 04/10/07	Wed 10/10/07	3
6	F	6 days	Wed 10/10/07	Wed 17/10/07	4
7	G	5 days	Thu 11/10/07	Wed 17/10/07	4,5
8	H	3 days	Thu 18/10/07	Mon 22/10/07	6,7
9	M-1	0 day	Mon 22/10/07	Mon 22/10/07	8

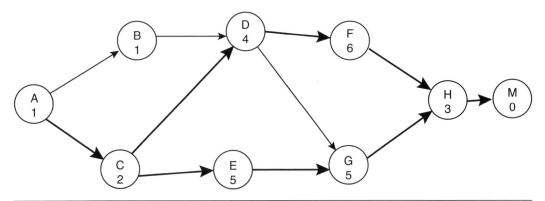

Figure 10.2 Task network representing a project schedule

(*continues*)

Example 10.5 (*continued*)

having the same total duration. A task that is included in a critical path is called a **critical task**. Any delay in the completion of a critical task leads to a delay in the project termination. A manager pays close attention to the monitoring of progress made on critical paths. For critical tasks, the earliest start date and latest start date are equal. No delays can be afforded on these tasks. Figure 10.2 highlights the two critical paths in the project schedule. These paths, whose durations are 16 days, are: A-C-D-F-H-M and A-C-E-G-H-M. However, non-critical tasks can have different earliest start and latest start dates without compromising the scheduled project termination date or milestone. The task **slack time** for a non-critical task is (latest start − earliest start). The slack time represents the flexibility that the manager has in scheduling non-critical tasks. The slack time for a critical task is 0. Table 10.16 shows three additional columns included in the project schedule table. The table shows that there is only one non-critical task with a slack time of one day.

Table 10.16 Project schedule table with additional task information

Task name	Duration	Earliest start	Earliest finish	Latest start	Latest finish	Pred	Slack
A	1 day	Mon 01/10/07	Mon 01/10/07	Mon 01/10/07	Mon 01/10/07		0
B	1 day	Tue 02/10/07	Tue 02/10/07	Wed 03/10/07	Wed 03/10/07	1	1
C	2 days	Tue 02/10/07	Wed 03/10/07	Tue 02/10/07	Wed 03/10/07	1	0
D	4 days	Thu 04/10/07	Tue 09/10/07	Thu 04/10/07	Tue 09/10/07	2,3	0
E	5 days	Thu 04/10/07	Wed 10/10/07	Thu 04/10/07	Wed 10/10/07	3	0
F	6 days	Wed 10/10/07	Wed 17/10/07	Wed 10/10/07	Wed 17/10/07	4	0
G	5 days	Thu 11/10/07	Wed 17/10/07	Thu 11/10/07	Wed 17/10/07	4,5	0
H	3 days	Thu 18/10/07	Mon 22/10/07	Thu 18/10/07	Mon 22/10/07	6,7	0
M-1	0 day	Mon 22/10/07	Mon 22/10/07	Mon 22/10/07	Mon 22/10/07	8	0

Project tracking is one of the critical tasks that have to be performed by a project manager. Tracking a project can either rely on a qualitative or quantitative assessment of the progress made during the execution of the project. Qualitative assessment is based on periodic reporting by the software developers and reviewing by the project managers. This assessment may eventually lead to changes to the project timeline chart or **Gantt chart**. A qualitative assessment is usually subjective in nature and, therefore, might not be accurate or precise in reflecting real progress. A periodic review of the project schedule by the manager might reveal new critical paths and consequently new critical tasks with a 0 slack time. The manager must then shift attention to the newly-identified critical tasks. This shows the dynamic and continuous nature of project management and requires a highly vigilant and dynamic manager.

Earned value analysis is a technique for the quantitative assessment and measurement of progress made in a project. It indicates the progress made as a percent of project completeness. During effort estimation in the project planning phase, estimation techniques are used to quan-

Example 10.6

Suppose that after 8 days, tasks D and E have just finished. This means that tasks A, B, C, D, and E have been performed. The new task network shown in Figure 10.3 indicates that the only critical path is now F-H whose length is 9 days.

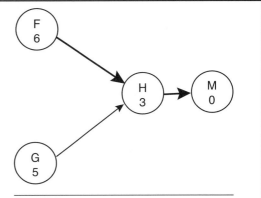

Figure 10.3 New task network with its critical path

tify the effort in person-months needed to complete each of the scheduled tasks. The budgeted cost of work scheduled for task t_i (BCWS$_i$) is the estimated effort for task t_i. The progress made at time T is the sum of all BCWS$_i$ values of all tasks that should have been completed at time T according to the project schedule included in the project plan. The sum of values of the BCWSs of all project tasks is referred to as the budget at completion (BAC). At time T, we can also compute the budgeted cost of work performed (BCWP). The BCWP is the sum of the BCWSs for tasks that have been completed at time T. The **schedule performance index** (SPI) is the ratio of BCWP/BCWS. SPI provides a measure of performance, indicating how the project execution is progressing compared to the project plan. The ratio BCWP/BAC indicates the percentage of work completed at time T. The schedule variance (SV) is the difference BCWP − BCWS. A negative variance implies that the project is behind schedule.

In addition, the manager can also assess the cost efficiency in the project at time T. Similar indicators can be used. The actual cost of work performed (ACWP) is the sum of the costs incurred on the tasks that have been completed at time T. The **cost performance index** (CPI) is the ratio BCWP/ACWP. A CPI < 1 implies that the project ran over budget. The CPI indicates whether or not the project is still within budget. The cost variance (CV) is the difference BCWP − ACWP. A negative variance implies an over-budget project.

Based on both the SPI and CPI, the manager needs to intervene and take the appropriate corrective actions according to the risk management plan developed for the project.

Earned value analysis can also be used to compute the estimate and variance at the completion of the project given the current situation at time T and the originally estimated efforts for the remaining tasks. The estimate at completion (EAC) can be computed using various methods. The most simplistic one is to compute EAC as the ratio BAC/CPI. A more detailed EAC can be computed as: EAC = (BAC − BCWP)/CPI + ACWP. This method projects that the future performance is correlated with the current performance up to time T. The variance at completion (VAC) is a projection of the final cost variance for the project. VAC is computed as the difference BAC − EAC. Finally, the schedule at completion (SAC) indicates a projection of the final cost of the project based on the current performance at time T. SAC is computed as the ratio BAC/SPI.

Example 10.7

A software project plan includes 20 tasks that are estimated to require 200 person-months. At time T, the 6 tasks of a software project plan that should have been completed are shown in Table 10.17. The table shows the effort in person-months that was estimated to complete each task and the effort that was actually needed. The table indicates that only 5 tasks were complete at time T.

Table 10.17 Project progress information at time T

Task	Effort planned	Actual effort
1	10	9.5
2	12	13
3	7	7.5
4	15	17
5	14	14.5
6	9	—

At time T, the BCWS is 67 person-months, the BCWP is 58 person-months. Therefore, the schedule performance index SPI is BCWP/BCWS $= 58/67 = 0.91$ and the schedule variance SV is BCWP $-$ BCWS $= 58- 67 = -9$, indicating that the project is behind schedule. The SPI indicates that the project at time T is behind schedule. The percentage of completeness is BCWP/BAC $= 58/200 = 29$ percent. The ACWP at time T is 61.5 person-months. The cost performance index (CPI) is $58/61.5 = 0.94$. The CPI indicates that the project is over budget at time T. The CV is BCWP - ACWP $= 58 - 61.5 = -3.5$, indicating an over-budget project at time T. The estimate at completion EAC is BAC/CPI $= 200/0.94 = 212$, according to the simplistic method, and EAC $=$ (BAC $-$ BCWP)/CPI $+$ ACWP $=$ (200 $-$ 58)/0.94 $+$ 61.5 $=$ 212. The variance at completion VAC is $200 - 212 = -12$, meaning that the project will require an additional 12 person-months. Finally, the schedule at completion SAC is BAC/SPI $= 200/0.91 = 219$, indicating that the project will be completed using the efforts of 219 person-months.

10.6 SOFTWARE PROJECT MANAGEMENT PLAN DOCUMENT

The IEEE has recommended a standard template for writing a **software project management plan** (SPMP). IEEE Std. 1058.1-1987 describes the format and contents of the SPMP. The template used is a generic one because it applies to software projects of all types and sizes. The project manager can tailor the SPMP according to the needs of the project at hand. The IEEE standard does not recommend or explain any specific project management technique, nor provides examples of use. The standard is the product of experienced contributors from both academia and industry. The use of a standard-based SPMP would help facilitate the communication among managers and other users of the document worldwide.

The SPMP document consists of eight main sections, describing in a comprehensive and generic way all aspects of a project. The level of detail that is included in a particular project plan document depends on the complexity of the project and the budget and time allocated to it. An experienced project manager tailors the plan accordingly.

The first section of the plan contains an overview of the project. The overview includes a project summary and a specification of how the plan will evolve and be maintained. The project summary describes the purpose, scope, and objectives of the project and the product to be developed. In addition, this section includes the project assumptions, the constraints imposed on the project, the project deliverables and their dates, and a summary of the project schedule and budget. The evolution of the plan describes the circumstances under which the plan will be updated and how the updates will be managed.

The next two sections include a list of referenced documents and sources used in the plan and a definition of terms and acronyms used in the project plan, respectively.

The **project organization**, in terms of its internal structure, external interfaces, and the roles and responsibilities assigned to the groups in the organization is included in the fourth section. The internal structure presents the organization's hierarchy and the lines of authority and reporting within the project. The hierarchy shows the various relationships among the development groups and the supporting groups within the organization.

The fifth section includes all the plans for the management processes that need to be enacted during the execution of the project, which include:

- **Project startup** plan includes the estimation, **staffing**, **resource acquisition**, and project staff **training**.
- **Project work plan** includes the work activities to be performed during the project, the schedule of these **work activities**, the resource allocation, and the budget details. Project management tools can be used to provide a graphical representation of this management process plan.
- **Project control plan** includes management plans for the control of requirements changes and their effects on the project work plan. In addition, it contains plans for control of the schedule, budget, quality, reporting, and the **metrics collection** plan.
- **Risk management plan** includes the identified risks, their priorities, and the risk avoidance, monitoring, control, and mitigation procedures should these risks occur. The identified risks include technical, business, environmental, and personnel risks among others.
- **Project closeout** includes the plans for the archiving of deliverables and metrics, the reassignment of project personnel, and the assessment of project success.

All the technical processes that need to be enacted during the execution of the project are contained in the sixth section and include:

- **Process model plan** describes the activities to be performed and their respective deliverables and supporting processes. It also describes the methods, techniques, and tools to be used for the execution of the activities of the project.

- **Infrastructure plan** describes the project development environment and the procedures, policies, standards, and facilities needed to operate and maintain the environment.
- **Product acceptance plan** describes the project deliverables acceptance criteria for the client acceptance. It also includes the tools and methods that will be used to verify the satisfaction of the acceptance criteria.

The seventh section contains the process plans that are needed to support the execution of the project work activities and includes:

- **Configuration management plan** includes the methods and tools used for release management and tracking and controlling project- and product-related changes.
- **Verification and validation plan** includes the methods, techniques, and tools needed to perform the verification and validation of the deliverables of the work activities.
- **Documentation plan** includes a description of the project- and product-related documents that will be produced during the execution of the project, and the procedures and tools for producing and reviewing these documents.
- **Quality assurance plan** includes the quality assurance activities that are needed to ensure that the project meets the quality criteria set for the product, the processes used, and the project activities.
- **Reviews and audit plans** include the procedures, resources, tools, techniques, and standards used to perform project reviews and audits.
- **Problem resolution plan** includes the procedures, resources, tools, and techniques used to capture and manage the software problem reports generated during the execution of the project.
- **Subcontractor management plan** includes the procedures and tools used to manage the relationship with each subcontractor as it relates to the project activities.
- **Process improvement plan** includes the procedures and tools used to assess the project activities and to pinpoint the areas and processes that can be improved while the project is evolving and later for future projects.

The final section includes descriptions of various other project- and product-related plans, such as safety, installation and deployment, user training, integration, conversion and transition, and maintenance and support plan.

Table 10.18 shows the template for the software project management plan.

Table 10.18 Template of a software project management plan

Title page
Change history
Preface
Table of contents
1. Overview
   Project summary
   Evolution of the plan
2. References
3. Definitions
4. Project organization
   External interfaces
   Internal structure
   Roles and responsibilities
5. Managerial process plans
   Startup
   Work
   Control
   Risk management
   Closeout
6. Technical process plans
   Process model
   Methods, tools, and techniques
   Infrastructure
   Product acceptance
7. Supporting process plans
   Configuration management
   Verification and validation
   Documentation
   Quality assurance
   Reviews and audits
   Problem resolution
   Subcontractor management
   Process improvement
8. Additional plans
Annexes
Index

SUMMARY

The proper management of software projects is key to their successful completion. A software project is considered successful if it meets all the specified customer requirements and is delivered on time and within budget. Various project management activities must be performed during the lifetime of a software project. These activities ensure that the product under development will meet its set quality requirements and will be developed on time and within budget. In this chapter, we have studied the main components of a software project plan. Metrics and estimation techniques such as function point, use case point, and COCOMO were studied and used to determine the milestones of the project schedule. Risk engineering techniques were studied and used to ensure the continuous identification, action planning, monitoring, and control of project risks. Project tracking techniques identifying the critical path in the project were also studied. In addition, earned value analysis for the quantitative assessment of project progress was discussed. Finally, the IEEE standard template for a software project management plan was presented.

KEY TERMS

COCOMO
configuration management
  plan
control plan
cost performance index
critical path
critical task
deliverables
documentation plan
earned value analysis
empirical estimation
environmental factors
estimations
feature point
function point
Gantt chart
infrastructure plan
lines of code (LOC)
metrics collection
milestones
people
problem resolution plan
processes
process improvement plan
process model

process model plan
product
product acceptance plan
project
project closeout
project control plan
project organization
project plan
project scope
project startup
project work plan
quality assurance plan
quality control
reporting
requirements-based
  estimation
resource acquisition
reviews and audit plan
risk acceptance
risk avoidance
risk control
risk engineering
risk exposure
risk identification
risk impact

risk likelihood
risk management
risk management plan
risk management planning
risk mitigation
risk transfer
schedule
schedule performance index
slack time
software metrics
software project management
  plan (SPMP)
specification-based
  techniques
staffing
subtractor management plan
task network
tasks
technical complexity
tracking techniques
training
use case point
verification and validation
  plan
work activities

REVIEW QUESTIONS

1. List three people-related software project failures.
2. List three process-related software project failures.
3. List three project plan-related software project failures.
4. List three product-related software project failures.

5. List the main project management activities.
6. List the various plans that can be included in a software project management plan.
7. List some software cost estimation techniques.
8. List some product-related metrics that can be collected.
9. List some process-related metrics that can be collected.
10. What are the risk engineering activities involved in software project management?
11. Why should risk management processes be performed continuously?
12. What are the main activities of a manager of a software maintenance team?
13. List a project schedule-related risk and possible avoidance or mitigation actions.
14. List a project staffing-related risk and possible response actions.
15. List a development environment risk and possible actions.
16. How can a risk be assessed?

EXERCISES

1. Table 10.19 gives a partial project showing all the tasks of the project, their durations, and interdependencies. Assume that each task is performed by one person working full-time.

Table 10.19 Table for Exercise 1

Task	Duration in days	Predecessor	Earliest start	Earliest finish	Latest start	Latest finish	Slack
A	3	—	1	3			
B	1	—					
C	5	—					
D	3	A, B					
E	3	C, D					
F	2	D, E					
G	3	F					
H	?	E					

What should be the duration of task H knowing that the project has 2 critical paths? There is a redundant (not needed) dependency, what is it? Draw the complete task network and show the 2 critical paths. Complete the table. What happens if task C is delayed by one day? What happens if task F is delayed by one day?

2. In Figure 10.4 you are given the task network for a software project.
What is (are) the critical path(s)? its duration? Fill the rows for tasks B, C, D, E and F in Table 10.20.

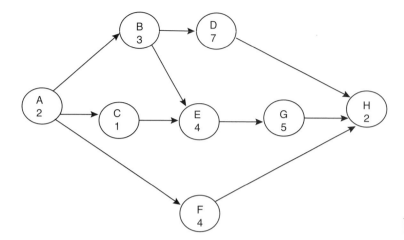

Figure 10.4 Figure for Exercise 2

Table 10.20 Table for Exercise 2

Task	Duration in days	Predecessor	Earliest start	Earliest finish	Latest start	Latest finish	Slack
B							
C							
D							
E							
F							

Suppose that after reviewing the plan we discovered that task F must be a predecessor for task G instead of being a predecessor for task H. What are the implications on the project? Why?

3. In Figure 10.5 you are given the task network for a software project.
   Given the following additional information:

   - All task durations are specified except that of F (for you to find out).
   - All task dependencies are specified except for one (for you to find out).
   - There are 2 critical paths each of 20 days duration.

   What is the duration of task F? What is (are) the critical path(s)? its duration? Where is the missing task dependency?

4, Estimate the function points needed for the problem described in Exercise 4.6.

5. A software development company is planning to commit itself to the development of software for controlling unmanned spacecrafts. The software development team is composed of experienced developers. However, the developers are not experts in the application domain. The manager has estimated that there is a 7.5 percent risk that the software will

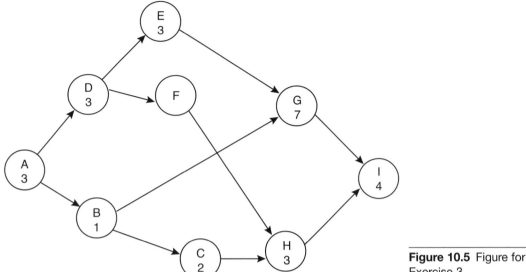

Figure 10.5 Figure for Exercise 3

have a critical error that will lead to the loss of the first launched aircraft at a cost of $2 million. There are five major options for the manager to reduce the risk:

- Train the team on the application domain at an extra cost of $200,000. The manager estimates that this will reduce the risk to 0.35 percent.
- Hire two application domain consultants at a cost of $250,000. The manager estimates that this will reduce the risk to 0.4 percent.
- Hire a third party to independently verify and validate the software at an additional cost of $100,000. It is estimated that this option will reduce the risk to 0.15 percent.
- Assume the risk and do nothing.
- Obtain special insurance at a cost of $350,000.

Determine the risk exposure for each of the five options and make the most appropriate decision.

6. Given the project table shown in Table 10.21, answer the following:
Draw the corresponding task network. List all the critical tasks. Show all the critical paths on the task network. What is the length of the critical path? What is the slack time for task B? task E? Give one milestone task. Why is it a milestone task? What is the total effort in person-days needed to complete all the project tasks? Give one constraint the manager has when scheduling the three parallel tasks C, D, and E.

7. Produce a function point-based estimation for the system described in Exercise 3.4.

8. Produce an LOC-based estimation using the COCOMO technique for the system described in Exercise 3.5.

9. Produce a use case point-based estimation for the system described in Exercise 3.6.

Table 10.21 Project table

Task #	Task name	Duration	Predecessors
1	A	1	—
2	B	4	A
3	C	3	B
4	D	2	B
5	E	1	B
6	F	2	C
7	G	3	D, E
8	H	0	F, G
9	I	3	H
10	J	2	H
11	K	4	I, J
12	L	0	K

Table 10.22 Project progress information at time T

Task #	Effort planned	Actual effort
1	13	11
2	12	11.5
3	7	7
4	15	13
5	14	15
6	5	—
7	12	8
8	3	—
9	4	—

10. A software project plan shown in Table 10.22 includes 30 tasks. It was estimated that 300 person-months will be needed to complete the project. At a given time T, 9 tasks were supposed to be complete, according to the original plan. Table 10.22 shows that only 6 tasks were completed at time T. Compute the BCWP, BCWS, SPI, CPI, CV, SV, VAC, and EAC at time T.

BIBLIOGRAPHY

Books

Bechtold, R. *Essentials of Software Project Management*, 2d ed., New York: Wiley 2006.

Boehm, B. *Software Engineering Economics*, Englewood Cliffs, NJ: Prentice Hall, 1981.

Brooks, M. *The Mythical Man-Month*, Reading, MA: Addison-Wesley, 1995.

Fenton, N. E., and S. L. Pfleeger. *Software Metrics: A Rigorous & Practical Approach*, 2d ed., London, UK: International Thomson Computer Press, 1998.

Humphrey, W. *A Discipline for Software Engineering*, Reading, MA: Addison-Wesley, 1995.

Jones, C. *Estimating Software Costs*, 2d ed, New York: McGraw Hill, 2007.

Karolak, D. W. *Software Engineering Risk Management*, New York: IEEE Computer Society Press, 1996.

Reifer, D. J., ed. *Software Management,* New York: IEEE Computer Society Press, 2002.

Thayer, R. H., ed. *Software Engineering Project Management,* New York: IEEE Computer Society Press, 1997.

Tsui, F. *Managing Software Projects*, Sudbury, MA: Jones and Bartlett, 2004.

Whitten, N. *Managing Software Development Projects: Formulas for Success*, New York: Wiley, 1995.

Papers

Adler, T. R., J. G. Leonard, and R. K. Nordgren. "Improving risk management: Moving from risk elimination to risk avoidance." *Information and Software Technology*, vol. 41, 29–34, 1999.

Albrecht, A., and J. Gaffney. "Software function, source lines of code and development effort prediction: a software science validation." 639–648, *IEEE Transactions on Software Engineering.* November 1983.

Boehm, B. W., and T. DeMarco. "Software risk management." 17–19, *IEEE Software*, May/June 1997.

Conrow, E. H., and P. S. Shishido. "Implementing risk management on software intensive projects." 83–89, *IEEE Software*, May/June 1997.

DeMarco, T., and A. Miller. "Managing large software projects." 24–27, *IEEE Software*, July 1996.

Grable, R., et al. "Metrics for small projects: Experiences at the SED." 21–29, *IEEE Software*, March/April 1999.

Hall, T., and N. Fenton. "Implementing effective software metrics programs." 55–64, *IEEE Software*, March/April 1997.

Jones, C. "Backfiring: Converting lines of code to function points." *IEEE Computer,* 28(11): 87–88, November 1995.

Kamer, G. "Metrics for objectory." *Diploma thesis*, University of Linköping, Sweden, No. LiTHIDA-Ex-9344:21, December 1993.

Kemerer, C. "Reliability of function points measurement: A field experiment." *Communications of the ACM*, 36(2): 85–97, 1993.

Kitchenham, B., and S. Linkman. "Estimates, uncertainty, and risk." 69–74, *IEEE Software*, May/June 1997.

Mackey, K. "Why bad things happen to good projects." 27–32, *IEEE Software*, May 1996.

Pfleeger, S. L., et al. "Status report on software measurement." 33–43, *IEEE Software*, March/April 1997.

Project Management Institute Standards Committee, *A guide to the project management body of knowledge (PMBOK)*, Project Management Institute, 2000.

Standards

IEEE Std 1058.1-1987 (R2002), *IEEE Standard for Software Project Management Plans*, IEEE, 1987.

ISO/IEC 15939:2002, *Software Engineering—Software Measurement Process*, ISO and IEC, 2002.

INDEX